TACTICAL CRIME ANALYSIS

Research and Investigation

TACTICAL CRIME ANALYSIS

Research and Investigation

Derek J. Paulsen | Sean Bair | Dan Helms

CRC Press
Taylor & Francis Group
Boca Raton London New York

CRC Press is an imprint of the
Taylor & Francis Group, an **informa** business

CRC Press
Taylor & Francis Group
6000 Broken Sound Parkway NW, Suite 300
Boca Raton, FL 33487-2742

© 2010 by Taylor and Francis Group, LLC
CRC Press is an imprint of Taylor & Francis Group, an Informa business

No claim to original U.S. Government works

Printed in the United States of America on acid-free paper
10 9 8 7 6 5 4 3 2 1

International Standard Book Number: 978-1-4200-8697-3 (Hardback)

This book contains information obtained from authentic and highly regarded sources. Reasonable efforts have been made to publish reliable data and information, but the author and publisher cannot assume responsibility for the validity of all materials or the consequences of their use. The authors and publishers have attempted to trace the copyright holders of all material reproduced in this publication and apologize to copyright holders if permission to publish in this form has not been obtained. If any copyright material has not been acknowledged please write and let us know so we may rectify in any future reprint.

Except as permitted under U.S. Copyright Law, no part of this book may be reprinted, reproduced, transmitted, or utilized in any form by any electronic, mechanical, or other means, now known or hereafter invented, including photocopying, microfilming, and recording, or in any information storage or retrieval system, without written permission from the publishers.

For permission to photocopy or use material electronically from this work, please access www.copyright.com (http://www.copyright.com/) or contact the Copyright Clearance Center, Inc. (CCC), 222 Rosewood Drive, Danvers, MA 01923, 978-750-8400. CCC is a not-for-profit organization that provides licenses and registration for a variety of users. For organizations that have been granted a photocopy license by the CCC, a separate system of payment has been arranged.

Trademark Notice: Product or corporate names may be trademarks or registered trademarks, and are used only for identification and explanation without intent to infringe.

Visit the Taylor & Francis Web site at
http://www.taylorandfrancis.com

and the CRC Press Web site at
http://www.crcpress.com

Table of Contents

Authors		**xiii**
	SECTION I	
1	**Introduction of Crime Analysis**	**3**
	Introduction	3
	Conclusion	7
2	**Understanding Criminal Behavior**	**9**
	Introduction	9
	Rational Choice	9
	Research Findings	11
	Routine Activities Theory	13
	Research Findings	15
	Crime Pattern Theory	16
	Research Findings	18
	Opportunity Makes the Thief	19
	Conclusion	23
3	**Behavioral Geography**	**25**
	Introduction to Behavioral Geography	25
	Spatial Behavior	27
	Mental Maps and Awareness Space	27
	Research on Mental Maps and Awareness Space	29
	Journey-to-Crime	32
	Journey-to-Crime Research	33
	Thinking Criminal	35
4	**Exploring Crime Types**	**45**
	Introduction	45
	Homicide	45
	Robbery	47
	Burglary	49
	Auto Theft	51

	Sexual Assault	54
	Conclusion	55
5	**Linking Crime**	**57**
	Introduction	57
	Linkage Blindness	58
	Jane Smith	58
	Sheriff Joe	59
	Who, What, Where, When, How and Why	60
	The Dresser Drawers Theory	60
	The Investigative Mindset: Fact and Inference	62
	Process Models: The IZE Method	64
	Process Models: Inductive Versus Deductive	68
	Process Models: Quantitative Identification	70
	Data Mining	71
	Data Mining: Regular Expressions	72
	Data Mining: Concepts	74
	Conclusion	75
6	**Temporal Analysis**	**77**
	Introduction	77
	Definitions	77
	Basic Assumptions	78
	Primary Time of Occurrence	79
	Multiple Times of Occurrence	79
	Aoristic Analysis	80
	Temporal Analysis Units	81
	T Coordinates	82
	Temporal Study Area (Range)	82
	Temporal Distribution	83
	Tempo	86
	Velocity	87
	Temporal Cycles	87
	Time Series Analysis	88
7	**Geographic Profiling**	**91**
	Introduction	91
	Background of Geographic Profiling	91
	Geographic Profiling Schools of Thought	92
	Criminal Geographic Targeting (CGT)	93
	Personalities and History	93

	Application	93
	Investigative Psychology (I-Ψ)	95
	Personalities and History	95
	Application	96
	CrimeStat	97
	Personalities and History	97
	Application	97
	Empirically Calibrated Decay Functions	100
	Wedge Theory	100
	Personalities and History	101
	Application	101
	Geoforensic Analysis	101
	Personalities and History	101
	Application	102
	Philosophical Foundations	102
	Individual Methods	103
	Research on the Accuracy of Geographic Profiling Systems	105
	Glossary of Terms	107
8	**Forecasting and Prediction**	**109**
	Overview	109
	Why Forecasts Work	110
	Why Forecasts Don't Work	110
	The Utility of Forecasts	111
	Temporal Forecasting	111
	Spatial Forecasting	112
	Why Predictions Work	112
	Decision Models	113
	Why Predictions Don't Work	117
	Methods	120
	Percent Change	121
	Correlation	123
	Autocorrelation	123
	Linear Trend Estimation (Regression)	125
9	**Intervention**	**127**
	Introduction	127
	Objectives	128
	Intervention Strategies	132
	Opportunity Cost	135
	Tactics	135
	The Action Plan—A Combined Approach	136

SECTION II

10 Getting Started   **141**

Goals of This Section:	141
Introduction	141
Accessing the Textbook Web page	141
Online Resources	141
Obtaining the Software	142
Open and Evaluate Data using ATAC	142
Lesson 1: Open the Sample Database in ATAC	142
Practice on Your Own: Evaluate Crime Data Using ATAC	142
ATAC and Microsoft Access	143
Lesson 2: Open a Microsoft Access Database in ATAC	143
Practice on Your Own: Evaluate Call for Service Data	144
ATAC and Microsoft Excel	144
Lesson 3: Open a Microsoft Excel Spreadsheet in ATAC	145
Lesson 4: Open the Sample Database in Excel	145
Practice on Your Own: Evaluate Data Using Microsoft Excel	145
Lesson 5: Import Data from Access into Excel	145
Practice On Your Own: Import Data into Excel	147
Review Exercise: Open Other Data	147
Review Questions	147

11 Identify Patterns Using the IZE Method (Process Models)   **149**

Goals of This Section:	149
Introduction	149
Layouts in ATAC	150
Lesson 6: Organizing a Layout Using ATAC	150
Lesson 7: Saving a Layout in ATAC	151
Layouts in Excel	152
Lesson 8: Organizing a Layout Using Excel	152
Practice On Your Own: Create a Robbery Layout Using Microsoft Excel	152
Sorting Data	153
Lesson 9: Organizing Data by Sorting in ATAC	153
Lesson 10: Organizing Data by Sorting in Excel	154
Review Exercise: Create Sorts for Three Crime Types	154
Review Questions	154

12   Minimize and Maximize—IZE method   155

Goals of This Section:	155
Introduction	155
Structured Query Language	155
Lesson 11: Minimize Using the Visual Query Module in ATAC	156
Lesson 12: Minimize Using the Filter Bar in ATAC	157
Lesson 13: Minimize Using the Filter Bar in Excel	158
Practice on Your Own: Minimize Data Using Excel	159
Practice on Your Own: Find the Twins	159
Practice on Your Own: Identify a Crime Series	160
Regular Expressions	160
Lesson 14: Create and Run a Regular Expression	160
Lesson 15: Create and Run a Proximity Search Regular Expression	161
Lesson 16: Create a Concept	162
Lesson 17: Create and Run a Proximity Search Concept	163
Review Exercise: Using RegEx to Perform the Inductive Method	164
Review Questions	165

13   The Behavioral Dimension: Describing the Problem   167

Goals of This Section:	167
Introduction	167
Archetypes	168
Lesson 18: Creating an Archetype from ATAC	168
Movement Logs	168
Lesson 19: Develop a Movement Log	169
Review Exercise: Creating an Archetype	170
Review Questions	170

14   The Temporal Dimension   171

Goals of This Section:	171
Introduction	171
Activity Schedules	172
Lesson 20: Creating an Activity Schedule	172
Lesson 21: Create a Temporal Topology Using Excel	173
Lesson 22: Create a Temporal Topology Using ATAC	174
Practice On Your Own: Evaluate Time of Day and Day of Week for Various Crimes	175

	Dynamic Temporal Analysis	177
	Temporal Distribution	177
	Tempo	178
	Lesson 23: Create a Tempogram in ATAC	178
	Lesson 24: Create a Tempogram in Excel	179
	Lesson 25: Create a Mean Interval Forecast with Excel	180
	Practice on Your Own: Calculate Mean Interval for Various Other Crimes	181
	Variograms	181
	Lesson 26: Create a Variogram Using Excel	181
	Lesson 27: Create a Variogram Using ATAC	182
	Practice on Your Own: Calculate Lag Variograms against Various Other Crimes	183
	Lesson 28: Study of Correlation Using Excel	184
	Lesson 29: Study of Correlation Using ATAC	186
	Review Exercise: Evaluate Other Crime Series Using Correlation	187
	Review Questions	188
15	**The Spatial Dimension**	**189**
	Goals of This Section:	189
	Introduction	189
	Preparing for Spatial Analysis	190
	Lesson 30: Launching ArcGIS and Exploring the Interface	190
	Lesson 31: Add the Gotham City Crime Series Using ArcGIS	191
	ArcGIS and the Spatial Analyst Extension	191
	Lesson 32: Loading Spatial Analyst	192
	ArcGIS and SPACE (Spatial Predictive Analysis of Crime Extension)	192
	Lesson 33: Loading the SPACE Tools in ArcGIS	193
	Preparing for Spatial Analysis Using Google Earth	193
	Lesson 34: Load Points in Google Earth	193
	Lesson 35: Export to Google Earth	194
	Preparing for Spatial Analysis Using ATAC	194
	Lesson 36: Loading Points in ATAC	195
	Point Distributions	196
	Frame of Reference	196
	Lesson 37: Frame of Reference	196
	Identify Point Distribution	196
	Mean Nearest Neighbor	198
	Lesson 38: Calculating Nearest Neighbor Statistics	198
	Density Fields	198

Lesson 39: Density Fields Using ArcGIS	199
Lesson 40: Calculating Density Analysis in ATAC	200
Minimum Convex Polygon	201
Lesson 41: Minimum Convex Polygon	202
Standard Deviation Ellipse	202
Lesson 42: Standard Deviation Ellipse	202
Spider Analysis	202
Lesson 43: Spider Analysis	203
Lesson 44: Establishing Offender Activity Space Using Spider Lines and Density Fields	205
Space-Time Analysis	206
Sequence Lines	206
Lesson 45: Sequence Lines	208
Geographic Profiling	208
Lesson 46: Calculate the Great Circle against the Beltway Sniper Series	208
Practice On Your Own: Are you a Marauder or Commuter?	209
Lesson 47: Create a Newton-Swoope Geoforensic Profile of the Beltway Sniper Series	210
Review Exercise: Using the Great Circle and Geographic Profiling	211
Review Questions	212
Bibliography	**213**
Index	**219**

Authors

Derek J. Paulsen is currently an associate professor in the Department of Criminal Justice and Police Studies at Eastern Kentucky University at Richmond. Dr. Paulsen has published numerous articles dealing with crime mapping and crime analysis issues that have appeared in such journals as *Policing: An International Journal of Police Strategies and Management, Journal of Investigative Psychology and Offender Profiling, International Journal of Police Science and Management,* and *Journal of Criminal Justice and Popular Culture*. A frequent presenter on crime mapping topics at both academic and professional conferences, Dr. Paulsen has been an invited speaker numerous times at the National Institute of Justice (NIJ) MAPS Conference, NIJ Conference, UK Crime Mapping Conference, and the International Investigative Psychology Conference. In addition to crime mapping and tactical analysis, Dr. Paulsen's research focuses on crime and urban planning, socially sustainable design, and geosimulation of crime.

Dan Helms is a private consultant working for various defense and law enforcement agencies. He is the former program manager of the Crime Mapping and Analysis Program (CMAP), a program of the National Law Enforcement and Corrections Technology Center, NIJ. Prior to his work at CMAP, Mr. Helms served as crime analyst for the Las Vegas Metropolitan Police Department, where he specialized in spatial analysis and prediction of serial crime. He is the chair of the Professional Applications and Measures Committee for the International Association of Investigative Psychologists. He currently develops professional software and advanced analytical methodologies for justice, defense, and intelligence organizations. Mr. Helms works closely with Bair Software, Inc., a leading consulting and software production firm in the crime and intelligence analysis community. He currently splits his time between Denver, Colorado and Washington D.C. Mr. Helms has made numerous appearances on television and radio, and has been featured in a television documentary. He has spoken at MAPS, IACA, CCIAA, NIJ, and ACJS conferences in the USA, and the International Investigative Psychology Conference in the UK.

Sean Bair is the president of Bair Software, Inc., a Colorado-based software company dedicated to providing consulting, training, and cutting-edge solutions to the law enforcement, intelligence, and defense communities. He is the former assistant director at the National Law Enforcement and Corrections Technology Center, as well as a former crime analyst and police officer for the Tempe (AZ) Police Department. He holds an MBA degree from the University of Denver. Mr. Bair has made numerous appearances on television and radio, providing commentary or instruction on the analysis of crime and other law enforcement related matters. He has trained thousands of analysts, officers and investigators around the world in the analysis of crime. The associated website www.bairsoftware.com contains supplemental material that provides a richer learning experience.

Section I

Introduction of Crime Analysis

Introduction

Crime analysis is an emerging discipline within the field of public safety. In its current state of near infancy, the functions, techniques, products, and even the nomenclature critical to this new profession are still being defined. When one becomes a police officer, one enters a standardized and accredited training program. Every department knows the specifics of each officer training each officer and knows that each officer demonstrated competency in core skills upon completion of the program. When an agency looks to hire an officer, it knows that the officer has the skills necessary to protect and serve the public. This is not the case for a crime analyst. The skills of crime analysts in the United States vary drastically from place to place, even within a single law enforcement agency. In one department, an analyst may only have the skills and functions necessary for data entry and yet hold the title of crime analyst. In another, the analyst may provide valid and useful spatial, statistical, and temporal analysis to the department, which in turn uses the analyst's results to make more informed and effective decisions. As in any emerging profession, efforts are being made to standardize the skills and training of crime analysts. Within the next decade or so, the skills and training of crime analysts and crime analysis units will be as commonplace and standardized as those of police officers.

Crime analysis is a collection of police functions that provide analytical and decision support to law enforcement and public safety agencies. Although the analysis of crime is implicit in the title, crime analysts also study police activity and may range farther afield in support of their mission. The crime analyst is a support unit, not a primary police unit. This is no trivial role, however. The crime analyst is no less vital to the sworn police officer than his patrol car or radio. When properly utilized, the analyst can provide direction and guidance that act as a force multiplier. A typical crime analyst can be expected to improve the efficiency of the investigators and patrol force; thereby effectively increasing the agency's ability to serve the community to a greater degree than a single new officer or detective.

The crime analyst's role is to support decision making by police officers and administrators through effective analysis and presentation of information. Although the analyst is seldom a decision maker, no part of police operations should be aloof from scrutiny by the crime analyst. The ability to effectively retrieve, analyze, and disseminate information means that the analyst acts as a decision supporter. It is the place of the analyst to recommend and advocate effective actions and strategy based on her or his professional expertise. While the analyst should not be giving orders to sworn personnel, decisions made without benefit of analytical support are unlikely to be the best decisions.

Crime analysts must not only be proficient at statistical techniques and mathematics, but specialists in technology as well. The typical crime analyst must have a comprehensive understanding of data and databases, the software used to retrieve those data and analyze them, but also the personality and credibility to present his or her finding to a group who does not understand either. An analyst must use technology and delve into disciplines that others make their careers from in order to provide the department with information that is timely, accurate, and operationally useful.

Most crime analysts now recognize four main divisions of the profession: tactical, strategic, operational, and administrative. Although many departments are beginning to see the importance of specialization, most analysts still must manage their day to provide service across all four areas. In doing so, analysts may be relegated to the role of jack-of-all-trades, but masters of none. In this introductory chapter, we will briefly explore various definitions that have been advanced for the four types of crime analysis. We will begin with the authors' own simple, albeit broad, definitions of these categories:

- Administrative analysis is the study of police efficiency and effectiveness.
- Strategic analysis is the study of crime trends and statistics.
- Tactical analysis is the identification, analysis, and resolution of crime incidents, patterns, series, and sprees.
- Operational analysis is the study and support of specific police activities.

Tactical crime analysis is the comprehensive identification, evaluation, analysis, and resolution of specific criminal activity problems. These problems are typically categorized as being incidents, patterns, series, or sprees. Tactical problems are characterized as being distinct from mainstream criminal activity due to the presence of recognizable identifiers which distinguish them as belonging to an identifiable category. Incidents are unique crime events unrelated to other events, but distinguishable from mainstream criminal activity because of their significantly unique properties. Incidents demand directed attention (i.e., a schoolroom spree-killing). Patterns are criminal activities that are related by a number of characteristics such as location, *modus operandi (MO)*, time, or day. However, critical incidents do not have sufficient suspect information to either confirm or refute the causality behind the related incidents. Series are sets of criminal activity that are believed to share the same causality. By causality, we mean that the same offender, group of offenders, criminal organization, gang, or enterprise is responsible for planning or perpetrating the involved crimes. The aim of the tactical crime analyst is to resolve each individual problem as quickly and decisively as possible for the immediate benefit of the public safety.

Strategic crime analysis is the comprehensive identification, evaluation, analysis, and resolution of non-specific criminal activity problems. These problems are descriptive of mainstream criminal activity; the strategic crime analyst, therefore, deals with those problems making up the vast majority of threats to the public safety. The aim of the strategic crime analyst is to increase public safety by reducing the level of crime throughout his or her jurisdiction.

Operational crime analysis is the comprehensive identification, evaluation, analysis, and resolution of specific police activity problems. These problems are characterized as being distinct from mainstream police activity because of the unusual and atypical nature of each problem. Police activity problems involve activities initiated and performed by police, law enforcement, and public safety authorities (e.g., patrol operations, traffic stops, surveillances, warrant services, etc.), as opposed to criminal activity, which are crimes perpetrated by offenders. The goal of the operational crime analyst is to resolve each individual problem as quickly and decisively as possible for the improvement of the public safety through the successful police operation.

Administrative crime analysis is the comprehensive identification, evaluation, analysis, and resolution of both non-specific police activity problems. These problems are characterized as being descriptive of mainstream police activity problems; the administrative crime analyst therefore deals with those problems making up the vast majority of problems relating to police activity. The aim of the administrative crime analyst is to increase public safety by increasing the efficiency of police activity.

In recent years, tactical and operational analysis have somewhat gained in ascendancy over the previously dominant strategic and administrative analytical paradigms. The prevalent acceptance of concepts such as problem oriented policing (POP), community oriented policing (COP), crime prevention through environmental design (CPTED), the recurrence of high-profile criminal incidents such as spree-killings and terrorist attacks, and the public and police fascination with serial offenders have all conspired to increase the focus on tactical and operational problems. This has resulted in a corresponding de-emphasis on strategic and administrative functions as resources are prioritized.

In the United States, tactical crime analysis has become a type of analysis where analysts are beginning to specialize. Many departments are hiring a tactical crime analyst because the functions require so much of an analyst's day. A typical tactical crime analyst in the United States spends the bulk of his or her day reading police reports, scanning for trends in criminal activity. The analyst plays a game of mental Mahjong while trying to remember key facts from each case as new cases are stored in his or her brain's database. This is obviously the least efficient and effective way to identify a trend.

It is in the area of tactical crime analysis that technological advances have occurred in crime analysis and specialized software has begun to emerge. Applications are now specifically written to identify trends in crime data. Once identified, software specific to tactical analysis enables the analyst to analyze and predict the possible next strike or optimal location to look for the offender. The analyst now plays a key role in the investigation and apprehension of a serial predator.

Statistical and geographical programs that enable an analyst to study activity for administrative and strategic analysis have existed for decades. Moreover, the techniques used to conduct these analyses for a department are proven statistical techniques. However, in the area of tactical crime analysis, as previously mentioned, there is no standard technique that is the agreed-upon means to identify crime patterns. In Chapter 5, the authors present a method they have developed that is beginning to gain recognition and has been adopted by many departments around the world.

In the area of prediction, analysts are using specialized tools to conduct next-event forecasting and geographic profiling. Next-event forecasting attempts to predict the next probable location of a strike in a crime series. Geographic profiling attempts to determine likely anchor points that an offender may have derived from the locations he or she has chosen to strike. Both techniques now have specialized tools and software that can be used to assist the analyst in performing these functions.

In the United States, crime analysis is a mandatory function if the agency wishes to become an accredited law enforcement agency. Accreditation enables a department to seek federal funding through grants and other financial assistance. Given the financial incentive, many departments are seeking to hire their first crime analyst, or to promote someone from within to that position. This has resulted in a number of departments promoting someone ill-qualified for the job.

Today, a number of colleges and universities provide curricula geared toward crime analysis. A decade ago, this was not the case. In fact, the vast majority of analysts in positions today have no formal training in crime analysis. Most have come from college with justice studies, criminal justice, or sociology degrees, but with no emphasis placed on crime analysis in their coursework. As a result, analysts may have an understanding of criminological theory and concepts, but no formal training on how to perform crime analysis.

Conclusion

Crime analysis and those who perform it are essential to a public safety organization. Decisions in an agency today are, or should be, guided by the crime analysis unit. Every function in an organization from officer acquisition, resource allocation, beat reconfiguration, identification of problem addresses or areas, comparison of crime from month to month, or year to year, and even identifying and predicting crime series falls within the realm and responsibility of crime analysis. The following chapters shed light on tactical crime analysis by providing a solid theoretical foundation and unique set of methods and procedures from which to draw upon to better prepare an individual charged with this tremendous responsibility.

Understanding Criminal Behavior

Introduction

For many students of criminology and criminal justice, the class they fear the most, besides statistics, is criminological theory. A myriad of theories proclaim to explain the actions of criminals. These include confusing hypotheses and more confusing research studies that either refute or prove research results that ultimately seem to contradict everything and prove nothing. For most students, one class is enough to turn them off to the study of criminal actions forever. Yet the study of criminological theory is essential to understanding crime patterns and developing effective police responses. While many within policing do not like to admit it, all police tactics are based on some form of criminological theory. Without a sound understanding of why criminals offend, we cannot develop effective responses to crimes or mount effective investigations of crime series. From a tactical crime analysis perspective, understanding criminal behavior and motivations provides assistance in determining potential victims, target areas, and response strategies. For this reason, a sound understanding of the main criminological theories is essential.

Rather than an in-depth discussion of all criminological theory, this chapter will focus on a few theories that are most relevant to understanding individual criminal behavior and tactical crime analysis. Specifically, this chapter will cover the opportunity theories of routine activities, crime pattern theory, and rational choice. The goal is to provide readers with a brief discussion of the theories most associated with serial crime and to show the importance of these theories to tactical crime analysis. At the end of this chapter, readers should have a better understanding of these theories and how they are applicable to offender behavior and tactical crime analysis.

Rational Choice

More than any other criminological theory, rational choice theory attributes crime to purposive behavior on behalf of the offender. In a nutshell, rational choice espouses the theory that offenders rationally think through the potential costs and benefits of committing a crime and then choose whether or not to the commit the crime based on this rational calculus. Offenders seek to maximize their pleasure and minimize their pain, and thus choose to commit crimes in which the risk of apprehension is outweighed by the potential reward (Taylor and Harrell, 1996). Heavily influenced by the research of economists such as Becker (1968), Heineke (1978), and Crouch (1979), rational choice is closely related to classical criminology as envisioned by 18th century philosophers Bentham and Beccaria with the exception that classical criminology focused more on laws and deterrence whereas rational choice focuses more on offender behavior.

Within rational choice, there are two main branches of the theory—pure models and bounded models of rational choice (Akers, 2008). The pure model is the more rigid and posits that an offender chooses to commit a crime with full knowledge and free will, taking into account all possible risks and rewards before making a decision. While this pure model receives the majority of discussion from critics of rational choice, it is rarely put forth by rational choice theorists (Akers, 2008) because purely rational decision making is a rarity in any decision-making process, legal or illegal. Such a decision-making process in which every probable consequence of an action is carefully weighed has yet to be fully documented by researchers. Completely weighing all possible consequences would not only make every decision a long and laborious process, it would be nearly impossible because knowing all possible outcomes is nearly impossible in every situation, especially when dealing with criminal actions. A more plausible theoretical framework is the one put forth by the bounded rational choice model, in which offenders think before they act, even if only for a moment, taking into account some of the benefits and costs of committing an offense (Felson and Clarke, 1998). Thus, bounded rationality provides a more realistic approach to rational decision making in which offenders weigh only some of the potential outcomes and for a limited time before choosing to commit a crime. In this model, the offender's decision making is based almost solely on that which is most evident and immediate, while ignoring costs and benefits that are more remote to the current decision (Felson and Clarke, 1998). An example would be when an offender encounters an individual who leaves his car running while he hurries into a store to make a purchase. An offender presented with this situation might look around and seeing no one, decide to steal the car. While this thought process appears to involve at least some rational thought concerning possible capture, it is limited to immediate capture and does not involve longer term consequences. In this bounded rational choice model, little thought is actually given to eventual punishment or the long-term effects of the potential crime.

From a tactical crime analysis standpoint, rational choice is often used to help explain how offenders choose victims, search areas for crimes and other elements associated with target selection. Offenders will choose victims that provide the greatest reward although not necessarily the least chance of getting caught. Crime analysts often use this theory to help determine what offenders desire in a crime target as well as to create response strategies that may remove the reward for the offender. While rational choice cannot explain why a particular offender thinks one target is better than another, it does provide insight into what offenders think is a suitable target and what areas are useful for searching for targets based on empirical findings. In particular, many researchers use crime data concerning burglary and commercial robbery locations to infer characteristics of a target that make it attractive for an offender. In many ways rational choice is a natural companion to discussions of behavioral geography (see Chapter 3) because it focuses on how an offender's knowledge of geography impacts his target selection.

Research Findings

The history of rational choice within criminological theory is shorter than other theories, but the amount of research that has been conducted is substantial. Research into rational choice has largely been split along the lines of pure and bounded rational choice models, with bounded rational choice receiving far more research than pure models. While this bias towards bounded rational choice models might seem cause for concern, it is mostly a factor of the reluctance of researchers to put forth a pure rational choice model for testing. Researchers have been more likely to develop models of rational choice that take into account limitations and constraints on choices through lack of information and other influences on criminal behavior (Akers, 2008). In terms of support for a bounded or limited rationality in criminal offending, ample support appears largely in the form of interview research. In a study of repeat property offenders, Tunnell (1990) found that offenders rarely thought about the risks associated with crime and instead focused on the anticipated rewards. While their actions indicated that they indeed did think about getting caught, as evidenced by planning of escape routes and techniques to minimize capture and arrest, concerns about negative consequences were minimized and put out of their minds. Offenders in the study were unable to make reasonable assessments of the risks of arrest and were largely uninformed about legal penalties in the state where they were offending, indicating an inability to make a purely rational decision about offending (Tunnell, 1990). Research by Cromwell and associates (1991) of residential burglary offenders also indicates a level of bounded rationality. In the Cromwell (1991) study, professional burglars were found to have engaged in partial calculations of risk and reward before deciding to burglarize a house and that their "careful plans" were anything but careful. While most burglars reported following careful plans when burglarizing homes, closer inspection revealed that most plans were loose guidelines that often gave way to opportunity and situational factors (Cromwell et al, 1991). Paulsen (2005), in his study of commercial robbery offenders, found that offenders were often contradictory in discussions of the rational calculus related to their crimes. Although offenders regularly stated that they were not concerned about apprehension or going to prison, their discussions of planning were often elaborate and included numerous methods designed to prevent capture. Similar findings have been reported in other studies of burglars and robbers (Rengert and Wasilchick, 2000; Wright and Decker, 1994; Wright and Decker, 1997). Overall, research into the bounded rational choice model provides ample support for the idea that criminals do, in fact, think rationally when deciding to commit a crime or not. However, rather than finding support for a pure rational choice model where all rewards and punishments are carefully weighed before a decision is made, criminals use a limited decision-making process.

Although a fair amount of research provides support for a bounded or limited rational choice model, there are many who have roundly criticized rational choice theory. Chief among criticism of rational choice is the idea that it is impossible to truly test a rational choice model of crime because offenders thoughts on choice decisions cannot be directly studied (Jeffery and Zahn, 1993). In particular, decision choices can only be studied through interview not through direct study, and interviews can only provide information on verbal behavior and not thought processes (Jeffery and Zahn, 1993). Thus, interviewing offenders about their decision-making processes only provides insight into what offenders say was their basis for decision, not the actual thought process involved in committing the crime. Moreover, rational choice researchers are often accused of using circular logic because researchers conclude offenders are rational based in their actions and then use the concept of rationality to explain the same behaviors (Akers, 2008). The other major criticism of rational choice is the lack of sound empirical studies employing only variables of expected utility or reward (Akers, 2008). Akers (2008) criticizes the research of Paternoster (1989a; 1989b) as an example of research that includes variables that make it indistinguishable from other nonrational choice research. Specifically, Akers (2008) claims that Paternoster and others employ enough sociological and psychological background variables to make empirical results indistinguishable from other theories that are in conflict with rational choice. These findings, while not casting doubt on the validity of rational choice theory as an explanation of crime, do raise doubts as to claims of empirical support for the theory.

Overall, there is ample evidence to indicate that offenders do employ limited models of rationality when making decisions about crime. The majority of the evidence in support of rational choice comes from interview research and indicates that most rational decision making occurs in the areas of target selection and search area strategies. While there has been criticism of the research on rational choice, researchers continue to support the idea that offenders employ some amount of rationality when making crime oriented decisions.

Routine Activities Theory

Closely related to rational choice theory is the routine activities theory, a theory that proposes crime is a result of the convergence in time and space of three simple elements: a motivated offender, suitable target, and the absence of a capable guardian (Cohen and Felson, 1979). In a nutshell, the theory proposes that crime victimization increases when a motivated offender converges in time and space with a suitable victim when no formal or informal guardians are present to deter the offender. Importantly, the theory takes its name from the original assumption that these three elements are directly related to the routine activities of potential victims and guardians (Cohen and Felson, 1979). In particular, Cohen and Felson (1979: 593) define routine activities as "recurrent prevalent activities which provide for basic population and individual needs, whatever their biological or cultural origins ... including formalized work, leisure, social interaction, learning ... which occur at home, in jobs away from home, and in other activities away from home."

In order to better understand this theory, it is best to further explore the concepts of motivated offenders, suitable targets, and capable guardians. First in the routine activities equation is the motivated offender. Of the three essential elements, motivated offenders and what constitutes a motivated offender has probably been the least discussed (Akers, 2008). Most theorists have taken from the writings of Cohen and Felson (1979) and later writings by Felson that motivation in an offender is an assumed characteristic to which there is no real cause attributed. In essence, the routine activities theory does not try to explain why there are motivated offenders, only that for whatever reason (insert your favorite theory here), offenders are motivated to offend and when they converge in time and space with the other elements a crime occurs. Routine activities is not concerned with why offenders are motivated only that they are.

Much more has been written and discussed about suitable targets, which are described as any person or thing that may evoke "criminal inclinations" in a motivated offender (Felson, 1983). In general, characteristics that evoke criminal inclinations include the value of a target, its visibility, ease of access and escape, and its portability (Felson, 1983). These characteristics have been refined into the popular routine activities acronym VIVA, which stands for value, inertia, visibility, and access (Felson and Clarke, 1998). Value refers to the worth, either monetary or symbolic, of the target to an offender with the higher value seen as making a target more desirable. Inertia refers to ability of the target to be taken, with targets that are small (jewelry) or easily movable (cars) being seen as attractive. Visibility refers to how visible a target is to an offender. The more visible targets are seen as more suitable. Finally, access refers to how easily a target can be accessed by an offender and those that are easily accessible are considered more suitable. While each of these elements on its own is important to the suitability of a target, it is the combination of them that makes it easier to determine relative suitability and helps to explain the increased victimization of some targets. In particular, targets that have high value, low inertia, and high visibility like iPods and their mugger-white headphones, are particularly attractive to motivated offenders and are a more suitable target than LCD TVs which, although high in value, are not as low on inertia due to their bulk. While these characteristics are usually applied to property crimes, suitability of human targets can also be determined to a degree by factors such as age, physical size, and gender. Importantly, Cohen and Felson (1979) claim that changes in the characteristics of these suitability elements (more things being highly valuable, low in inertia and easily visible and accessible) can result in increases in crime without any change in the offender population.

The last element is capable guardians, which refers to anyone or anything that can protect a target from victimization (Eck and Weisburd, 1995). Capable guardians range from formal guardians such as police to informal guardians such as friends, family and neighbors, and mechanical guardians such as alarms, guns, and other protection devices. While many people think of capable guardians as police only, Felson (1994) actually downplays the importance of police as guardians in favor of informal guardians who provide protection through normal daily interaction and presence. This means that the routine activities of potential victims may not only facilitate criminal victimization, but they may also prevent it as well. Specifically, streets that are active and full of people are less likely to be the scenes of victimizations because the normal flow of foot traffic acts as a capable guardian.

From a tactical crime analysis standpoint, the routine activities theory is similar to rational choice in that it is often used to help explain how offenders choose victims, search areas for crimes and other elements associated with target selection. According to routine activities, offenders will converge with suitable targets in the process of their daily routines. Thus, factors such as travel routes, work locations, and residence locations will all be areas where an offender will find seek and find suitable targets. On a basic level, these ideas, when flipped theoretically, provide the basis for basic geographic profiling. In particular, if you know where offenders find their suitable targets, you should in a sense know their routine activity locations as well since the crime locations are probably along routes they travel on a routine basis. These ideas and their full implications will be explored further in the discussion of crime pattern theory as well as the chapter on behavioral geography.

Research Findings

Overall there has been a wealth of empirical research into routine activities and its major claims, much of which has found support for the relationship between victim lifestyles, routine activities, and criminal victimization. In particular, research has indicated that the risk of criminal victimization varies according to the circumstances and locations in which people place themselves and their property (Cohen and Felson, 1979). Those whose routine activities are concentrated in and around their homes will be less likely to interact with offenders and will experience lower levels of both property and personal crime than those whose routine activities take them away from home (Messner and Tardiff, 1985). Similar studies have revealed that victimization varies by age and gender as well as the extent to which people stay at home or go out at night. Those who go out at night are more likely to be victims (Kennedy and Forde, 1990).

In addition to the lifestyles and routine activities of individuals, research has found that certain locations within a city are also likely to be the site of a convergence of offenders and targets in the absence of capable guardians. Sherman (1989), in his study of hot spots of crime in Minneapolis, found that most crime reports came from only 3% of all locations within the city. While Sherman did not have an explanation for why those locations were so attractive to crime, he hypothesized that something about them related to the convergence of offenders and targets in the absence of capable guardians (Sherman, 1989). Other researchers have explored attractive targets, with findings indicating that unoccupied residences contribute to higher burglary rates and that even mundane things such as good weather (sunny and warm) can contribute to increased crime by getting people out and away from home (Hipp, Bauer, Curna, and Bollen, 2004).

Despite the generally positive research findings regarding the routine activities theory, there are a couple of general criticisms of the theory. First, and perhaps most important from a theoretical standpoint, is the fact that there have been few if any full tests of the entire theory. While numerous studies have looked at different aspects of routine activities (victims, offender, and capable guardians), only a few have ever directly measured the key concepts of the theory (Robinson, 1999). Most studies have used proxies for one or more of the elements of routine activities. For example, Cohen and Felson (1979) created a household-activity ratio associated with activities away from home in order to measure the level of guardianship at home and its impact on burglary and other crimes in the home. Others have measured criminal opportunities using aggregate measures of employment and housing data as well as measured guardianship using measures of police expenditures and employment figures (Stahura and Sloan, 1988). The other major criticism is the lack of discussion as to what constitutes a motivated offender (Akers,

2008). Specifically, if all people are potentially motivated offenders, is the presence of a motivated offender assumed by the presence of any one individual near a potential target? This lack makes testing the theory difficult as well as determining the true levels of capable guardianship and the vulnerability of targets.

Overall, routine activities has been shown to have strong empirical support as well as clear policy implications for both crime prevention and tactical crime analysis. While the general propositions of routine activities theory are largely common sense, Cohen and Felson and others have taken these "common sense and empirical realities and woven them into a coherent framework for understanding the variations in criminal victimization by time and place" (Akers, 2008).

Crime Pattern Theory

As with routine activities, crime pattern theory focuses on the elements that converge to create a criminal event, although with more emphasis on how offenders select and search for suitable targets. Leaning heavily on rational choice, routine activities, and environmental criminology, crime pattern theory focuses on the convergence in time and space of offender motivation and target characteristics across an opportunity structure (Brantingham and Brantingham, 1993). In particular, the theory focuses on how once the desire to commit a crime is triggered an offender uses a mental template to choose targets from within a search area that is highly influenced by an offenders' own spatial knowledge. Similar to routine activities, the majority of the focus of crime pattern theory is not on the triggering of criminal motivation, but rather on the creation of an offender's template and the search process that lead to a criminal event. This target selection process of an offender "depends on mental templates used to shape searches for targets of victims and to predefine the characteristics of a suitable target or suitable place for finding a target" (Brantingham and Brantingham, 1993). These mental templates guide an offender in determining what is a suitable or good target as well as what is a bad target (Felson, 1987). These templates are then applied by offenders to search for targets across an area that is largely determined by an offenders routine activities and activity space (see Chapter 3). Thus the routine activities of an offender, as well as those of victims, will shape the distribution of crime and will have a pronounced impact on the pattern of crime over time and space (Eck and Weisburd, 1995; Brantingham and Brantingham, 1993).

Unlike other theories that are fairly simple in their logic and propositions, crime pattern theory offers a detailed series of propositions that help to define the theory and understand criminal events. The propositions of crime

Understanding Criminal Behavior

pattern theory as laid out by Brantingham and Brantingham (1993:261-264) are as follows:

1. Criminal events are best viewed as the end points in a decision process or sequence of steps. This process may not always involve conscious and explicit decision making, but in almost all cases results in rational behavior (Brantingham and Brantingham, 1993: 261).
2. The decisions themselves are neither random nor unpredictable and are reconstructable (Brantingham and Brantingham, 1993: 261). While these decisions may be part of an unconscious or subconscious process, they are not random in nature.
3. The decision process leading to a crime begins with an offender who is ready for crime and has sufficient motivation and knowledge to observe and act upon an available criminal opportunity (Brantingham and Brantingham, 1993: 261).
4. Criminal motivations and states of readiness come from diverse but understandable sources (Brantingham and Brantingham, 1993: 261).
5. Whether the offender's general state of readiness leads to crime is a function of psychological, social, and cultural background of the individual offender as well environmental factors such as available opportunities (Brantingham and Brantingham, 1993: 262).
6. The number and sequence of decision points in the process that lead to a criminal event vary with the type and quantity of crime (Brantingham and Brantingham, 1993: 262). Thus, the decision process involved in committing a crime is crime specific and goes beyond simple divisions into property and violent crimes.
7. The level of crime readiness in any offender varies over time and place given his or her background and site specific features (Brantingham and Brantingham, 1993: 262).
8. Neither motivated offenders nor opportunities for crime are uniformly distributed in space and time (Brantingham and Brantingham, 1993: 262). Locations of targets and potential offenders vary greatly by time of day, characteristics of the target, and the site of the target (Brantingham and Brantingham, 1993: 262).
9. The suitability of a target is a function of the characteristics of the target and the characteristics of the target's surroundings (Brantingham and Brantingham, 1993: 263).
10. The identification of what makes a good or suitable target is a multistaged process contained within a general environment that can involve either a few or many stages (Brantingham and Brantingham, 1993: 263).

11. Individuals develop images about what surrounds them, which make up templates of what constitutes a good target and includes more than simple characteristics of the target but also includes issues of location and surroundings (Brantingham and Brantingham, 1993: 263).
12. Templates vary by specific crimes, offenders, and the general context for the crime such that what makes a good target for one type of crime and offender, may not for another offender (Brantingham and Brantingham, 1993: 264).

Importantly, although Brantingham and Brantingham (1993) view crime as complex, they claim that there are discernable patterns for crimes and criminals at both detailed and general levels of analysis. Specifically, they state that "crimes are patterned; decisions to commit crimes are patterned; and the process of committing crimes is all patterned" (Brantingham and Brantingham, 1993: 264). From a tactical crime analysis perspective, crime pattern theory has numerous implications regarding how to "read" a criminal and his template and search strategy in order to develop investigative strategies. Specifically, criminals search for crimes in areas determined largely by their routine activities and select targets consistently based on their mental templates. Moreover, crime pattern theory also reinforces the idea that while individual criminals and crime series differ in motivations, templates, and search strategies, there are discernable patterns that can be determined through analysis. These patterns can be used both to assist in developing crime prevention strategies as well as to develop leads and strategies in ongoing investigations.

Research Findings

While the various different propositions of crime pattern theory are based on extensive research for which there is enormous support, at this point there has been no formal test of the accuracy of the theory as a whole. Although good at "theoretically" explaining any crime, the theory and its individual propositions are based on expansive research, but no researcher has empirically tested the theory on any individual crime (Ratcliffe, 2006; Tita and Griffiths, 2005). While Brantingham and Brantingham (1993) in laying out the theory discuss how it can explain theft of office supplies, residential burglary, and serial rape, they provide no empirical evidence of how well the theory actually explains these different crimes. While this lack of empirical research is indeed a major drawback, it does not diminish the importance of the theory in explaining criminal events. Rather, most would argue that the lack of empirical research in support of the theory is because of both the complex nature of the theory and the difficulty in testing the theory's key aspects. While criminals undoubtedly employ some manner of mental template in choosing suitable targets, empirically verifying those mental templates is exceptionally difficult. As Jeffery and Zahn (1993) pointed out, testing for such mental templates requires interviews and verbal discussions, which is not the same as the internal thought process that researchers seek to understand. Overall, while there is a complete lack of research findings in support of the "complete" theory, the fact that crime pattern theory is based on well researched and defensible propositions makes it a viable and useful theory of explaining both crime series and crime patterns.

Opportunity Makes the Thief

Guided by rational choice, routine activities, and crime patterns theory, Marcus Felson and Ron Clarke conducted a research project for the British Home Office in 1998 to look into how these theories impacted opportunities for criminals to commit crimes. In particular, they looked to show that by understanding criminological theories and the ways they influence offender choices and opportunities, police can have a dramatic impact on crime prevention. Within this research, Felson and Clarke (1998) came up with 10 principles of crime opportunity that they felt were particularly important to reducing opportunities for crime and reducing crime. While some of these 10 principles are more geared toward situational crime prevention techniques, overall there are many implications for crime analysis in general and tactical crime prevention in particular.

The first of the 10 principles is that opportunity plays a role in causing all crime (Felson and Clarke, 1998). Traditionally, researchers have thought that opportunity only plays a role in property crimes such as burglary, theft, and robbery because the earliest examples linking opportunity to crime all dealt with property crime (Felson and Clarke, 1998). Recent research has indicated that all crimes, including crimes of violence, are influenced by levels of opportunity and design factors. Research by Felson (1998) found that fights in bars are strongly influenced by design and management issues, with larger bars that serve predominantly young male clients who do not know each other being more likely to have fights break out than other bar configurations. Results are attributable to the anonymity of the customers, the large numbers of young and potentially aggressive clients, and the high possibility of incivilities between customers who have been drinking. Results also indicate that opportunity is a factor in sexual offenses, homicide, aggravated assaults, drug dealing, and even white collar crime (Felson and Clarke, 1998). From a tactical crime analysis aspect this finding is important because it reinforces the idea that serial crime is largely a crime of opportunity and not an idiosyncratic decision by individual criminals. Importantly, investigative and response strategies can be developed that focus on reducing opportunities and on potential targets that produce similar opportunities as prior victims. Examples include target profiling where potential targets are profiled to determine the degree to which potential targets have similar levels of opportunities and investigative strategies are then focused on those potential targets.

A second principle dealing with opportunity and crime is that crime opportunities are highly specific to the individual crime (Felson and Clarke, 1998). Rather than a common set of opportunity characteristics that apply to all crimes, opportunities for crimes vary by each type of crime and each offender subset (Felson and Clarke, 1998). The implication from this finding is that it is important to focus on evaluating the opportunities for each type of crime in order to determine what crime prevention and investigative tactics might help reduce crime. Thus, prevention tactics will be different for commercial robbery than for street robbery, with analysis helping to determine the differences and providing guidance in programs that may be successful. From a tactical crime analysis perspective, this finding points to the need to determine if an offender is seeking particular opportunities in order to tailor investigative strategies toward that offender.

The third principle is that crime opportunities are concentrated in time and place (Felson and Clarke, 1998). Influenced heavily by routine activities, this principle points out that despite the seemingly uniform distribution of people throughout an urban area, crime is not uniformly distributed, but clustered in time and space. Examples clustering include the presence of increased crime around crime attractors and crime generators, spatial patterning of commercial robberies on main arterial roads, and temporal changes in crime volume. Research by Paulsen (2005) found that commercial robbery offenders were more likely to select targets that were isolated geographically even over other factors such as potential value from the robbery. From a tactical crime analysis standpoint, this principle is important in that it reinforces the need for analysis of opportunity structures and determining what areas are "hot" and what areas "cold" in terms of potential targets.

The fourth principle is that crime opportunities depend on everyday movements of activity (Felson and Clarke, 1998). As stated by routine activities, crime patterns are heavily influenced by our normal and legal patterns, be they patterns of travel, work, or behavior. Offenders are keen observers of these patterns and use them to determine suitable targets for crime. For example, residential burglary spikes upward when people leave for work and downward when the workday is ended (Felson and Clarke, 1998). Implied in this principle is the need to analyze the mundane and routine for the clues it can provide about patterns of crime and suitable targets. Specifically, this indicates the need to analyze road layouts and traffic patterns, zoning and land use patterns, temporal and seasonal changes, all of which impact patterns of crime and victimization. From a tactical crime analysis perspective, these ideas underlie the practice of geographic profiling and its understanding of how offenders select targets along their routine travel routes and near their routine nodes. Thus, understanding the routine and mundane can provide valuable insight into seemingly random and highly unusual crimes.

The fifth principle of opportunity and crime is that one crime produces opportunities for another (Felson and Clarke, 1998). This principle points to the fact that in committing one crime an offender is often exposed to opportunities to commit many other crimes. An offender committing a burglary may, through opportunity, have the potential to commit a weapons crime, assault or even a sexual assault, all by entering a residence for the purpose of burglary. As can be seen, most opportunities that spring from a crime are random in nature and difficult to identify beforehand. From a tactical crime analysis standpoint, the implication is to use analysis to determine the opportunity a criminal event may produce, such as a chance for repeat victimization of a particular location. Using this analysis to guide crime prevention and investigative strategies can be highly beneficial in developing leads and determining where to put assets in ongoing crime series.

Opportunity and crime principle number six is that some targets offer more tempting crime opportunities than others (Felson and Clarke, 1998). In addition to the VIVA method for determining the attractiveness of consumer targets, several researchers have explored this idea in relation to property and violent crime. Paulsen (2005) interviewed commercial robbery offenders to determine what characteristics make a target attractive from both spatial and financial perspectives. In the research, Paulsen (2005) found that isolated, convenience stores with back road access, single cashiers, and windows obstructed by posters are the most attractive targets. In addition, Rachel Armitage (2007) has explored characteristics that make residences attractive targets, even going so far as to create a vulnerability checklist for use by analysts. Residences that are near an open space, have signs of desertion, and access in the rear from paths or alleys are the most attractive residential targets. These findings are consistent with crime pattern theory that states that the suitability of a target is a function of the target's characteristics and surroundings (Brantingham and Brantingham, 1993). Not only do some targets offer more opportunity than others, but individual offenders value some targets more than others based on their own templates for crime and their search areas. From a tactical crime analysis perspective, determining the attractiveness of targets can be useful in ongoing crime series investigations because it helps identify potential targets.

The seventh principle is that social and technological changes produce new crime opportunities (Felson and Clarke, 1998). While seemingly a simple idea, this principle actually helps to chart the temporal changes in crime victimization. Specifically, victimization related to new products is inversely related to the length of time an item has been sold and the cost of the item.

When goods are first developed, they are generally very expensive and of limited quantity and market, making them an attractive target financially. However, the longer a product is around the less expensive and more saturated it becomes within the market, the less attractive it becomes as a target. An example of this phenomenon is the CD player. When first introduced, it was very expensive, but as time has passed the cost declined and market saturation increased, making it less attractive as a target. From a tactical crime analysis perspective, this principle is important in determining target attractiveness for prevention and investigative purposes. As with almost all targets, there will be a discernable spatial pattern in their distribution, particularly when they are first introduced. Analyzing these patterns can help determine areas of highest target availability, something that can be used to focus both crime prevention and investigative resources.

The eighth opportunity and crime principle is also the most well known; crime can be prevented by reducing opportunities (Felson and Clarke, 1998). This principle has such a strong empirical basis that it is the basis for several well known crime prevention and design-oriented crime reduction strategies including defensible space, Crime Prevention Through Environmental Design (CPTED), and situational crime prevention (Felson and Clarke, 1998). While each technique is different in its methods, all focus on using natural, practical and simple methods (Felson and Clarke, 1998). Traditionally, these techniques have been employed mostly within crime prevention, but their use in tactical crime analysis is currently being explored.

The ninth principle is that reducing opportunity does not usually displace crime (Felson and Clarke, 1998). While many practitioners and academics believe that any type of opportunity reduction strategy simply causes displacement of crime, research has shown this not to be the case. Because criminals commit most crimes within their activity spaces, most will not displace their offending unless there are ample opportunities available to them in another geographic area of their activity space. Simply put, most offenders will not move to completely different geographic areas because they do not know the locations, even if there area targets appear to be attractive. Moreover, those cases where displacement has occurred have shown that crime levels were lower in the "new" area as compared to the original location, resulting in a net reduction in crime (Felson and Clarke, 1998). From a tactical crime analysis perspective, these opportunity reduction strategies can prove to be beneficial investigative strategies because when attractive targets are eliminated, criminals may be forced to search in areas outside their comfort areas.

The final opportunity and crime principle is the principle that focused opportunity reduction can produce wider declines in crime (Felson and Clarke, 1998). Closely related to the previous principle, opportunity reduction strategies not only do not induce displacement, they often produce reductions in crime across a city at large. Rather than crime displacing to new areas, research has shown that the benefits of opportunity reduction are displaced or diffused to other areas. Specifically, the implementation of opportunity reduction programs often results in other crimes declining or in benefits or reduction expanding outside the focused area. While this principle does not have a great impact on tactical crime analysis, it reinforces the importance of reducing opportunities as a crime prevention strategy.

Conclusion

Although many practitioners have a deep pathological fear of criminological theory, much can be learned from theory that can be of practical use in policing in general and in tactical crime analysis in particular. While this chapter did not provide an in-depth discussion of all criminological theory, it did provide a solid discussion of those theories most relevant to tactical crime analysis. In particular, the discussions of this chapter provided the tactical analyst with an expanded set of tools through which to work on analyzing criminal behavior and active crime series. Rather than going about analyses atheoretically, analysts now have the ability to understand and analyze crime series differently and apply theoretical principles that have true practical implications.

Behavioral Geography 3

Introduction to Behavioral Geography

One of the most important tools in the arsenal of a tactical crime analyst is a sound understanding of both criminological theory (why criminals commit crime) as well as behavioral geography (spatial decision-making process). In combination, these two areas can help tactical crime analysts to better understand not only the rationale of an offender's motive, but also his decision-making process in terms of why he selects targets in certain areas over others. Behavioral geography is a subfield of geography that focuses on the individual's spatial decision making, or why and how people make decisions about where to go for everything from shopping for groceries to crime targets. The behavioral geography field is often divided into two categories of research and study—behavior in space and spatial behavior (Rengert, 1989). While both areas have different focuses and empirical realities, they have implications for crime analysis in general and tactical crime analysis in particular.

Behavior in space is a research approach that "considers the geographic distribution of opportunities for crime and the social, economic, physical, and physiological constraints on criminal spatial behavior" (Rengert, 1989). As implied from the definition, this area of crime research deals with how the spatial structure of opportunities for crime shape the distribution of crime. In simpler terms, behavior in space focuses on how the locations of crime opportunities (single family homes) impact the distribution of crimes (burglary). Thus, behavior in space research is more place specific and looks at how the mix of opportunities and constraints within an area impacts patterns of crime. Criminological research strongly influenced by this area of behavioral geography includes the crime pattern theory and opportunity structure models.

An example of how the geographic distribution of opportunities for crime affects crime patterns is the spatial distribution of commercial robbery. In most cities, commercial robberies tend to cluster on the major arterial roads of the city, with highest concentrations often centering in areas of greatest cash based commercial activity. Figure 3.1 shows the distribution of commercial robberies in Lexington, Kentucky and illustrates the concentration along major arterial roads.

Figure 3.1 Commercial Robbery Distribution in Lexington, KY.

Paulsen (2005), in his research on commercial robbery and opportunity structure, found there were several factors that helped explain the location of commercial robbery locations. In particular, Paulsen (2005) found that businesses that were cashed based, located in high population density areas, and near crime attractors were more likely to be robbed. Using these and other basic factors associated with commercial locations, Paulsen (2005) was able to predict the likelihood of a location being robbed with an accuracy of 97%. Moreover, these factors were better predictors than traditional prediction methods such as whether a location had been robbed previously or the type of business location. Other opportunity structure research has dealt with crimes such as burglary. In analyzing how opportunity structures impact the distribution of burglary in Philadelphia, Rengert (1991) found that the number of residential housing units in an area was a strong measure of "criminal attractiveness." In particular, areas within a city that contained large numbers of residential dwellings were more likely to experience higher concentrations of burglary incidents, than those with lower densities of residential dwellings or mixed use areas. While the findings of this area of research may seem relatively obvious, opportunity structure and its impact on crime distribution are nonetheless important to criminal justice practitioners and crime analysts. In particular, crime analysts can use opportunity structure as a forecasting method by performing basic spatial analysis

Behavioral Geography

(residential dwelling density, commercial business density, crime attractor locations) within their jurisdictions and using these results to guide crime prevention tactics.

Spatial Behavior

The other area of behavioral geography is spatial behavior, an area of research that focuses on the person and how his spatial knowledge impacts his individual criminal behavior (Rengert, 1989). While behavior in space was more concerned with place issues and how spatial constraints impacted crime patterns, spatial behavior is interested in an individual's spatial knowledge and how it impacts his or her spatial activities. In particular, spatial behavior deals with the issues of offenders' mental maps, awareness space, activity space, and journey-to-crime, all of which have important implications for crime analysts and tactical crime analysis. Whereas research into behavior in space concepts has been rather limited, criminological research on spatial behavior has been much more robust. Because of this larger body of research, the different concepts of spatial behavior will be discussed separately.

Mental Maps and Awareness Space

While the concepts of mental maps, awareness space, and journey-to-crime are all highly interrelated in terms of their impact on an individual's spatial knowledge, mental maps are the building blocks from which the other concepts are derived. A mental map can best be described as "the internal representations of the world that we use to find our way and make decisions about what we will do and where" (Canter and Hodge, 2000). In simple terms, a mental map is a mental image and the general geographic knowledge that an individual has of a particular area. Importantly, a mental map does not necessarily imply detailed knowledge of an entire area, only that an individual is familiar with the geographic extent of an area. In the city where I grew up, I have a mental map of the geographic extent of the entire city and its boundaries; however, I have detailed knowledge of only those parts of the city with which I am familiar because of personal experience. Figure 3.2 is an example of a basic mental map drawn by a commercial robber during an interview about his offending behavior.

While the mental map is crude in terms of geographic details, it provides valuable insight into the offenders' spatial knowledge and how this knowledge impacted his chosen crime locations within the city.

Most often people have mental maps that are highly detailed in some areas and only vague understandings of other areas, largely due to the variation in the amount of activity they conduct in the different areas. Those areas

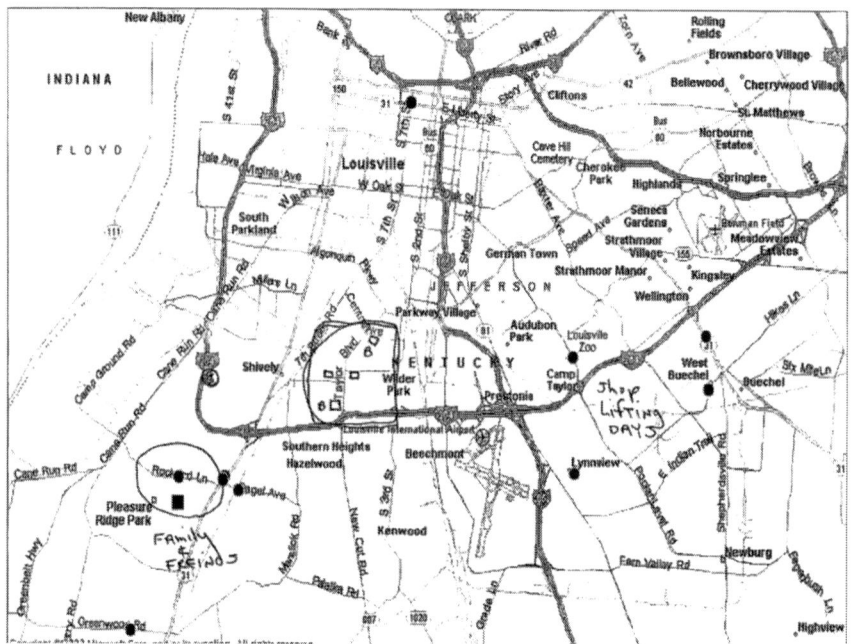

Figure 3.2 Mental Map of Commercial Robbery Offender.

where an individual has a more detailed knowledge are generally those places he has had more experience. These are called an individual's awareness space. In a practical sense, an individual's awareness space is nested within a larger mental map of an area. People conduct the vast majority of their normal daily activities (work, shop, home, recreation) in a relatively contained area, known as their activity spaces (Brantingham and Brantingham, 1993). The size and shape of an individual's awareness and activity space, and his resultant knowledge of the area, is extremely dependent on the amount, direction, and distance of that individual's daily routine activities. Individuals who travel only short distances from home in daily routine will have a much more compact activity and awareness space than an individual who must travel farther and in more directions. This will also result in a mental map with a smaller area of detailed knowledge and understanding. Moreover, since research has shown that offenders choose crime victims almost exclusively from within familiar areas, it will also results in a much smaller target selection area.

The main determiner of the size and shape of an individual's activity space is the location of that individual's nodes and the paths taken between them. Nodes are places central to an individual's life, such as home, place of work, school, shopping areas, and favorite recreation spots (Brantingham and Brantingham, 1993). The places an individual travels to and from essentially make up the extent of that individual's activity space and act as anchor points for an individual's legitimate and criminal activities. Specifically, nodes form mental boundary points within which criminal offenders search for criminal opportunities. Connecting individual nodes are paths, the everyday routes people travel. While nodes act as anchor points for a person's activity space, paths determine the areas that individual will learn about through the routes he or she travels on a regular basis. Because people spend long hours in routine paths traveling to and from activity nodes, paths will determine the areas along which criminals will search for potential victims (Brantingham and Brantingham, 1993). Awareness space, activity space, nodes, and paths are very important concepts for tactical crime analysis because research has shown that an offender's main search area in terms of criminal activity is within an awareness space containing his key nodes and paths (Brantingham and Brantingham, 1991). More specifically, offenders are most likely to search for criminal targets within an awareness space bounded by their key activity nodes and connected by their normal paths.

In addition to normal nodes and paths, a criminal's search area can be impacted by the presence and location of two specialized nodes—crime attractors and crime generators. Crime attractors are places, areas, or neighborhoods where criminal opportunities are well known, and to which motivated offenders are subsequently attracted as a source for criminal activity (Brantingham and Brantingham, 1993). Examples include known drug markets, college housing areas, nightclub districts, and prostitution areas, all of which provide ample criminal opportunities for different offenders. Importantly, crime in these areas is often committed by people who live outside the area, but who travel to these areas specifically because of the criminal opportunities that exist there (Brantingham and Brantingham, 1993). In contrast, crime generators are areas and locations to which large numbers of people are attracted for legitimate reasons, but which provide criminal opportunities because of the sheer number of potential victims (Brantingham and Brantingham, 1993). Examples of crime generators include shopping centers, entertainment districts, college campuses, and sports stadiums, all of which generate crime by providing large numbers of potential victims at specific times and within concentrated areas.

Research on Mental Maps and Awareness Space

While often brushed aside by crime analysts, research on mental maps and awareness has several implications for tactical crime analysis and for understanding crime patterns. Mental map research has focused mainly on spatial perceptions and can be broken down into citizens, police, and criminals. Research into the perceptions of normal citizens has revealed that there are many differences in how people perceive crime and where people perceive crime to be high. Perhaps the best research on spatial perceptions of crime was conducted by Pyle (1980), which studied the city of Akron, Ohio to discern how various social and location factors impacted perceptions. Findings from the study included: minorities have more accurate perceptions of crime patterns than whites; females tend to have less accurate perceptions than males; those who have lived in the area longer have more accurate perceptions of crime patterns; wealthier, more educated residents overestimate the amount of crime in the city center; and suburban residents have exaggerated perceptions of crime in the city center. In general, the findings point to the fact that those who live closer to the city center (poor, lower educated, minorities) have more accurate perceptions of the reality crime than those who live in the suburbs (wealthier, educated, whites). This shows the importance of proximity and experience in driving accurate understandings of crime patterns; those who live near supposed high crime areas understand the reality better than those who live farther away.

Research into the perceptions of crime patterns by police officers has also produced important results. In particular, research has found that officers' perceptions of crime patterns in general are not that accurate, but that accuracy sometimes varies by crime type (Paulsen, 2004; Ratcliffe and McCullagh, 2001). Paulsen (2004) found that police officers perform poorly at indicating high crime areas within their jurisdiction and that even when given daily, weekly and monthly crime maps, their performance does not improve. In contrast, Ratcliffe and McCullagh (2001) found that the accuracy of officers' perceptions vary by crime types with officers being most accurate in their perceptions of those areas prone to burglaries and less accurate in their perceptions of other crimes such as auto theft and non-residential burglary. It was theorized that the geographic knowledge of burglary was attributed to the seriousness of this crime and the officers' increased desire to reduce and prevent these types of crimes over other crime types (auto theft and non-residential burglary).

The final area of research on mental maps is in the area of perceptions of the criminals, which in contrast to the research on citizens and police officers, focused on those areas of a city offenders felt were good for crime. While criminals and non-criminals were found to have similar perceptions of crime patterns, criminals viewed the city differently than non-criminals, dividing the city into "dimensions of evaluation" (Carter and Hill, 1980). These dimensions of evaluation are based on criminals' "work" centered view of a city in which criminals evaluate different areas based on their potential for criminal activity, splitting the city into good and bad areas for work (Carter and Hill, 1980). The two most important criteria for criminals when evaluating whether an area is "good," are familiarity and knowledge of the area and potential strategy for an area (Carter and Hill, 1980). In general, criminals viewed areas in which they had in-depth spatial knowledge and "felt comfortable" as being attractive locations for crime, even more important than factors such as potential take. In addition, criminals viewed wealthy areas as attractive places for crime unless they did not know the area well (Repetto, 1974; Petersilia, Greenwood, and Lavin, 1977). In interviews with commercial robbery offenders, Paulsen (2005) found offenders avoided potentially lucrative targets unless they felt comfortable with their spatial knowledge of an area. As with research on citizens and police officers, differences in perceptions of suitable targets and areas for crime were also based on age and race of offenders. In particular, younger offenders and minority offenders tended to put more emphasis on familiarity than older or white criminals when determining areas to offend (Carter and Hill, 1980; Repetto, 1974).

Similar to research on mental maps, research on awareness space has focused on both citizens and criminals, with important findings in each area for tactical crime analysis. In terms of citizens' awareness space, research has found: females have more limited awareness spaces than males (Rengert and Monk, 1982); younger people have more limited awareness spaces than older citizens (Ley, 1983); those who are employed have more expansive awareness spaces than the unemployed (Orleans, 1973); and those who live in central city areas have a more limited awareness space than those in suburbs (Orleans, 1973). Most of these differences can be attributed to activity space, nodes, and path issues and how they vary based on the nature and size of the activity space. Those who have larger activity spaces (older, employed, suburbanites) have larger awareness spaces and, in return, larger areas of spatial knowledge. From a crime standpoint, this indicates that criminals who are younger or live in city centers have more limited awareness spaces and will commit crimes in smaller areas than their older, suburban counterparts. Research supports this assertion. Repetto (1974) found that criminals tend to operate in neighborhoods they know well despite having identified other neighborhoods as having more opportunities. In addition, Rengert and Wasilchick (1985) found that burglars usually choose crime sites only a limited distance from their normal travel paths, usually along the path between home and work. Other research has found that nearly all robberies, burglaries, serial rapes, and serial murders are committed within the awareness space defined by offenders' nodes and paths (Maguire, 1982; Rengert and Wasilchick, 1985; Gabor et al., 1987; Canter and Larkin, 1993; Alston, 1994; Rossmo, 1994; Wright and Decker, 1994). In conclusion, research has found that most criminals commit crimes exclusively within their awareness space, usually centered around their routine nodes and paths and that spatial exploration for the purpose of criminal activity is a rare event (Rengert and Wasilchick). From a tactical crime analysis perspective, these findings are extremely important as they indicate that in most crime series, offenders will choose crime locations near their anchor points. Practically, this research forms the basis for both geographic profiling and next event forecasting and helps to explain the criminal's journey-to-crime.

Journey-to-Crime

The last behavioral geography concept that will be discussed is journey-to-crime, perhaps the most commonly known yet most misunderstood behavioral geography concept. In a nutshell, journey-to-crime research is interested in the distance that a criminal travels to commit a crime. While a fairly simple idea, journey-to-crime impacts most major criminological theories (see Chapter 2) and has a significant impact on both geographic profiling and next-event forecasting (Rengert, Piquero, and Jones, 1999). Specifically, journey-to-crime, and the factors that drive offender travel, target attractiveness, spatial attractiveness, and target backcloth, all have a major impact on crime analysis and crime series analysis because of their theoretical and investigative implications.

The first of the three factors behind offender travel distance is target attractiveness, which refers to the number of high value targets available in an area (Rhodes and Conly, 1991). Proponents of target attractiveness argue that criminals travel to an area to commit crimes based on the number of perceived high value targets within that area. The higher the density of high value targets, the more likely it is that criminals will be driven to offend in that area. Factors considered as evidence of target attractiveness include high income, significant numbers of potential victims, significant numbers of single family dwellings, crime attractors, and crime generators (Rhodes and Conly, 1991). In many ways, this factor is associated with behavior in space concepts, in that how opportunities, such as residential land use, are structured within a city can determine the areas of highly attractive targets. In interviews with offenders, researchers have repeatedly found that target attractiveness ranks as the least powerful of the three factors and that other spatial factors are more important (Paulsen, 2005; Rengert and Wasilchick, 1991).

The second of the factors that drive offender travel behavior is spatial attractiveness, or the distance or proximity of targets to an offender's residence or major anchor points. Simply put, spatial attractiveness states that a major factor in the attractiveness of a target is the proximity of the target to an offenders' residence, with offenders choosing to commit crimes closer to home in areas where they feel comfortable. Spatial attractiveness finds support in two major laws of criminal and geographic behavior: 1) that all things are related, but closer things are more related, and 2) that criminals are generally lazy. Taken together, these laws indicate that criminals will have a strong desire to strike at targets nearest their homes no matter how attractive a more distant target may be. Importantly, there is ample support within the interview research to indicate that spatial attractiveness is indeed an important driving factor in the distance criminal will travel to offend (Paulsen, 2005; Rengert and Wasilchick, 1999).

The last major factor influencing offender travel behavior is target backcloth or opportunity structure, a concept very similar in many ways to behavior in space. The idea behind target backcloth is that the locations of suitable victims may not be uniformly distributed within a given area, particularly when a criminal is looking for a particular type of victim. In cases in which the criminal is seeking a specific type of victim, the journey-to-crime and offense locations will be influenced more heavily by the victim's activity spaces and locations than by the offender's activity spaces (Rossmo, 1994). An example of where target backcloth heavily influences offender travel behavior is in bank robberies. While offenders who wish to commit a street robbery can most likely find suitable targets near their residences, the locations of banks to victimize is determined by the individual bank's opportunity structure and thus offenders may have to travel a great distance to commit the desired crime. As with both target and spatial attractiveness, interview research suggests that target backcloth has a significant impact on offender travel behavior (Paulsen, 2005; Rengert and Wasilchick, 1999).

Journey-to-Crime Research

In contrast to the research on mental maps and awareness space, a great many studies have been conducted on journey-to-crime of offenders. Moreover, that research has produced two important, consistent findings that have significant implications for tactical crime analysis. The first major recognized finding is the concept of distance decay. Distance decay states that offenders will select targets closer to home and that the farther they go away from their home the fewer crimes they will commit (Phillips, 1980). As Figure 3.3 indicates, distance decay approximates a curve where the greatest amount of crimes will occur close to an offender's residence and fewer crimes will occur the farther you move away from the offender's residence.

Closely related to the idea of distance decay is the theoretical buffer zone, which is in essence a self imposed "no-crime" zone employed by criminals in which they will not commit crimes too close to home (Rossmo, 1993). When taken together a buffer zone states that offenders will not offend too close to home for fear of being recognized and caught and they will not offend too far away from home because of their lack of knowledge or the increased effort required. Importantly, while Rossmo and others support the idea of a buffer zone, there is increasing evidence to suggest that it is a statistical anomaly more than an empirical reality (Paulsen, 2005; Rengert, Piquero, and Jones, 1999). However, irrespective of the discussion of buffer zone existence, the findings regarding distance decay have major implications for tactical crime analysis in that they in essence form the basis for geographic profiling.

The other major finding related to journey-to-crime, is that offenders' journeys to crime vary greatly based on the type of crime and offender. These findings include the following: offenders travel farther to commit property crimes than personal crimes; female offenders travel shorter distances to commit crimes than males; minority offenders travel shorter distances than white offenders; younger offenders travel shorter distances than older offenders; criminals living in rural areas travel farther to commit crimes than those living in urban areas; criminals in more compact cities travel shorter distances than those in more sprawling cities; inexperienced offenders travel shorter distances than experienced criminals; offenders committing unplanned (rape, murder) crimes make shorter crime trips than those making planned (robbery, burglary) crimes. While, many of these findings are based on simple realities such as ability to travel, victim-offender relationship, and city type, these factors are important to crime series investigations. Knowledge of these facts can help form geographic profiles, suspect lists, and forecasting results.

However, for all the research on journey-to-crime and its importance to geographic profiling and tactical crime analysis, there are serious criticisms of the research that need to be discussed. First, and perhaps most important, is the fact that almost all journey-to-crime research is based on official data involving only offenders who have been arrested and prosecuted for an offense. While it can be informative and insightful in some cases, official data only provides a record of crimes known to the police (Robinson, 2002). Not only are many crimes not reported to the police in the first place, fewer still result in arrests and convictions such that an offender addresses can be recorded. Bureau of Justice statistics indicate that only one in three property crimes is reported to the police and that clearance rates for property crimes are well below 20% (BJS, 1997). The importance of this reliance on official data, is that we are making assumptions about offenders' travel based on small and quite likely unrepresentative samples of the criminal population. As Paulsen and Robinson state (2009), journey-to-crime research can best be described as research on the travel behavior of only the criminals who were inept and got caught and prosecuted.

A second criticism of the journey-to-crime research is that it is overly "domocentric" in its focus. In particular, journey-to-crime research relies far too heavily on the assumption that the origin of all offender travel is the offenders' homes when measuring distances to offense locations. Support for this criticism comes from research that indicates that many criminal's journeys-to-crime start from other anchor points (work, friend's home, etc.) or other locations a significant distance from home (Rengert, Piquero, and

Jones, 1999; Pettiway, 1995). The impact of this domocentric approach is that we fail to measure the actual distance criminals travel to commit their crimes, instead measuring distances that may provide insight into actual travel patterns.

The final criticism is closely related to the domocentric criticism, and revolves around the actual measurement of offender travel distances. Currently, offender travel distance is measured using one of three different methods, Manhattan, crows' flight, or wheel distance, all of which merely approximate the distance. Police do not collect data on actual trips, and thus the different measures are simply approximations. Most importantly, it does not provide an accurate measure of actual offender travel distance. Taken together, these three criticisms provide a grim reality about journey-to-crime data which is made even more disconcerting given its use and implications in tactical crime analysis.

Thinking Criminal

The ultimate goal of studying behavioral geography issues such as mental maps, awareness space, and journey-to-crime is to provide a better understanding of how an offender selects targets within a geographic space. Having a sound understanding of behavioral geography concepts and research can help crime analysts make better informed judgments about serial offender behavior and provide insight into both anchor point locations and potential crime targets. In a sense, a sound understanding of behavioral geography helps crime analysts to think like a criminal and to read a crime series for the geographic and behavioral clues that crime locations provide.

While knowledge of behavioral geography can come from many different sources, one of the best is interviews with actual offenders. Several studies include interviews conducted with burglars (Cromwell and Olson, 2004; Rengert and Wasilchick, 2000; Wright and Decker, 1994) street robbers (Erickson, 1996; Wright and Decker, 1997), and even commercial robbery offenders (Gill, 2000; and Paulsen, 2006). These studies enable tactical crime analysts to learn more about the actual processes that offenders go through in selecting locations, acquiring mental maps and awareness space, and generally learning to think like a criminal. Included below is the text of an interview with "Tim," a commercial robbery offender convicted of 16 commercial robberies, although admittedly a perpetrator in many more than that. Tim was interviewed while serving a 25-year sentence for commercial robbery in the Eddyville penitentiary in Kentucky. During the interview, questions dealt with target selection factors, journey-to-crimes, awareness space, and other geography based issues dealing with offending. Rather than an unabridged version of the interview, the text below provides insight into those issues most pertinent to a discussion of behavioral geography, anchor points, awareness space, and target selection processes.

Q: Would you consider yourself an amateur or a professional criminal?
Tim: Amateur.
Q: Despite robbing more than 25 commercial stores, you would consider your self an amateur? Why is that?
Tim: Well, it's because of the way I did things. I did things that no professional would do. I did robberies with no gloves, and burglaries with no gloves, the only thing I ever thought of to use was a mask when I did my armed robberies. It was pretty much amateur all the way.
Q: Did you prefer any one type of target over another, such as commercial targets to residential?
Tim: Yes. The reason I started robbing was because with thieving you had to fence things off to get money, so I just thought that I would just go straight to the cash money. That was the only reason I got into it. I was making good money stealing cars, I had a guy who would buy my cars I would steal. However, it was so tedious going out of state, coming back and all that, so I just bought me a shotgun and started robbing instead. What I would look for when I was out cruising, was for a convenience store or gas station where there was only a lady there, if possible that was what you would want. Then you would kick back and watch them until the time was right.
Q: Did you ever worry about getting caught?
Tim: Nope.
Q: It never crossed your mind that you would get caught?
Tim: Nope not even once. I never worried about it.
Q: What kind of things did you look for in a target?
Tim: A convenience store that sits off by itself, with no other connecting stores or anything, and either one or two women is all that's working there. When I found a place I'd park somewhere that I could watch until the traffic slowed down and soon as I got my break I would run up in their with my bandana around my neck and pull it up over my face and run in there and rob them.
Q: Why did you like stores off by themselves?
Tim: Well you don't have to worry about someone in the other stores coming in, like a guy who works in a liquor store next door. Usually a liquor store is armed and if they see me come running in next door with my mask on, they may come over and try to help. You don't want nobody getting hurt, if you can keep the people to a minimum and control the situation it makes it easier. That's what I looked for.
Q: So in general you tried to avoid convenience stores that were attached to other stores?

Tim: In general I would avoid them if they were connected to any others kinds of stores. Now I have done it. One time I robbed a convenient store and when I was coming out I just happened to run down in front of a liquor store and the guy was opening up the liquor store, it was early in the morning, and he was just standing there, so I robbed him too. It was an opportunity, I could make a double hit.

Q: Were there types of neighborhoods that you liked more than others when looking for targets?

Tim: I would go anywhere I felt comfortable. But I liked to be in places that I knew, because once I did the robbery I would get away through the neighborhoods to stay off the main roads. First chance I got I would get off the highways and start zig-zagging through the neighborhoods, because they (police) are going to come down those roads first, just in case somebody got a description.

Q: Were there places that you avoided looking for targets because of knowledge of the area or anything?

Tim: No, not for me, because I knew all of Louisville real well. I would avoid places near a police station, but besides that I had a lot of knowledge of everywhere so I felt comfortable.

Q: Would you rob stores on major roads?

Tim: I wouldn't want to, but I have done it. If I found the perfect isolated convenient store. If it was isolated but still on a main road I would do it as long as the traffic was light.

Q: Traffic patterns were real important in choosing a location?

Tim: Yes. If it was too busy you wouldn't want to do that.

Q: What about lighting? If the store was well-lit did that matter to you?

Tim: No that didn't bother me at all. But one thing that I did look for was stores that had neon sign and advertisements in the windows, because if someone is passing by on the road they can look in the store and not be able to see what is going on. They just wouldn't be able to see in and see me robbing the place. They put all those things up in the windows they were just asking for it.

Q: If you had to choose one thing that was most important in selecting a target for robbery, what would it be?

Tim: A lone female working the store. Very important. They wouldn't fight back like the men.

Q: Did you ever hit the same place twice?

Tim: I hit one three times. It was a convenient store by my mom's and what I would do is stop by my mom's house and see what she was making for dinner. If she was making something good for dinner I would tell her that I would be right back and I would go and jump across the fence and go across the street and rob the convenient store and go back and eat dinner at my mom's. The police would come while I was eating and by the time I was done they would be long gone.

Q: Of the different types of stores was there a type of store you liked to rob best? Such as fast food, gas station, etc.?

Tim: I liked convenient stores because most of the time there was just one person in there and if they are next to someplace else they are usually closed down by the time I get there.

Q: Was there a time of day you liked to rob places?

Tim: Not really. Some times I would do it in broad daylight. Sometimes I would get so hard up for cash that I would just go and rob a place. I would sometimes sit there for 3 hours just watching a place.

Q: Did any security measures matter to you in terms of deterring you from robbing a place? Such as a video camera, alarms, protective glass.

Tim: Cameras didn't bother me because I wore a mask when I robbed a place. Alarms didn't bother because I never knew that they were there. I would by-pass places where cashiers were behind protective glass, because you couldn't do anything there.

Q: Was number of employees very important to you?

Tim: Yes. Two at the most and I would hope that they were both women. If it was men they would maybe get a macho attitude and try and stop me. I am not there for a murder, I just want the money, but some people try to be a hero and get macho, and I don't understand that.

Q: If they were armed would you rob the place anyway?

Tim: No way. I wouldn't touch it, wouldn't go near it if I knew they were armed.

Q: Did you ever rob a bank?

Tim: No, but I have thought about it lots of times. The only reason I didn't rob one was because of dye packs. The alarms didn't scare me, the amount of people in there didn't scare me, it was just the dye packs. I was afraid I wouldn't be able to get away with it. I wouldn't know what to look for, like I said it was amateur hour.

Q: How did you learn to pick out targets? Did you learn from someone or did you figure it out by yourself?

Tim: I figured it out all by myself. One day I just got tired of having to fence everything so I decided I would go straight to where the money was. I just started cruising and looking for different isolated spots and just waiting for the right time.

Q: How important was it to plan an escape route from the target?

Tim: Very important. You wanted to make sure you knew the escape routes from the place.

Q: Did you ever plan it out or drive the escape route before you committed the crime?

Behavioral Geography

Tim: No. This is because I was robbing stores in places I knew already and so I didn't need to drive any routes. I already knew how to get out of there and knew all the back roads already. I would usually avoid the major roads because that was the route where the police would be coming to the robbery. If someone got a description of my car and called it in the police would know what to look for when they were driving there to the robbery location. It happened to me twice where a cop saw me as I was going down the same road they were and they radioed one of their buddies to pull me over.

Q: When you went out to commit a robbery where were you usually coming from? Work, home, girlfriends?

Tim: Home, just about every time, unless I happened to be out late partying and I just happened to cruise past a place and it looked good, a perfect opportunity, then I would pull over and rob it. But these were rare, I usually went out looking when I needed some cash.

Q: When you went robbed a place were you going out for that specific purpose, or were you already out with friends and running errands when you decided to rob a place?

Tim: Almost always I was going out to rob and rob only. Every now and then I would be coming from somewhere and I would just see an opportunity I couldn't pass up, but mostly I was just going out to rob.

Q: Did you ever pick locations and then hit them at a later time?

Tim: Most of the time I had already picked a place a couple of days before then I would sit back and wait for the right time. Sometimes I wrote them down and would just go and rob them when I thought the time was right.

Q: So would you find places when you were out doing your normal daily routine?

Tim: Yes, I would be out doing whatever and if I saw a place I would make a mental note that it looked like a good place, or I would write it down and go back later. Most of the time this is how I picked my locations. When I ran out of money or needed some quick cash I would just go to those places I already knew about. I wasn't a hawk, when I started to need the money is when I would go rob.

Q: When you would go to rob these places would you go straight there or would you drive around for a while first getting ready?

Tim: I would go straight there. I would park the car a little bit away from the place, maybe a quarter of a mile because I didn't want to run too far. I wanted the car where I could get away quick and where they wouldn't get an ID on it. But sometimes if I pulled up and there was no one in the parking lot I would just park right out front and rob it. But majority of the time you just can't do that you have to sit and watch the place to wait for the right time.

Q: When you finished robbing a place where would you go? Home or would you drive around looking for more locations?

Tim: Most of the time I just went home and counted the money, maybe put some of it up if I got enough and then go out and party a little. There was once or twice that on the way home I saw other places and stopped and robbed them. I thought it was pretty smart because the cops are responding to the first robbery so they ain't going to be ready for this robbery.

Q: In regard to the map of your crimes, how did you learn about these places? Why did you rob them?

Tim: Most all of them were near my house where I knew I could get back home without having to be on any main roads for long. But this one I remembered from my car thieving days. A couple of these places I learned about from when I was young and I used to shoplift by the mall areas. There are a lot of places that I remember from when I was car thieving or shoplifting that I remembered were good opportunities and so I would go back and scope them out and wait for a good time to rob them.

Q: Did you ever shop at any of the places you robbed as a way to check them out?

Tim: Sometimes. It was usually just places that I saw that I robbed. It's weird but there were a couple of places that I would stop at to buy beer or something and then say I got to rob this place because it looks good. Any place that was on the highway was dangerous because it was too lit up and too much traffic all hours of the day and night. Most of the time I would check them out, but I didn't always stop in and shop first.

Q: Were there any places in town that just avoided?

Tim: Any parts of town that I didn't know I wouldn't do them, especially if I didn't know the back ways out. I didn't really go down too far into the city, because there were a lot of cops down there and I really didn't know my way around. I wasn't ever that concerned with cops, but if I didn't know my way around I wasn't going near it. There were parts of town that I robbed that I only knew because I used to steal there and I hated to rob some of the places near home, but they were just too pretty to pass up.

Q: Did you ever commit a robbery in a part of town you didn't know?

Tim: (after a pause) No. Even the one I did in Hardin county I knew from my car thieving days when I used to stop there on the way to sell the cars. I wouldn't want to do it because there are too many things I didn't know. I tried it once. I went up to Indiana because I did so many in Louisville, and I went up there and got lost. So that nixed that idea. I even went back during the day to try to map out my way, but it still got too confusing, it's just not a place I hung out or ever traveled a lot. I don't like a place where I don't know the area. There is no need to go to places I didn't know well. There is too many places out there to rob to have to go some place where you are going to get friggin' lost.

Q: I know you robbed most of the places because they were close to home, or you knew them from car thieving or shoplifting days? Did you ever go out and learn new areas?

Tim: Yea, after you hit so many places in an area you know the police are going to be out looking for more robberies. I did start looking for new places to rob that were still near where I knew. I would go out in the day and drive around and get a feel for the area and map it out. First I would try to find my place, just cruising, and you would see a big isolated place and then you would drive around and figure out a way to get out of there without having to hit main roads. I was working so I had all day to kill anyway, so I would drive around a little looking for back roads to help me get around. I still wasn't in areas I didn't know, it was just I didn't know them as well as the places where I robbed the most.

Q: If you couldn't find a good route out would you still rob it?

Tim: Nooooo. I would stay clear of it.

Q: Did you ever get tips from someone else about where to rob? Like from a partner?

Tim: No. Even the few times I did have a partner it was always me that suggested the places to rob.

Q: Were there any areas of town that you really liked to rob in for whatever reason?

Tim: The area over where I used to go from my shoplifting days was a good place for me. I would just go out there and just go. I didn't really plan a way back because I knew I could get back on the Waterston (highway) and I knew my way around from the shoplifting days. This is the area where I first got the idea to start robbing. I stopped into a store to get a pop and some chips before I went back to work (shoplifting) and I was getting tired of all this hassle and that's when it dawned on me to start robbing. I thought that this place would be perfect for robbing, and I filed it in the back of my head and came back and robbed it later.

Rather than an area I really just liked an isolated spot, with just a woman working or an old couple would work too. If it was possible, plenty of posters and advertisements on the windows to block the view from the street. I never worried about cameras or alarms or any of that. I just wanted to get in quick and get the money and hope nobody got hurt and then get back home quickly.

Q: Were there any types of stores that you avoided? Did you prefer chain stores to little local stores?

Tim: No, pretty much if it was isolated and looked like a good location I would hit it. A lot depended on the set up of the store, if the counter was near the door and I could get in and get behind the counter quick it was a good location. Also if they had the signs and everything in the windows I liked it because it was harder to see what was going on from the street.

Places I wouldn't touch, if it was surrounded by other stores, if it was anywhere near a police station, because the cops could get there too quick, if there was a man and a woman behind the counter, because the man would be macho and it would end bad. There were a couple of places that I wanted to rob, they were good and isolated and everything, but they were too close to the police station and I never would touch them.

Q: Were the places you robbed in more business or residential locations?

Tim: I preferred residential areas where it was a little store that everyone in the neighborhood would go to for things. Not too many in business areas at all. I can't remember any of them in big business areas.

Q: Did your target selection process change over time as you got more experienced?

Tim: A little, but not much. When I started this was just something new that I was going to try because I was tired of having to fence things. I would remember a place that looked easy and looked like it would be easy to get away from and go back and rob it. In time, I started to map out how I was going to get away. At the time (I started) I wasn't thinking about how I was going to get away it was just like a snatch and grab, but after I did a couple of robberies I started thinking to myself I need to find a better way to get away from this place. I was going on the highway too much.

Q: From when you first started committing crimes as a juvenile, did how far you traveled to commit a crime change?

Tim: Absolutely, once I got a driver's license I went a lot farther. When I didn't have a license I stayed much closer to home.

Q: Did you ever avoid committing crimes too near to home?

Tim: No. I didn't want to commit crimes near home, but like I said about that one convenient store that was right near my mom's. I just couldn't pass it up. The main reason I hit that one was when I just didn't want to drive real far to hit a place, I could just get that one. That's why I hit them three times.

Q: Did you ever worry that you were so close to home people would know you?

Tim: No. Especially with the neighborhood I lived it, they aren't going to pick out one certain person. That neighborhood I lived in was full of criminals, that's all that lived there. We all grew up together. But I tell you what, the neighborhood I lived in you wouldn't have any burglaries. People didn't want to burglarize a bunch of criminals. Plus we was most of the burglars and robbers. It was a good neighborhood, but it was a breeding place for thieves is all it was. You never had a problem in the neighborhood of us stealing from one another, because we would go to other places. It was one of the safest neighborhoods out there.

Overall, the interview with "Tim" provides an excellent example of the thought process employed by criminals when they choose both types of places and general areas to victimize. Moreover, Tim's comments provide valuable information concerning how criminals evaluate locations including what they consider good qualities (isolated, ease of escape on back roads, obscured view on windows, lack of traffic, few customers, one cashier), what they find bad about a location (business areas, busy traffic areas, proximity to police, lack of back roads for escape, lack of knowledge of the area), and what security features don't seem to matter (cameras and alarms). All this information can be beneficial to police in analyzing a crime series, determining anchor points, future crime locations, and potential suspects.

Exploring Crime Types 4

Introduction

While much of the book to this point has dealt with theory and conceptual information, this chapter offers an in-depth discussion of the most common types of serial crimes and of offense, offender, and victim characteristics for homicide, arson, robbery, burglary, auto theft, and sexual assault. This chapter's ultimate purpose is to provide useful information about specific crime types that could be used to assist in criminal investigations. Designed to be used in concert with the information provided in the chapters on criminological theory, and behavioral geography, this chapter will be a resource for crime analysts about both types of offenders and offenses.

Homicide

If Hollywood's depiction of crime was a realistic portrayal of actual crime trends, serial murder would be one of the biggest problems facing modern society. Luckily, Hollywood highly exaggerates the incidence of serial murder. In reality, serial murder is one of the most rare crimes. Only 337 reported serial offenders were reported in the United States between 1800–1995, or about 1.7 cases per year (Hickey, 2002). In contrast, there were approximately 224,000 homicide victims in the United States from 1986–1995, a number that dwarfs the approximately 3,800 victims of serial murder from 1800–1995 (FBI, 2007; Hickey, 2002). In general, overall homicide rates in the United States have declined since the early 1990s. For example, the homicide rate in 2005 was 5.6 victims per 100,000 (FBI, 2007). Hickey (2002) reports that if it were possible to create a serial murder rate for the United States, it would be somewhere around 0.02 per 100,000 for the period of 1975–1995, the most active of all time periods of serial murder. Furthermore, if all of the serial murder incidents that occurred between 1975–1995 were treated as if they happened in the same year it will only increase the serial murder rate to 0.04 per 100,000. However, despite the extremely rare nature of serial murder, when it occurs, it causes a media sensation.

In looking more closely at serial murder, there are several important characteristics about the offense, offenders, and victims that can be useful in tactical analysis. According to an exhaustive study by Hickey (2002), the majority of serial murderers are male (90%), white (73%), kill intra-racial victims, and are local hunters as opposed to travelers. In addition, Hickey (2002) notes that the majority of victims of serial murder are strangers (73%) and that of those stranger victims, the most popular victim is a young female alone, followed by prostitutes and hitchhikers. Possibly of most importance to tactical crime analysts is the fact that the majority of serial murderers are local in nature, a fact that flies in the face of the media driven picture of serial murder. In particular, Hickey (2002) found that only around 27% of all serial murderers could be characterized as travelers, with another 63% being local hunters and a final 10% being place specific. Taken in conjunction with the victimization data, the profile of serial murder target selection would be a local offender looking for female victims who are either out alone or in employment positions (prostitution) that put them in risky situations.

In contrast to serial murder, homicide in the United States is more mundane, although much higher in volume. In general, homicide statistics are similar to serial murder, with the majority of offenders being male (88%) and the victim–offender relationship is predominantly intra-racial in nature (FBI, 2005). However, in many other ways, homicide in general is very different from serial murder. In particular, the typical homicide victim is likely to be male (77%) with both victims and offenders more likely to be black than white, and with only about 14% of victims being strangers (FBI, 2005). In contrast to the typical media portrayal (Paulsen, 2002), homicide is more likely to be the result of an argument than a gang or felony related cause, with arguments far out numbering any other known cause (FBI, 2005). Combining both victim and offender data reveals that the typical homicide in the United States is between males of the same race who have a known relationship, caused by an argument or other trivial motive.

Using this information about homicides in a tactical situation leads to several considerations. First, most begin simply as fights that end in homicide, so that both victim and offender travel distances are relatively short. In the majority of homicides, the incident occurs in the spur of the moment, leading to victim selection mostly based on convenience and familiarity (Miethe, McCorkle, and Listwan, 2006). Thus, from an investigative standpoint, it is essential to first rule out those nearest to the victim both geographically and relationship wise. This is particularly important in cases where the victim is female, because females are most likely to be killed by intimate partners in or near places of work or residence (FBI, 2005). Where no relationship can be determined for female victims, either interpersonal or geographic, the likelihood of the victim being a serial offender victim increases.

Robbery

While not generally as newsworthy as homicide, robbery is a more common crime in the United States, with over 400,000 incidents reported every year since 1974 (Miethe, McCorkle, and Listwan, 2006). Recently, robberies have been on the increase, jumping more than 7% from 2005 to 2006 (FBI, 2008). While many people think of banks as the primary victims of robbery, in reality the majority of robberies occurred on streets (45%), followed by commercial locations (24%), and residential robberies (14%) (FBI, 2008). In looking more closely at robbery, the average amount taken was approximately $1,200, with a high of approximately $4,300 for bank robberies and a low of less than $800 for convenience stores and street robberies (FBI, 2008; Miethe, McCorkle, and Kistwan, 2006). As with most crimes committed in the United States, robbery offenders tend to be male (90%) and a member of a minority group (54%) (FBI, 2008; Feeney, 1986; Gabor et al., 1987; Rainville and Reeves, 2003). However, in contrast to other crimes, robbery offenders tend to be more than 25 years old (62%) with prior felony arrest records (64%), making them older and more experienced than many other types of offenders (FBI, 2008; Feeney, 1986; Gabor et al., 1987; Rainville and Reeves, 2003). While the general public thinks of robbery in monolithic terms as the previous data indicate, robbery is comprised of two types of victims, individuals, and business locations. While commercial and individual robbery victims share characteristics, other factors including offender characteristics, travel distances, and target selection processes can be quite different.

In looking at commercial robbery, the assumption is that these types of robberies involve a great deal of planning and advanced thought. However, research has shown this is not necessarily the case. Interviews with convicted robbery offenders have shown that the typical robbery offender (commercial or individual) is an opportunist who does little advanced planning and thinks little about actually being caught (Feeney, 1986). While some research has shown that those robbers involved in commercial robbery are more likely to plan than those involved in individual victimization, the level of planning is still very basic. Planning activities for commercial robbery are most likely to focus on getaway cars, escape routes, and target selection (Feeney, 1986; Wright and Decker, 1997). It is important to note that research has shown that as the number of robberies committed increases, the likelihood of planning increases (Miethe, McCorkle, and Kistwan, 2006). In interviews with commercial robbery offenders, Paulsen (2006) found that as offenders committed more robberies they developed a pattern that involved the types of victims they robbed as well as the manner in which they committed the robbery. Important in this research was the fact that the offenders were as likely to attribute these regular patterns to "routine and tradition" as they were rational selection criteria (Paulsen, 2006). In most cases, offenders continued committing crimes in the same pattern because it had worked before and "changing things up may bring bad luck" (Paulsen, 2006).

In terms of target selection, there are several factors that research has shown influence commercial robbery victimization, including

- **Land Use**: Stores located next to commercial property were less likely to be robbed than stores near residential property (Hunter and Jeffery, 1991).
- **Building Type**: Stores that are isolated are more likely to be robbed than those surrounded by other buildings (Crow and Bull, 1975).
- **Activity levels**: Stores located near areas with evening commercial activity were less likely to be robbed (Hunter and Jeffery, 1991).
- **Road Type**: Stores located on streets with speed limits above 35 mph were more likely to be robbed (Jeffery, Hunter, and Griswold, 1987).

In addition, research has determined several neighborhood characteristics associated with where robbery is more likely to occur. In particular, robbery is more likely in neighborhoods with high levels of heterogeneity, population turnover, unemployment, single parent homes, and low family incomes (Miethe and Meier, 1994). While commercial robbery locations are more often dictated by the locations of potential victims (banks, convenience stores, etc.) these neighborhood characteristics still play an important role. Research by Paulsen (2006) found that a combination of both neighborhood and individual level factors was the best predictor of commercial robbery victimization. Thus, commercial store locations that had several of the individual level characteristics (land use, building type, etc.) were more likely to be robbed if they were in neighborhoods high in heterogeneity, population turnover, and other neighborhood characteristics associated with robbery.

In contrast to the numerous different target selection criteria associated with commercial robbery victimization, street robbery is most highly associated with convenience (Feeney, 1986). Research has consistently found that despite the risks of recognition, most street robbers offend within their own neighborhoods (Feeney, 1986). Journey-to-crime research supports these assumptions, with offender's journey-to-crime distances being dramatically shorter for street robbery offenses than for commercial robbery offenses. In a nutshell, robbery offenders who wish to rob an individual usually have ample targets within their neighborhoods, whereas offenders who wish to rob commercial establishments must travel to the location to commit their crime. From a tactical crime analysis standpoint, these findings are important, in that incidents of street robbery should have offenders living in much closer proximity to the offense location than those of commercial robbery. Thus, investigative support systems such as geographic profiling should be of more use in street than commercial robbery incidents.

Burglary

One of the most common crimes that any crime analyst deals with on a regular basis is burglary, both residential and commercial. According to FBI (2008) statistics, there were approximately 2.18 million burglaries in the United States in 2006, which is fairly consistent in number with previous years. Overall, burglary is declining from historic highs in the 1980s, although in the last few years there has been a slight increase (FBI, 2008). While burglary can be generally divided into residential and commercial types, the vast majority of all burglary (66%) is residential (FBI, 2008). In contrast to many opinions, the average take from a burglary is significantly higher ($1,834) than the average take in a robbery ($1,200), while the burglary cleared-by-arrest rate is much lower than for robbery (FBI, 2008). This would appear to make burglary a much more attractive crime type than robbery, and may in part account for its much higher number of victimizations.

While burglary is considerably more numerous in terms of yearly victimizations than homicide or robbery, the exact number is difficult to determine. Although the FBI (2008) reported approximately 2.18 million burglary victimizations in the United States in 2006, evidence indicates that actual victimization numbers are higher than reported to police. National victimization data indicate that more than 3.4 million burglaries occurred in the year 2003, far more than the number reported that year (Catalano, 2004). Reports indicate that only around 60% of burglaries are reported to the police and less than 15% of all burglaries are cleared by an arrest (NCVS, 2002; FBI 2008). The overall impact of these findings is that research on the "typical" burglar may be somewhat skewed by the subjects relied on for information. Specifically, research on target selection, offender profiles, and other information that comes from interviews may be more indicative of the few burglars that are caught than burglary offenders at large. However, numerous studies have been conducted on active burglars, thus avoiding problems with research being skewed by only those bad enough to get caught.

The typical burglary offender is a male (86%), white (70%), younger than 25, and has a prior felony arrest record (70%) (Bennett and Wright, 1984; Chaiken and Chaiken, 1982; FBI, 2008; Rainville and Reeves, 2003). The young age is often attributed to the gateway nature of burglary. In particular, burglary is often considered a crime that offenders start with and branch out to other types of crime that may be more serious (Miethe, McCorkle, and Listwan, 2006). As such, research has shown that burglars are usually nonspecialists and often involved in other crimes such as robbery, assault, theft, and drug dealing (Chaiken and Chaiken, 1982). Moreover, when offenders do specialize in burglary, research has found that it is usually only for short periods of time when victimizations are particularly profitable or convenient for the offender (Maguire, 1982; Shover, 1991; Wright and Decker, 1994).

In addition to being non-specialists, research indicates that most burglars are afraid of confrontation with victims and thus choose locations and times to avoid this possibility (Cromwell, Olson, and Avery, 1991). Research by Bennett and Wright (1984) found that the majority of burglars never purposely enter occupied residences and that encountering a resident is one of their greatest fears. This desire to avoid confrontation has a significant impact on both the temporal and spatial selection patterns and provides a clue into the reasoning and planning of burglaries. In looking at residential burglaries, 63% of incidents where time of occurrence was known or could be accurately estimated occurred during the daytime (FBI, 2008). Moreover, the most popular victimization times are weekdays from 10:00–11:00 a.m. and from 1:00–3:00 p.m., when most residents are at work (Cromwell, Olson, and Avery, 1991; Rengert and Wasilchick, 1985). This avoidance of confrontation also impacts commercial burglary patterns, which are most likely to occur in the middle of the night when vacancy is most assured.

While similar to robbery in that victimization can be categorized into commercial and residential, burglary is different in that target selection and offender planning characteristics are consistent across offense type. Whereas robbery offenders were found to use minimal if any planning before committing their crimes, burglary offenders are more likely to use detailed planning. Bennett and Wright (1984) categorized all burglaries into either opportunistic or planned based on the difference in time from when the offender made a chance discovery of a suitable target and when the offender committed the crime. Specifically, only if an offender happened upon a suitable target by chance and committed the crime *at that time* would the burglary be categorized as opportunistic in nature (Bennett and Wright, 1984). Based on this categorization, Bennett and Wright (1984) concluded that the majority of burglary offenders are one of two types of planners, opportunistic-planners and search-planners. Opportunistic planners are those in which there is a chance discovery of a potential target and the victimization takes place later, whereas search planners make more conscious efforts at target selection (Bennett and Wright, 1984). Importantly, while most burglars are planners, convenience and familiarity with the locale are two of the most important criteria in determining where offenders look for victims (Miethe, McCorkle, and Listwan, 2006). Thus, offenders often have short journey-to-crime distances, as they search or happen upon victims close to their anchor points.

The more planned nature of burglary has led to numerous important findings relating to target selection and offending strategies of burglars. Specifically, research has found the following factors to be important in target selection:

- **Surveillance**: Those locations that are easily observable and seen by neighbors or passersby are less likely to be victimized (Cromwell, Olson, and Avery, 1991).
- Fences that are too high (6-8 feet) allow burglars cover from neighbors and allow them to commit crimes easier once the fence is defeated (Miethe, McCorkle and Listwan, 2006).
- **Occupancy**: Those locations that exhibit signs of occupancy (cars in driveway, lights on, etc.) are less likely to be burglarized (Cromwell, Olson, and Avery, 1991).
- **Accessibility**: Houses located on cross streets or continuous roads are more likely to be burglarized than those on dead-end or cul-de-sacs (Rengert and Wasilchick, 1985).
- **Permeability**: Locations that have multiple means of access (roads, sidewalks, footpaths, trails) in and out of a neighborhood, are more likely to be burglarized (Armitage, 2006).
- **Target Hardening**: Houses with extra locks on doors and windows are less likely to be burglarized (Rengert and Wasilchick, 1985; Scarr, 1973).

In addition to these findings, crime prevention works such as CPTED, Defensible Space, and Secured by Design also point out other target selection factors associated with burglary. In general, burglary offenders are more likely than most other offender types to engage in planning for their target selection. Because of this, there is a greater chance that the incidence of burglary can be predicted based on the spatial patterns of target characteristics than in other crimes. In particular, using target selection characteristics discussed above along with creating a target profile based on previous incidents in an active series can help narrow likely offense locations within a jurisdiction.

Auto Theft

While not as common as burglary or larceny, auto theft is one of the most common major crimes in the United States. More than 1.1 million cars were stolen in 2006, a slight decline from the more than 1.23 million that were stolen each year from 2002–2005 (FBI, 2008). While these numbers are down from historic highs of the late 1980s and early 1990s, they are an increase from earlier in the decade. Estimated losses from auto theft approach $7.9 billion dollars a year, with the average property loss per theft being approximately $6,600 (FBI, 2008). As with other property crimes, only about 13% of auto thefts are cleared by arrest, despite the fact that more than 85% of all auto thefts are reported to the police (Miethe, McCorkle, and Listwan, 2006). Importantly, despite the low cleared-by-arrest rate, the majority of stolen cars are recovered. This is largely because joyriding and temporary transportation are major sources of auto theft (Miethe, McCorkle, and Listwan, 2006). Although this low rate of arrest and clearance has little impact on property loss totals, it severely impacts the knowledge available about the typical offender. Specifically, research on typical auto theft offenders is based on about 10% of all offenders, and thus the validity of offender profiling is suspect at best.

Despite the issues concerning the validity of auto theft offender profiles, much is known about victims and victim types. In their research on auto theft victimization, Clarke and Harris (1992) created a three-part categorization scheme for auto theft comprised of cars stripped for parts, cars used temporarily, and cars stolen for permanent retention and resale. Important to this categorization scheme is that victim characteristics varied greatly among these three groups. Automobiles stolen to be stripped for parts tended to be foreign made cars such as Mercedes Benzes, BMWs, Volvos, and Saabs, while those stolen for temporary use tended to be American-made muscle cars such as Camaros, Dodge Chargers, and Corvettes (Clarke and Harris, 1992). Finally, those cars stolen for permanent retention were a mix of expensive sports cars such as Porsches and Ferraris and less expensive foreign-made cars such as Nissans and Toyotas (Clarke and Harris, 1992). Increasingly cars stolen in the United States are being exported to other countries such as those in Eastern Europe, the Middle East, and Central and South America (Blake, 1995). This theft-for-export business model has become a growth industry of late for professional auto thieves, with estimates of upwards of 200,000 cars being stolen and shipped overseas or driven across the border (Blake, 1995). These victimization categories and their disparate victim types can be extremely useful when analyzing auto thefts in general and auto theft patterns and series in particular. Knowledge of the type of car stolen and the circumstances surrounding the theft can provide valuable information about the type of offender. For example, expensive cars stolen from wealthier neighborhoods that are not recovered within 24 hours are most likely resale thefts committed by professional auto thieves, whereas late model cars taken from working class neighborhoods are more likely to be temporary transportation.

This three-part categorization and its resulting victim characteristics underlie the nature of auto theft being driven by two disparate groups, juvenile joy riders and professional auto thieves. In contrast to previous crimes analyzed in this chapter which are neatly categorized based on victim type, auto theft is more readily categorized by offender type. In particular, auto theft is dominated by two types of offenders, professionals and joy riders. Although movies such as *Gone in 60 Seconds* have glamorized auto theft as a crime committed by fashionable, professional car thieves stealing exotic cars, the reality is different. Auto thieves are predominantly male (83%), white (61%), and younger than 18 (Chaiken and Chaiken, 1982; FBI, 2008; Ranville and Reeves, 2003). These offender characteristics indicate that auto theft is very similar in many ways to other property crimes, with the exception that offenders are more likely to be under 18, with arrests for auto theft peaking at the age of 16 (Miethe, McCorkle, and Listwan, 2006).

Obscured within these general offender characteristics are two very different categories with different offender characteristics and target selection methods. Joy riders are more likely to be very young males who take cars from local areas and use them for temporary transportation. These offenders often commit numerous other crimes in addition to auto theft and their offending involves little planning and more chance opportunism. Rather than engage in elaborate searches for potential victims, juvenile joy riders rely on opportunity and most often find targets either in their local neighborhoods or the neighborhoods of friends. The general lack of technical skills (hot-wiring, crack ignition switches) leaves juvenile joy riders to pick only those cars where victims leave the keys in the car. In contrast, professional auto thieves are older, far more advanced in their target selection methods, and skill sets. Probably the most striking difference between a professional car thief and a joy rider is the amount of advanced planning that goes into the theft. While joy riders more often base their search for targets only on convenience, professional thieves employ advanced tactics to find their targets. Examples include using DMV records, following drivers home from car dealers, and using informants and scouts to assist in target location. Once professionals find a target they are also far more likely to have the skills necessary to steal a car, regardless of the level of security. Not only are the skills required to steal cars professionally more advanced than those employed by joy riders, but the knowledge of how to dispose of the car is also crucial to a professional's success.

Despite these obvious differences, joy riders and professional thieves do share some target selection criteria in common. First, the vast majority of all auto thefts occur at night as opposed to during the work day (FBI, 2008). This is largely due to the fact that surveillance of vehicles is much more difficult at night when most people are asleep and that alcohol is more likely to be consumed. Alcohol is often associated with car theft in that victims are more likely to forget to be safety conscious when drinking, and offenders are more likely to take chances when drinking (Miethe, McCorkle and Listwan, 2006). A second common target selection characteristic is that most cars are stolen from streets near an owner's home. Research indicates that more than two-thirds of all car thefts occur within one mile of a victim's home and that few occur from either personal or public garages (NCVS, 2002). Automobiles are less vulnerable when in either public or private garages because of the increased security measures at garages as well as decreased visibility of automobiles. This decreased level of victimization in garages is particularly important given the widespread use of public parking garages in urban areas.

Sexual Assault

The last crime to be analyzed is that of sexual assault. Rather than a type, sexual assault is actually a class of crime that encompasses rape, sexual assault, incest, and exposures. Importantly, these crimes, although lumped together, are actually quite different in their victims and target characteristics. In this discussion, focus will be only on rape and sexual assault. Statistics indicate that there were 92,455 forcible rapes in 2006, down approximately 2% from the previous year (FBI, 2008). Overall, sexual assaults, which include rape, attempted rape, and sexual assault, numbered approximately 272,350 incidents in 2006, not including victims under 12 (NCVS, 2006). Thus, after removing forcible rapes, there were approximately 179,895 attempted rapes and sexual assaults in 2006 (FBI, 2008). While these numbers are high they are down from historic levels in the late 1970s (NCVS, 2006). As with other crimes analyzed in this section, the validity of data on offenders is often questionable due to the low number of reported crimes that end in arrest and the reliance on these arrest statistics to generate offender profiles. Compounding this problem is the fact that sexual assault victims have a low rate of reporting to official sources. Specifically, results from the NCVS (2006) indicate that only approximately 50% of victims reported their crimes to the authorities. Factors influencing the reporting of sexual assaults include whether the act was completed versus attempted, victim–offender relationship, use of weapons, and occurrence of injuries during the attack (Dorbinm et al., 1996).

Further exacerbating the creation of good offender profiles in sexual assaults is the volume of seemingly contradictory research concerning the offenders' motivation. Much of the research on sexual assault offenders deals with personality traits, personality disorders, emotional states, and childhood background, rather than common behavioral characteristics or MO features. Because of this line of research, the majority of the reported findings on sexual assault offenders focus on psychological conditions, with much of the information being contradictory. Findings from this line of research indicate that most sexual assault offenders have anti-social personalities, are emotionally weak and insecure, have a history of high exposure to violent pornography, and a history of sexual abuse in their childhoods (Greenfeld, 1997; Longo and Groth, 1983; Rainville and Reaves, 2003). While this information is beneficial in the prosecution or treatment stages, it is not always useful during the investigation of a crime series. Of more use is information on outward offender characteristics, target selection patterns, and behavioral characteristics. As such, research has found that most sexual assault offenders are male (99%), white (64%), younger than 25, and rarely attack victims of different racial categories (FBI, 2008; Greenfeld, 1997; Longo and Groth, 1982; Rainville and Reaves, 2003). Also of importance in understanding sexual assault offenders is that most offenders specializing in this crime type begin with more minor sex-related crimes before progressing to violent sexual assaults (Miethe, McCorkle and Listwan, 2006). Investigatively, this information is important in that it provides guidance into potential suspects. For example, in developing suspect lists for incidents of stranger rape or sexual assault, police should look at those individuals who have prior records involving minor sex offenses (exposure, peeping, etc.) and who live near the offense location or those individuals who have a history of sexual assaults and numerous other crimes.

In analyzing sexual assaults, it is important to focus on victim–offender relationships because those incidents involving strangers are quite different from those where the offender is known to the victim. Although accounting for less than one-third of all sexual assaults, incidents involving offenders who are strangers to the victim have longer journey-to-crime distances, are far more likely to involve the use of weapons, more likely to result in injury, and are less likely to be based on convenience factors (FBI, 2008; NCVS, 2006; Miethe, McCorkle, and Listwan, 2006). While in general sexual assaults involve only rudimentary planning and are opportunistic in nature, stranger based sexual assaults are the exception, often evidencing a degree of planning in terms of target search areas or MO (Miethe, McCorkle, and Listwan, 2006). Perpetrators who are strangers to their victims often conduct searches in areas they feel may contain victims and also may use tactics such as drugs or weapons (Rossmo, 2000). This information is particularly useful, in helping develop investigative strategies and determine suspect lists.

Conclusion

Overall the purpose of this chapter was to provide the reader with a better understanding of the realities of crime types that are commonly dealt with in tactical analysis situations. In particular, this information was designed to provide a better understanding of the nature and extent of the crime problem, as well as specific information about offender and victim types. When used in tactical analysis, this information can provide assistance in determining offender types, suspect lists, and prevention strategies. Taken together with the information provided in the chapters on behavioral geography and criminological theory, this information provides a thorough understanding of the reasoning and rationale of an offender. This information is particularly useful as we begin the next part of the book, which deals with investigative strategies such as geographic profiling, temporal analysis, linking crimes, and forecasting criminal events.

Linking Crime 5

Introduction

Historically and routinely today, officers respond to and investigate crimes. Those crimes are recorded on police reports usually then sent to a sergeant for approval. Once approved, the official police report is uploaded to the department's Records Management System (RMS). Once in the RMS, the detectives are assigned cases based on solvability factors: recovery of evidence, confessions, witness statements, possible suspects, severity of the crime. In most departments, those crimes are assigned to detectives categorically. That is, a detective specializes in a crime type and is only assigned those cases. Robbery detectives get the robberies whereas burglary detectives receive the residential and commercial burglaries. Depending on the size and focus of the department, the categories may be further subdivided by sub-crime classification, geographically, or based on the number of cases carried.

Once a detective is assigned a crime, he further prioritizes the case based on those solvability factors. If there were no witnesses, suspects, evidence, etc. the detective may actually just close the case virtually never to be reopened. If the detective notices information in the report that may be actionable, he will do what is necessary to solve the case. In many police organizations, the detective is responsible for the identification of patterns in their data. After all, he is the one reading each report, he knows that type of crime better than anyone and has only that one particular type of activity to focus on. Many detectives are proficient at finding crimes seemingly committed by the same person. Once a person is arrested for one of their crimes under investigation, the detective will sift back through his case load and determine what other, unsolved and similar cases could have been committed by the person arrested. At that point, the detective attempts to get the suspect to confess to the additional cases and thus, clear more cases.

This routine occurs daily in departments around the world. It is often the detectives in an organization who are the principals in identifying and resolving crime series. And, they are often very successful. However, they often lack the tools or training required to find those patterns in the first place. In investigator's school, instructors do not actually teach the future detective how to find crime series in data. The focus of the investigation is the crime, not the crimes. It is by sheer coincidence that the detective finds patterns in data at all, rarely employing specialized techniques and rarely utilizing "pattern detection" software.

Within the last few decades, departments have begun to embrace the crime analyst as an individual in a department who has the tools and techniques to assist in the identification and resolution of crime series (Bair, 2002). Similar to the situation detectives face, however, many analysts also have not been taught how to find these patterns and as such, rely on similar investigative methods to find similarity among crime.

Linkage Blindness

The Italian economist Vilfredo Pareto in his 80/20 rule (Lemberg, 2008) and Marvin E. Wolfgang in his theory of juvenile delinquency (Norval, 1972) bring us two theories that help define the purpose behind crime series analysis. If there is adequate evidence to suggest that clustering of factors does occur in most phenomena and that a small cohort of individuals are responsible for a disproportionate number of criminal events, then we can be confident there are crime series in our data. It is imperative that someone in the organization identify this cohort of crimes or persons. If these crimes or persons can be identified, then it stands to reason that the organization can reduce their crime rates dramatically by focusing on the few who impact the many. Why do so many crime series go unnoticed for so long? We call this Linkage Blindness.

Jane Smith

An analyst from the Midwest shared a story and it illustrates this phenomenon of linkage blindness. Jane Smith had recently downloaded the Automated Tactical Analysis of Crime (ATAC) software application and wanted to evaluate how well it did in assisting her with the identification of crime series and patterns. In ATAC, she hand-entered every single auto theft from the last year into her database. She took great care to properly enter and describe each event.

Smith stated that after she, and only she, completed the entry of the events, she began using the methods and tools within ATAC to look for patterns in her data. Within the first hour, she uncovered a pattern that had been in her data for several months; an auto theft series. Now aware of this series, she was able to analyze the group of cases, make a prediction, and watch as patrol caught the suspect on the date and time she predicted. The big question is: why did not this analyst notice the pattern when she was hand-entering all those records? The answer is: our brains do not function in this way. Our brains can identify uniqueness better than routine, everyday events (Restak, 2001). Her brain did not pick up on the hidden pattern within the data because there was nothing so unique or similar about those cases to draw her attention to it. Only when we apply a process model such as the "IZE" method do we see patterns emerge.

Sheriff Joe

Another example of how we often overlook crime series in our data comes from the Midwest. Joe Robertson (a pseudonym), a sheriff in a very small town, was responsible for public safety in his community. The town was so small ("How small was it?") that emergency 911 rang to his home phone! Sheriff Joe had kept an Access database (his Records Management System) of every incident that had occurred in his jurisdiction from the time he became sheriff. Not only did he enter every report, he personally wrote each of the reports and conducted the investigations. There were several hundred records in this database spanning three years.

One day, Sheriff Joe sought the help of his long-time friend, Dan Helms, with a problem he was having in his database. Apparently it had become corrupt. While Dan was fixing Sheriff Joe's database, Dan decided to spend a few minutes scanning the data looking for crime patterns. Within a few minutes, Dan uncovered a five-case horse tack series spanning more than a year. When Dan returned Sheriff Joe's database to him Dan asked, "Did you ever catch that horse tack thief?" Sheriff Joe replied, "What thief?" Dan explained what he found. Sheriff Joe later commented, "I never saw that." It turned out to be a valid series Sheriff Joe was unaware existed in his data.

How did Sheriff Joe miss this series? He was an excellent investigator. In fact, he had personally investigated each of those incidents in the series. And, he personally entered them into his database. The reason Sheriff Joe did not identify this series in his jurisdiction has to do with the fact that officers and investigators are not trained to look for patterns; their job is to investigate and solve "a" crime. As stated previously, our brains are not wired to find patterns in common elements. They are best at identifying uniqueness. If you are an analyst or an officer, how many times have you sat in briefing only to hear the most recent "exceptional" crime orated to the squad? Do the sergeant or officers describe in detail the "routine" burglary they took yesterday? Of course not. We remember uniqueness, things outside normal, events that are not like other events. The elements that we routinely identify patterns on are lost in the noise of everyday crime. Unless we employ the right tools using the right methods, our crime patterns remain hidden in our data. In the following section, we will introduce the types of data necessary to avoid linkage blindness.

Who, What, Where, When, How and Why

On a recent trip to instruct a dozen analysts on crime mapping, we noticed a unique set of placards on the wall of the department's training room. Each placard had a word across the top in bold, black lettering and then a set of cartoon-like images on the plaque. The five words across the top of each placard were who, what, where, when, and how. Underneath each were images that illustrated the information to be gathered regarding these five categories. The placards were reminders to officers about the information they should gather when investigating crimes. Most interesting was the absence of one of the more important placards—why. Knowing the "why" of a crime can often be the single factor that leads the investigator or analyst to the perpetrator.

Some might ague that why someone commits a crime is irrelevant; the fact that they committed the crime is what is important. For prosecution, this argument seems reasonable. However, to uncover what led someone to commit the crime, and perhaps others like it, trying to infer the "why" of a crime is extraordinarily useful. Inferring the why of a crime is the hardest of the six and requires a deeper look at the other five.

The Dresser Drawers Theory

Kevin Johnson was an analyst and then became an officer for the same department. He carried his understanding of crime and criminology from behind the desk into the field. Officer Johnson investigated countless residential burglaries. To him, each seemed similar with only slight variations in the five categories, usually a result of the environment. During one of his investigations of a typical residential burglary on a particularly slow day, Officer Johnson decided to spend a bit more time in the residence trying to understand as much as he could about the crime and suspect from the clues left at the scene. At first the effort was yielding little other than what was already noted—after all, he had been trained to investigate the who, what, where, when, and how of a crime. Officer Johnson decided to try and understand the why. Why did the burglar choose this house? Why did he enter the way he did? Why did he take what he took? Why did he commit the crime the way he did?

One thing that Officer Johnson wondered was why the suspect left all three drawers open on the dresser ransacked during the crime. After all, in order to leave all three open, the suspect would have had to start at the bottom and work his way up. If he started at the top and rummaged the top drawer, Officer Johnson began to see how the suspect would need to first close the top drawer if he wanted to continue searching subsequent lower drawers. Was this a conscientious act on the part of the burglar, or an interesting fact not entirely useful in the investigation? Officer Johnson noted

Linking Crime

this fact in his notebook and continued throughout the day until later that afternoon when he was dispatched to another residential burglary. In this burglary, the suspect targeted a similar three-drawer dresser in the master bedroom, but left only the bottom drawer open, closing the top two drawers. The types of property taken in this burglary were slightly different as well. In this burglary, the suspect seemed to take inexpensive property. Additionally, the suspect took several video games from the living room. Officer Johnson remembered that in the earlier burglary, the suspect had taken jewelry. In fact, the suspect left behind certain jewelry the victim remarked was costume jewelry and not worth much.

The question of why began to drive the way Officer Johnson investigated subsequent burglaries. Of particular interest to him was the question of why the suspects in the two different burglaries rummaged through the dressers differently.

Officer Johnson decided to study how a person would rummage through a set of dresser drawers if simulating the actions of a burglar. He asked his wife to pretend she had just broken into a person's house, had run to the master bedroom, and was about to go through the dresser drawers in an attempt to find items of value. His wife stood at their dresser as Officer Johnson shouted, "Go!" Mrs. Johnson frantically grabbed for the top drawer, opened it, and moved clothes around simulating looking for property. She then closed the top drawer and hurriedly opened the middle drawer. At this drawer, she even threw a few things on the ground as she pretended to rummage through the drawer as quickly as she could. Finally, she closed the middle drawer to gain access to the final, bottom drawer. She again moved clothes around looking underneath whatever was inside the drawer. She got up and told her husband, "Done." She left the bottom drawer open.

Officer Johnson had his wife repeat this exercise and on the third attempt, his wife did something differently. This time, his wife opened the bottom drawer first. She then went on to open the middle and then top drawer leaving all three dresser drawers open at the end. Officer Johnson asked, "Why did you start with the bottom drawer this time?" She replied, "It seemed more efficient."

After testing the process on several of his friends and fellow officers in addition to his wife, Office Johnson began to theorize that those who chose to open the drawers in reverse order, bottom to top, had learned that this method was more efficient than opening from top to bottom. Later arrests and comparisons against the property taken led the officer to theorize that those who started at the top were the less experienced burglars. Those who started at the bottom and worked their way upward were the more experienced and wiser burglars.

The "dresser drawers" theory led the officer and other investigators, as well as the analysts, to direct their investigatory efforts based on the number of drawers left open in a burglary; assuming the burglar targeted the dresser. For instance, if the burglar left all drawers open, the team would search known offenders;, those who might have previous criminal records, or those who would be willing to drive a greater distance or might be an older suspect. If the bottom drawer was left open, they theorized that perhaps this was an inexperienced burglar, someone young, someone not on probation or parole. This would lead the investigators to first search local schools, talk to neighbors regarding deviant juveniles in the neighborhood, etc.

Why were the dresser drawers left open? Officers are not taught to ask the why, just to note that they were left open. It is left up to the analyst to ask these questions. So there exists a disconnect between those who gather the data and those who use the data. Good analysts or researchers will understand their data collection methods. In order to find the right answer, someone must first ask the right question.

The Investigative Mindset: Fact and Inference

Another example of how asking why can provide other useful categories of data comes from Daytona Beach, Florida. Officer Mike Kerney was investigating a series of residential burglaries where window screens had been cut to allow the suspect to reach through to unlock a window. This was neither a new nor unique MO in his jurisdiction, but Officer Kerney noticed something different. In a handful of the burglaries, Officer Kerney noticed that the way in which the screen was cut indicated that he was dealing with a left-handed person. The cuts in some of the burglaries were shaped like the letter C whereas in other burglaries, the cut was shaped like a reverse C. Officer Kerney concluded that the logical and comfortable manner in which a left-handed burglar would cut the screen would follow the letter C pattern. Because of his observation and this one simple fact, he was able to clear a number of cases, while excluding erroneous cases. Instead of only noting on his reports that the suspect cut the screen to gain entry, Officer Kerney thought deeper about the crime and tried to answer the "why" of the crime. Why did the suspect cut the screen having this particular pattern? By simply looking at the why, Officer Kerney narrowed his burglar suspect population from 100% to a mere 7% (the approximate population of left-handed individuals in the United States).

In addition to the evidence-based data we capture about the incident and the data we develop from theories about why a crime was committed, we can also infer data from the crime itself, such as in the case of Officer Kerney.

A main distinction between the data that our RMS currently capture and those data we would like them to capture is in inferential data; most of which comes from the how question. One might argue that we can not guess or make up data where data is missing. That is not entirely true. Let us take the following residential burglary for example.

Linking Crime

A residential burglary against a single family dwelling occurred in Springfield on January 1 sometime between 0800 and 1700 hours. A 37-inch standard television, Sony DVD player and a six pack of Pepsi removed from the pantry were the items noted by the victim as being stolen. From the evidence left at the scene, we learned that entry was gained through the front door by means of a pry tool as indicated by the pry marks next to the lock. No other MO information was readily available. Or was it?

Once again we are confronted with the *how* of the crime. A television was taken, that is all we know. But, how did the suspect take the 37-inch television? First, we know the sheer weight of a 37-inch television set would require a strong adult to move it. So, we might rule out young kids. Second, the dimensions of the television set were such that it probably required two people to carry. It was just too bulky to wrap one's arms around. Moreover, how much did the television weigh? The size and shape of the television set were such that no one person could have carried it out the door. Hence, we can infer, given the weight and dimensions of the television, that there must have been two suspects. We can also infer that they used a vehicle. They certainly were not taking the bus or hopping on their bicycles for a quick escape! In fact, we can even go further to say that the type of vehicle was probably a SUV or truck, given the dimensions of the television. After all, the television would not have fit through a standard passenger vehicle door opening or in the trunk.

These inferences provide valuable insights into how our criminal committed his crime. Yet, nowhere on a police report will these categories of data be found. Case in point, remember the five placards? It is up to the analyst to analyze the crimes in an attempt to gather these elements that give insight into the act. With this insight, an analyst can do more with the limited data available.

In addition to the inference of data, it is often the enhanced observation that adds that valuable insight into the crime. Many residential burglaries committed around the world begin with the suspect kicking open the front door. In such a case, the officer will note that the point of entry was the front door, and that the method of entry was forced or even "kicked open." Less often, the officer notes the size, shape, pattern, direction, and possible handedness of the offender. Simply looking at the shoeprint on the door to identify which shoe was used, left or right, can help us to guess the offender's handedness. Right-handed persons would most likely use their right, dominate foot to kick open a door. The opposite is true for lefthanders. Likewise, where is the toe in the shoeprint? If the toe is pointing upward, the suspect was facing the door. If the toe is pointing downward, the suspect used a heel kick. This small fact in itself will not resolve the crime; however, it can be useful when comparing and contrasting other residential burglaries for inclusion or exclusion of cases into a series and helps avoid linkage blindness.

Process Models: The IZE Method

Tactical crime analysis is the comprehensive identification, evaluation, analysis, and resolution of specific criminal activity problems. Technologically, tactical crime analysis has advanced just as much as the other components of crime analysis. However, in tactical analysis, new techniques and advances in methodology have also developed. One is the IZE method for finding crime series in tabular data; so named because every word in the acronym ends in "ize" (Bair, 2005).

Traditional methods for identifying crime series include reading all the police reports and playing a mental matching game of finding like cases. Using IZE, analysts have a standardized methodology that, when used, can enable the analyst to identify more crime series than before. The IZE method instructs analysts to Categorize, Generalize, Organize, Minimize and Maximize their data in such a way that patterns begin to emerge. The general steps are outlined below:

- Categorize: Create variables conducive to finding crime trends (hair, race, sex, point of entry, weapon type, vehicle make, etc.).
- Generalize: Create general values for your categories (handgun, rifle, male, female, brown, black, blonde, etc.).
- Organize: Group certain MO variables and person categories together; sort data.
- Minimize: Query for clusters in your data identified by organizing it.
- Maximize: Query features salient to the identified crime series.

The first step in this process model is to *categorize* your data. This means that you create variables for the different types of data that you wish to capture. In looking for trends in crime data you might want to study a person's race or gender, the crime's point of entry or the weapon that was used. These are your categories. You probably would not want to study "date of last medical exam" as a category about a person because it would not necessarily help you in matching crimes or people responsible for the same crime.

Once you have identified a set of categories that you wish to use, you would then *generalize* the values that you store in those variables. If you wanted to find commonalities in the property taken, it would not be effective to have every conceivable value possible as in the following example:

- diamond ring
- heart-shaped diamond band
- diamond ring—marquee cut

Linking Crime

Instead, you would want to *generalize* the values in your variables to describe a category, in this case—jewelry.

Now that your data is in order, you can *organize* it. This is where you will spend the bulk of your time. As simple as it seems, identifying crime trends is a matter of organizing vast amounts of data so that similarities in data will emerge. Because of the large amount of data in law enforcement, particularly when dealing with crime trends, it becomes laborious and time consuming to scroll back and forth between a table or spreadsheet to check the value of one variable against the value of another using traditional applications like Microsoft's Excel, Access or SAS. To avoid this, simply reduce the number of variables captured, thus reducing the amount of information to analyze. However, limiting the information is obviously not the best approach.

Another, more efficient method is to organize the variables in a way that enables you to identify patterns in the data more effectively. Certain crimes have key variables that are more important than others to its patterning. For example, if you wish to analyze residential burglaries, suspect descriptors will prove less fruitful than looking at point of entry, method of entry, property taken, location type and the suspect's actions against the property. Conversely, if analyzing a robbery, you will focus more on the suspect's race, height, weight, age, eye color, hair color, weapon type, actions against persons, than point of entry and method of entry. In order to analyze different types of crimes and the variables conducive to identifying patterns in those crimes, we want to organize our variables (categories) so that those containing the most relevant data are co-located. This displays those variables containing the most useful data and reduces the need to scroll through variables comparing less useful values.

Once you have organized your categories horizontally across a matrix, you can organize vertically. Organizing data vertically is simply a matter of sorting the values in those variables you identified as relevant to the identification of a certain type of pattern. By sorting the variables, you group like values together vertically in the same way that you grouped like variables horizontally. The purpose of sorting the data is to identify similarities or clusters of similar data.

Once organized, you will see similarities emerge in your data, including particular data values or salient features in your data that you will want to query to further analyze a subset of data. This brings us to the fourth IZE in finding patterns—*minimize*.

Minimizing your data is reducing the data through queries. If you identify a group of location types as they relate to burglaries that seem similar, you query for those data and then delve deeper into the other variables related to that type of crime. For example, if you notice a group of dog door points of entry for residential burglaries, you may want to select just the dog door points of entry for residential burglaries. Once queried, you then look closer at the other variables to see if any other similarities exist in your data.

If so, you further reduce your data set by querying for those similar values. This process of organizing and then minimizing your data eventually leads to a core of cases you believe to be related—a pattern or series.

Most analysts stop here. The trend has been identified and thus the work is done. Not necessarily. It is at this point that the analyst can have the greatest impact on the investigation. In addition to the obvious statistical and analytical processes you should now perform, one often overlooked IZE step is *maximize*.

Maximizing your data involves using those values in those variables significant to your trend and expanding your search on each of them. Take the dog door residential burglary example. One of the salient features of this trend is the fact that the suspect entered through the dog door. So, to maximize your search, you would search for only dog door in all of your crime data. You may discover that a criminal trespass shared this point of entry in common and provided the single clue to identify the suspect and unlock the series.

Using the IZE technique, let us work through a mental exercise to see it in action. Suppose you want to identify a set of twins within the population of the United States. First, let us assess the magnitude of this query. There are approximately 300 million people living in the United States.

Your task is to identify two of those 300 million who are biological twins. You have been provided with a database, your RMS, of every person containing a few standard variables: race, gender, height, weight, date of birth, and eye color. Beyond these variables, you are entitled to a few more. However, it is up to you to determine which variables you need in order to find a set of twins. Would you want any more than were already provided? How many? What are they?

Let us use the IZE method to find a set of twins. Our first task is to identify those categories that are most conducive to identifying patterns in people. What are they? The obvious category is date of birth. In most cases, twins are born on the same date. You might also select name as another category. With just these two variables you could probably begin identifying twins. Unfortunately, you would also falsely identify people sharing the same date of birth and the same name. How many Jane Smiths born on the same date would you suspect there are? In a pool of approximately 150 million, there are probably thousands. More variables are needed. Identify the categories that you think help identify the twins. Once you have a set of variables, move on to the next step, generalize.

In the generalize step, we generalize the values for the variables you selected. If you select hair color as a category, you are on the right track. Hair color is a category that might assist you in finding "like" people. How many different hair colors are there to describe a person's hair? The Clairol Corporation believes that a person has 120 different hair color choices. Clairol produces more than 100 color choices for men and women. That is an astounding number of choices one could make when entering each unique person's hair color. Let us take blond as an example. A person could describe his or her hair as: blond/blond, dirty blond, dishwater blond, flaxen, fair, golden, honey, platinum blond, sandy blond, champagne blond, strawberry blond, yellow, tow-headed, etc. Clairol lists 37 colors alone in the blond category (Clairol, 2008)! Under the brown hair category, Clairol provides 53 colors. Shades of brown hair include brown, brunet/brunette, chestnut, chocolate, cinnamon, dark, mahogany. Would you ever have imagined there were so many ways to describe brown? Interestingly, Clairol breaks all 120 hair color choices into four general values: brown, blond, black, red. You might want a few more generalized values to account for persons who are bald, grey or silver, or who use specialized colors.

Did you select race or ethnicity as a category? Ethnicity will be a useful variable to have to later organize your people into similar groups. How many unique ethnic groups are there? What general values might you elect to use? The CIA World Fact book (CIA Web site, 2007) reports that there are 231 different ethnic groups in the world. The ethnicities you focus on may even depend on the part of the world where you are located. For instance, in the Southwest United States, analysts are wise to understand the various differences between Hispanics and American Indians. If you are an analyst in Hawaii, you need to know the various island races. If you ware an analyst in Florida, you need to know how a person from Mexico differs from a person from Puerto Rico.

Perhaps you decide that you do not want to use race or ethnicity but skin tone as a means to generalize and classify people. That is perfectly reasonable and actually has already been done. Felix Von Luschan's Chromatic Scale is a method of classifying skin color. The equipment consists of 36 opaque glass tiles which are compared to the subject's skin. Instead of race, Von Luschan thought that classifying persons would be much simpler by just using the color of their skins. But, just as identifying a person's race can be subjective to the outside observer, so too was Von Luschan's scale (Wikipedia, 2008).

The purpose of the generalize step in the process is simply this: if everything is unique, nothing is the same. Ergo, we must group our data values by generalizing them into smaller, manageable sets.

The next step in finding our twins is to organize. We organize those variables to the left of the grid that are conducive to identifying patterns in twins (people) and then organize those same variables vertically so we can identify like data in those variables. What variables are useful for finding patterns in people? You might select gender, race, date of birth, hair color, and perhaps one or two more. If you move those variables to the left of the grid and then sort by those variables, you wll notice, for example, that all the females who are white and who share the same date of birth and hair color appear next to each other in the grid.

With these clusters of data, you begin minimizing your data set. First, select only white females. Then, re-sort on the remaining variables. What other similarities emerge? Continue minimizing the data by selecting those values that are similar until you believe you have two cases that are the same—twins.

Now that you've identified the twins, you are not done, you must maximize. You take those attributes about your twins that made them similar and then query into the database looking for their likenesses. You might have identified a set of twins who shared these traits: white, female, brown hair, green eyes, date of birth of 9/16/1988, last name of Smith, home address of 1234 E Main St. Using these elements you query the database for most of these values while leaving out one or two. In other words, you query the database looking for white, brown hair, green eyes, date of birth of 9/16/1988 and a last name of Smith. In this example, you omitted the address and the gender. By doing so, you might find another person who has almost all those same characteristics shared by your twins—their brother!

The second part of the maximize step is to query on salient attributes. Given the information about your twins, if you query on the address, you may find a relationship between last name of the homeowner and the address of the house—their mother. The string of connections continues as you query on these salient attributes into other data sources. The purpose is to find all those individuals or events that might have some link or relationship to the items of interest.

Perhaps there are other categories that would enable you to find the matches without finding false positives. In fact, using only three variables, you could successfully identify most of the twins in the United States without identifying similar, but biologically unrelated individuals. The three variables are: date of birth, mother's maiden name, and hospital where born. Three simple variables could easily filter 300 million people and enable you to identify almost every pair of twins in the United States. Having the right categories initially is of upmost importance. The mental process of identifying a set of twins in a large data set is analogous to identifying two crimes sharing similar MO, persons, and vehicle descriptors.

Process Models: Inductive Versus Deductive

The IZE method overcomes linkage blindness by providing a standardized methodology for identifying patterns in data. In this section, we introduce the deductive and inductive method, two other process models that have been used to find patterns in data for years.

The deductive method starts with axioms or *postulates* (true statements) with the goal of providing *theorems* (many true statements) that logically follow from them. The inductive method begins with many observations of

Linking Crime

nature with the goal of finding a few, prevailing tenets about how it works (laws and theories) (Boba, 2007)

In crime analysis, we take observations about crime and attempt to identify and define a set of records as "the way it works." If this one crime and related records are different from other crimes, we believe we have a series or pattern based on their similarity among the crimes and dissimilarity to other crimes. Inductive reasoning goes from the specific to the general. Deductive reasoning goes from the general to the specific.

Both methods are applied to crime linkage as follows. With an inductive approach, the analysts begin with a single case or something they wish to find related to it. With a deductive approach, the analyst starts with all the data and begins to organize the data so that specific cases having like values emerge as in the IZE method. Both approaches are acceptable and encouraged as methods of identifying patterns. Investigators primarily follow the inductive method whereas analysts will use both.

With the inductive approach, it is usually a lone or anomalous case that prompts the analyst to inquire as to other similar cases. For instance, a recent case might emerge involving the theft of copper from houses under construction. This may be the first case the analyst sees having this particular MO. Thus, the analyst begins to search for cases where other houses under construction have had copper stolen. The analyst identifies that there are several other cases having this MO and begins to develop a pattern using this inductive approach.

Conversely, with a deductive approach, the analyst begins with all the data and attempts to organize the data so that patterns emerge. The deductive approach is very much like panning for gold where the prospector continues to sift out dirt and unwanted elements until what is left is either a nugget or nothing. The analyst pans through the data sifting out the typical and unwanted data until what is left is often something unusual or not like data seen before.

The analyst begins by sifting out all property related crimes focusing instead on person crimes. He then removes all persons who are white and Asian, but leaves in Hispanic, African American, and Middle Eastern. He then removes those crimes not occurring against single family residences. Finally, the analyst removes all cases where a weapon was not noted in the MO. What is left may be a set of robbery or criminal trespass cases where the suspects were identified as black or Middle-Eastern and used weapons against occupants of their home. In other words, a series of home invasion crimes possibly related.

The benefit of a deductive approach is that you avoid the loss of data due to missing, incomplete or slightly different parameters. In the example above, we removed suspects who were White and Asian but left all other races because the suspects may have been described as African American,

Middle-Eastern, Hispanic or the race was not noted at all. Using a deductive approach eliminates the possibility of excluding cases that may be related because, as compared to the inductive method, we only select the ones we think we want.

As an analyst, you may be following a robbery series involving a white male with red hair, but inadvertently remove a potentially useful related robbery because you queried for data for suspects only having red hair. In one of those cases, the suspect's hair may have been noted as "unknown" or "other."

The deductive approach is difficult and time consuming, but can often provide a related case that holds the key that will unlock an entire series. Holmes, the quintessential detective created by Sir Arthur Conan Doyle, knew that by eliminating all other factors, the remaining one must be the truth. This is the essence of the deductive process.

As stated previously, the inductive approach usually begins with an anomalous case or interesting factoid about a crime that prompts the analysts to inquire to see if there are other like cases. Numerous tools are available to inductively identify patterns in our data. When looking at data from an inductive approach, the analyst will leverage his understanding of Structured Query Language (SQL) and other data mining techniques as described later in this chapter.

Process Models: Quantitative Identification

Another way to look for the emergence of a crime series or pattern in data is to use threshold analysis. Threshold analysis uses historic data to identify and establish norms in one's data and then develops mechanisms to be alerted when those norms are broken.

Chief Burns in agency "A" gathered data for a year's worth of robberies in his jurisdiction. He noticed that the robberies had seasonal norms as well as minimum and maximum number of robberies during any given week. Factoring for the seasonality of robberies, Chief Burns discovered that his jurisdiction had, on average, between 35 and 45 robberies per week. For Chief Burns, having between 35 and 45 robberies was considered normal for his department. Therefore, if the department experienced more than 45 or less than 35 robberies one week, it would break their norms.

Threshold analysis attempts to discover norms in the data and alert you when you break a threshold. The threshold need not be only the minimum and maximum values. In fact, most analysts will buffer the minimum and maximum values to account for slight variations in counts. Chief Burns chose to buffer his average number of robberies each week by one standard deviation. Therefore, if Chief Burns' jurisdiction experienced less than 31 or more than 49 robberies in a given week, he considered that atypical and investigated to determine why the norms were broken.

Linking Crime

Chief Burns also used threshold analysis to uncover the emergence of a robbery series at fast food restaurants. The norms he had set for what his department expected of fast food robberies was exceeded by more than one standard deviation. This atypical rise in robberies prompted Chief Burns to query for and analyze fast food robberies that week. In doing so, Chief Burns noticed that several robberies shared similar MOs and suspect descriptions in a particular part of town. Chief Burns eventually refined the collection of robberies to a crime series and worked with his department to eventually apprehend the suspects.

Threshold analysis can be used not only to identify crime series, but also to uncover emergent patterns, increases or decreases in any activity. Threshold analysis can also be used in spatial analysis to uncover areas experiencing above average or below average levels of activity.

Bob, a crime analyst for the Westbrook Police Department, developed a threshold map to study the percentage of change from one week to another in residential burglaries by census layer. Each week Bob would develop a map that compared this week's residential burglary totals for each census tract against last week's residential burglary totals. The census tracts were shaded based on the percent of change from one week to the next. Those that experienced a statistically significant increase in burglary counts from one week to the next would show up on the map in bright red. Those tracts where residential burglary counts fell significantly were displayed in blue. Using his threshold map, Bob could visually identify those areas that might have a burglary series or pattern emerging as well as those areas that might have been impacted by neighborhood watch programs, CPTED implementation, or the arrest of a suspect.

Data Mining

One pattern that you might have seen emerge thus far in this chapter is the common thread that analysts need in order to have a firm grasp of their data. Not only must analysts be proficient in statistics, temporal analysis, and spatial analysis, they must also be experts at databases and the means used to mine their data. Analysts are beginning to learn more of data and databases, but rarely hold the mastery of the language used to query the data. SQL is the common and basic language used to mine data. Using SQL, analysts can query the database for information, perform statistics, and even modify their data to better meet their needs. The analyst's ability to mine data enables him or her to perform the various process models described herein against the varied types of data they encounter.

A simple SQL statement written to extract all the robberies committed with a handgun might look like this:

SELECT * from MO where [Crime] = "Robbery" and [Weapon] = "Handgun"

This statement would be analogous to "See Dick Run" in a child's development and understanding of the English language. A more robust understanding of SQL would enable the analyst to perform a query such as this:

SELECT MO.*,PERSONS.*,VEHICLE.* FROM (MO LEFT JOIN PERSONS ON MO.[IR Number] = PERSONS.[IR Number]) LEFT JOIN VEHICLE ON PERSONS.[IR Number] = VEHICLE.[IR Number] WHERE [First Date] >=NOW-30 AND [Synopsis of Crime] LIKE '%copper%' AND [Synopsis of Crime] LIKE '%construction%' AND [Synopsis of Crime] LIKE '%pipe%' AND ([Make] LIKE 'Ford' OR [Make] LIKE 'Chevrolet') AND [Color] LIKE 'Blue'

In this query, the analyst is querying the database for all crimes committed in the last 30 days where the words "copper," "pipe," and "construction" are found within the police narrative and where a blue Ford or Chevrolet vehicle was seen leaving the area. The inquiry itself is not complex, but the language required to extract that information from the RMS is.

A thorough understanding of SQL is essential to an analyst in his or her quest for patterns in the data. Just as a mastery of a foreign language will enable you to communicate better with those who speak it, a mastery of SQL enable you to communicate to the fullest with your data.

SQL is but one language that can be used to perform the myriad of data mining techniques necessary for pattern identification. Regular Expressions or RegEx is another language that can be used to extract information from data. From data comes information; out of information comes knowledge. With knowledge, we are on our way to understanding and we can use our understanding of the data to make the most effective and informed decisions regarding police operations. The RegEx language provides a means to extract more relevant and meaningful information from our data.

Inherent in the name itself, SQL is "structured." You must adhere to certain rules and stay within those rules to use SQL. RegEx is also a structured language, but provides more flexibility when it comes to designating which data to search.

Data Mining: Regular Expressions

RegEx enables us to perform such queries as: find the word "green" within five words of "motorcycle." It provides an ability to query for data not possible using traditional SQL. Unfortunately, not only do analysts now have to master SQL, they must also master RegEx to be mine data most effectively. Whereas SQL is a structured language used against any data structure, RegEx must be written in specialized application and can be much more confusing

Linking Crime

and complex than SQL, requiring a completely new set of rules to learn to perform even the simplest of queries.

The financial industry has been using regular expressions for years to uncover complex patterns and relationships in financial data. When you receive catalogs or unsolicited items in the mail, it is most likely due to some pattern uncovered in your spending habits using regular expressions.

Below is a table showing various syntax for RegEx. With an understanding of a few simple RegEX building blocks, you can begin to construct statements to mine your data.

Simple "or" expression

- Explanation: Finds WORD1 or WORD2
- Expression: WORD1|WORD2
- Example: JACK|JILL
- Results: Finds text containing the word JACK or JILL.

Simple "and" expression

- Explanation: Finds WORD1 before and included in the same variable as WORD2
- Expression: WORD1.+WORD2
- Example: DOOR.+FOOT
- Results: Finds text containing the word DOOR and FOOT in order.

Proximity search

- Explanation: Finds WORD1 within 10 words of WORD2 and no words in between.
- Expression: \b(?:WORD1\W+(?:\w+\W+){0,10}WORD2\b)
- Example: \b(?:CRACK\W+(?:\w+\W+){0,10}PIPE\b)
- Results: Finds data containing the word CRACK before and within a ten word proximity of the word PIPE and separated by zero words.

Using the reference table, let us construct a few expressions to perform a few fairly typical searches in data. Suppose your agency is experiencing a rash of thefts where suspects are taking copper from various sources to be used or sold. In order to use SQL, you will be required to specify the tables, fields and tables you wish to query for cases that fit a certain criteria. For instance, you may query the "Property" field for the word "copper." You might refine the query by specifying "construction, pipe, tube or wire" in the narrative or synopsis field. Of course, there may be cases that elude this query. What about the case where the officer noted that "copper tubing" was removed? Perhaps he or she noted "copper" in the property field, but you forgot to search for "tubing" in addition to "tube." Using RegEx we can construct a simple query that searches all variations of this inquiry: "COPPER" within 20 words of "TUBING" in either direction and separated by zero words.

\b(?:COPPER\W+(?:\w+\W+){0,20}TUBING|TUBING\W+(?:\w+\W+){0,20}COPPER\b)

In this example, we want to also search for those expressions containing PIPING. Therefore, by incorporating a simple "or" statement using the pipe separator, we can now search for COPPER within 20 words of TUBING or PIPING

\b(?:COPPER\W+(?:\w+\W+){0,20}(TUBING|PIPING)|(TUBING|PIPING)\W+(?:\w+\W+){0,20}COPPER\b)

RegEx opens the door for analysts to perform sophisticated data mining against their structured and unstructured data. Despite its complexity, with a little effort, an analyst can begin to construct simple expressions that can be a force multiplier for pattern identification and case investigation.

Data Mining: Concepts

Advancements in the way we query for information has taken us from SQL to RegEx and now to Concepts. Concepts hold the future for law enforcement and their use is only beginning to emerge in a handful of departments around the world. A concept is developed using RegEx that describes an item or action. Once the concept is developed, the analyst can combine concepts using RegEx to uncover almost anything imaginable. Taking our previous example, a concept might be used to find where a "green motorcycle" was used in a crime. The analyst first develops a concept for the color green. In a simple example, synonyms are used to develop the concept. The "green" concept may look for synonyms of green such as green, turquoise, teal, and even bluish. The concept of a motorcycle may include "motorcycle," "moped," "chopper," etc. Once the concepts are developed, the analyst simply tells the program to conduct a search using these concepts. In this case, the analyst might instruct the software program to search for the concept "green" within 20 words of the "motorcycle" concept. All of this is accomplished using RegEx.

More complex and advanced concepts can be developed with a mastery of RegEx. For example, the military might want to identify references to "tanks" in data. A concept developed that looks for tanks might instruct the program to look for tank but that the word cannot occur within a certain

Linking Crime

number of words of "fish," "gas," or "propane." This concept reduces the possibility of false positives when searching for tanks and improves an analyst's efficiency and effectiveness.

Let's take a look at an example concept. Suppose you wanted to create a concept around weapons that could be used by itself to find any mention of a weapon in a report, but also as a building block with other expressions. The concept developed to find weapons may look like this:

(GUN|FIREARM|WEAPON|RIFLE|GAK|GLOCK|SEMI-AUTO|SEMIAUTO)

Once this RegEx is developed, it will be saved as "WEAPONS."

To use this concept in combination with other expressions or concepts, simply replace the search expression with the concept's name. We might search for all robberies where a weapon was used by writing the following:

ROBBERY.+<WEAPONS>

Or, to search for weapons within proximity of the word ROBBERY, we might do this:

\b(?:<WEAPONS>\W+(?:\w+\W+){0,20}ROBBERY|ROBBERY\W+(?:\w+\W+){0,20}<WEAPONS>\b)

Small variations in the RegEx software engine will exist, but the general principle behind concepts remains. An analyst may develop a library of concepts to be selected and used when the need presents itself. Using all the prior examples, an analyst might develop a concept to find "copper" and another called "wire" to find "wiring, tubing or piping" and still a third that combines the "copper" concept with the "wire" concept to search for cases also containing air conditioning units. Armed with this library of concepts from which to draw, the data mining possibilities are endless. We could later use the air conditioning unit concept, which looks for "A/C, AC, air cond, Trane," along with a residential burglary concept to identify all the residential burglaries where entry was made by removing the window air conditioner.

Conclusion

The crime analyst has the tools, techniques and methods to accelerate an agency's ability to indentify crime series and patterns. An analyst becomes a force multiplier for an agency by bringing a unique set of abilities and perspective to the problems a department faces.

Departments will continue to identify patterns in data, to analyze and investigate them, and to find resolutions to the problems they face. As of late, the analyst has begun to assist the investigative effort by bringing to bear these abilities and perspectives to identify, analyze and resolve crime series more efficiently and effectively. Today's investigator has become overwhelmed with the volume and complexity of the data. What used to be done with hand searches and memorization must now be done with sound methods and powerful tools to enhance the investigator's ability to conduct the investigation. Using the methods and techniques presented in the chapter, the analyst and investigator can once again get the upper hand in the fight against crime.

Using the list of cases from the Excel file from the Bair Software website, identify the twins using the methods described in this chapter. Answer the following questions:

1. Which method worked best for identifying the twins?
2. How many factors or variable values did they have in common?
3. Within the original dataset and before any methods were used, did the two records appear easily or did they get lost in the noise of the data?

Temporal Analysis

Introduction

Temporal analysis is the analysis of time—when events occur, how long they last, their frequency, and regularity. Many types of temporal analysis have been practiced by researchers, scientists, and professionals from hundreds of various disciplines for many centuries; however, the temporal analysis of serial crime events presents special difficulties that can be particularly challenging. Fortunately, the timing of crimes is the result of human behavior and that means that it is potentially both explicable and predictable. In this chapter we will learn how to determine when a crime (or other event) has occurred, how to analyze the timing and tempo of events, the different distributions of events in time, how criminals (and others) move and act in time, and how temporal analytical information can be used to defeat a serial criminal. In this chapter we will begin our approach with the analysis of time by first defining a few terms and grasping some critical underlying assumptions about time; next, we will discuss some relevant and practical techniques and compare their merits and detractions; we will then discuss the success and failure of these methods in research and practice; finally, we will conclude with some examples of how these techniques have been put into practice.

Definitions

First, let us examine some relevant definitions.

Event: An event is a discrete incident in space and time. For example, a traffic accident is a discrete occurrence in space (located at a particular intersection) and time (the minute of its occurrence), so it is an event: If you looked at the same intersection at a different time, you would not see the accident (it has not happened yet, or else it is cleared away); likewise, if you looked at a different place at the same time, you would not see the accident (it is happening somewhere else). Therefore, an event can only be plotted using at least three coordinates on a flat map: An X and Y coordinate to display it is spatial location, and a T coordinate to pinpoint the time at which it occurred. A building is not an event (it is a discrete point in space, but not in time) nor is a holiday (a discrete point in time, but not in space, although a particular holiday party might qualify as an event).

Dimension: A dimension is a direction in which one can measure. For example, the "dimensions" of a physical object can be described by measurements of its height, width, and depth. The location of a point on a map can be pinpointed by a horizontal measurement (along an X axis) and a vertical measurement (along a Y axis), so two dimensions are needed to position an object on a flat map. In the real world, we need to add a third dimension, elevation (measurement along a Z axis) to show how high something is above ground, above sea level, or above the center of the earth. Time can be measured in one direction, based on how long an interval exists between two events, making it one dimensional.

T Coordinate: A T coordinate is an interval or ratio measure of where an event is located on a timeline. X and Y coordinates, which measure spatial position, use spatial units of measurement such as "meters," "feet," "decimal degrees," or "miles." T coordinates work the same way, but because we are measuring intervals in time we use measures such as "seconds," "minutes," "hours," "days," or "centuries." An X coordinate tell us how many units to the right of an arbitrary starting point some location falls along the X (horizontal) dimension. A T coordinate does the same thing; it tells us how many units to the right of an arbitrary starting point some event falls along a timeline.

Calendar: A calendar is an instrument for measuring units of time greater than one day. Most people today use the Gregorian calendar, but not all.

Clock: A clock is an instrument for measuring units of time smaller than or equal to one day.

Date: A date is the formatted position of a specific day on a calendar (e.g., January 1st, 2008; 01/01/2008; 01-JAN-08).

Time: A time is the formatted position of a specific second (or fraction thereof) on a clock (e.g., 2145; 9:45 PM; 9:45:20 AM).

Date time: Also called a *Date-time-group,* or *DTG,* a date time is the formatted combination of a date and a time (e.g., January 1st, 2008 21:45; 01/01/08 21:45:20; etc.). In this lesson, for clarity, we'll usually use the abbreviation DTG.

Basic Assumptions

The first—and most seriously flawed—assumption we must make when we perform temporal analysis is that we know when an event has actually occurred. This is particularly pernicious when dealing with crime. The majority of crimes are committed against property: theft, burglary, auto

Temporal Analysis

theft, larceny, embezzlement, fraud, forgery, identity theft. Because these crimes are not witnessed, we usually cannot know for sure precisely when they happened. On some rare occasions, perhaps a clue— such as the records of a burglar alarm or a barking dog in the middle of the night—might give us a strong indicator of a particular time, but this is unusual.

Sometimes it can be difficult to pin an exact time to the event that *is* witnessed. For example, a woman is drugged at a bar, taken to the offender's home and sexually assaulted, then left on the street where she awakens the next day. The crime is witnessed, but does the victim know the timeline? Moreover, can such a complex set of actions be said to have a single time?

Even though a witness tries to notice the time, he or she can still make mistakes. It is difficult for anyone to accurately judge the passage of time, particularly when a gun is pointed at him or when he is locked in a back room.

Therefore, the analyst's first challenge is to assign a temporal position to each event.

Primary Time of Occurrence

Most police agencies think of crimes as occurring at one specific time. This is because many crimes have relatively short durations. A robbery may take only a few seconds, for example, and a burglary only a few minutes. This can result in complications, however, when crimes span more than a few minutes.

Consider a bank robbery that turns into a hostage standoff. When can we say it occurred? Normally in such a case, the police analyst will use the known time at which the robbers announced themselves to the bank teller as the "time" of the event. This standard is relatively easy to understand and to work with, but has some obvious deficiencies. What about when the robbers first met and agreed to commit the crime together—that is a crime all by itself, "conspiracy." When did this conspiracy take place? What about when the robbers "cased the joint" hours or days in advance, checking for guards, cameras, and planning their crime? Is that not part of the event, too? What about the long hours of the standoff, while negotiations and threats pass back and forth until the situation is somehow resolved?

Unfortunately, many crimes—the great majority—have a lot of temporal complexity, and trying to pin a single time to these is like trying to represent the location of the Pacific Ocean on a globe by drawing a dot.

Multiple Times of Occurrence

One way in which analysts might deal with the timing of complex events is to assign multiple times to each crime. The analyst first breaks the crime into phases or actions (e.g., planning, casing, practice-run, encounter, attack, dump, escape) and then assigns a time to each. This method definitely captures more information than trying to use one time to describe a whole crime, but it can result in problems, too. For one thing, the analyst has to use her own judgment when deciding what phases occurred in the crime. How does she know if a planning phase actually ever occurred, much less when it happened? Also, each of these phases can be broken into smaller elements, and each has duration, so the basic problem of using one single time hack to describe when a complex event took place still remains.

Aoristic Analysis

In the case of crimes that are witnessed, such as robberies and sexual assaults, the chance that we will have accurate temporal information about each event is fairly strong. Usually the victims know approximately when they were attacked. Sometimes, however, even this is not true. Consider the case of a sexual assault committed using a date-rape drug such as Rohypnol? The victim may have no idea of the time of the attack, except perhaps for the time of initial contact in a bar or on a date. If a crime such as a robbery occurs in a remote area, the victims may need to travel for long periods before they can report their crimes, and may not be able to accurately time their victimization.

But the most troubling crimes from a temporal standpoint are also the most commonplace in law enforcement. These are the unwitnessed crimes, targeting property: larceny, burglary, auto theft, and vandalism. In these, we have almost no temporal information at all.

If we do not know when crimes have occurred, what use are all these techniques we have discussed? The answer is that although we do not actually know when unwitnessed or poorly-recorded crimes precisely occurred, we might be able to infer when they happened with a little bit of science and a little bit of luck.

Practically every police agency in the world times unwitnessed crimes by utilizing "Earliest Possible" and "Latest Possible" date/time stamps. So, the timing of a crime such as a burglary could be defined as falling between 0800 Monday and 1730 Monday, for example. Police personnel are accustomed to thinking about the timing of crimes in terms of this boundary-based format, which we can use as a starting point to perform what some innovative analysts term, "aoristic analysis" (Ratcliffe & McCullagh, 1998). Although methods for solving aoristic problems are as old as police work itself, the term aoristic—derived from the Greek and meaning not fixed in time—has only recently been applied to the police world (A`o`ris´tic a. Indefinite; pertaining to the aorist tense [OED, 2002]).

There are two common ways in which a working time can be interpolated for cases having no known exact time of occurrence; these are the *Midpoint* and the *Weighted Methods*.

Temporal Analysis

The Midpoint Method, also known as the Split Time method, involves identifying the midpoint between the bounding "earliest" and "latest" possible date/times. To calculate the midpoint of an aoristic time, divide the difference between the two bounding date/times (in hours) by two, then add this to the earliest date/time. The strengths of this method are that it is fast and easy to use; also, by definition, its mean observed error will be smaller than any other method. As a result, if this method does guess wrong, on average it will guess less wrong than other methods. Drawbacks are that it is somewhat arbitrary. The accuracy of this technique is measurable in inverse proportion to the time span between the two bounding date/times—when there is a long range, this method is weak; when the range is narrow, it is stronger.

The Weighted Method is a much more creative approach. Here we evenly divide the "risk" of each crime among each temporal unit across its bounding span. That sounds complicated, but it is not. We just assign an increasing probability to each temporal unit (usually the hour of the day) based on the percentage of the chance that a crime occurred there. We sum up all the probabilities, and the result is a smoothed jeopardy curve that shows where the highest probabilities of crimes have landed. To calculate the weighted risk, for each case in your collection, divide 1 by the number of hours spanned, then add this fractional value to each hour as a "risk" score. Repeat the process for every case, adding fractional scores when they overlap. This method is far less arbitrary than the midpoint process and is particularly well-tuned for strategic applications. Weaknesses include the fact that the timing of cases influence one another, therefore "outliers" which do not fit the rest of the temporal series are heavily de-emphasized and may lead to chaotic results.

Temporal Analysis Units

Mappers use spatial units of measurement such as feet, meters, inches, miles, kilometers, or yards to describe the distance between things. Instead of distance in space, temporal analysts must measure intervals in time, but the principle is exactly the same. So, we must choose a temporal unit of measurement to use for all of our numeric work. When choosing a unit of measurement for mapping, we pick one that is convenient and sensible for the scale at which we are operating. In other words, if we are examining an individual crime scene in an apartment, we might measure in inches, centimeters, perhaps even millimeters for high precision; but if we are analyzing crimes across an entire city, we will probably use kilometers or miles instead. The same holds true for temporal analysis. The analyst must choose a unit of time measurement that makes sense with the data she is using and the time periods that must be studied. In general, tactical crime analysts use hours. In the past, days were used, but as the precision of tactical analysis methods has increased, a smaller, higher-resolution unit has become desirable. Few analysts use anything smaller than hours; the nature of police record reporting makes it very unlikely that the timing of crimes is known down to the minute most of the time.

T Coordinates

Just as the location of an object on a two-dimensional map can be described using an X and Y coordinate pair, the location of an event can be described on a one-dimensional timeline using a single T coordinate.

The use of T coordinates rather than date-time groups to describe when an event happens offers many benefits to the analyst. Because calendars and clocks use different mathematical systems (sexigesimal minutes and seconds, duodecimal hours, septinary days of the week, duodecimal months of the year, and a varying number of days within the month), it is extremely complicated to perform even such simple procedures as calculating the interval between two events. When one introduces additional problems, such as Daylight Savings Time changes, movement from one time zone into another, or the use of different calendars, the complexity becomes exponentially greater. By transforming the date-time groups into interval-ratio numbers along a timeline, determined by measuring how far each event is from the same arbitrary starting point, we can eliminate a huge number of difficulties and use simple, decimal math to calculate any relationship we desire between events in time.

Moreover, by treating events in time as being identical to the location of events in space (albeit described using only one dimension, rather than two or three), all the techniques used for analyzing spatial relationships can be applied to temporal relationships with equal effectiveness. In other words, processes usually performed against dots on a map, such as cluster analysis, "hotspot" analysis, autocorrelation, centroid analysis, and others, can also be applied against a timeline. Instead of comparing the X and Y coordinates of the dots, the T coordinates of the marks on the timeline can be analyzed.

Temporal Study Area (Range)

When we look at dots on a map that represent crimes, we obviously need to be using a sensible frame of reference—in other words, the extent of the map (its scale and focal point) should reflect the geographic area in which we are interested. We would not use a neighborhood-level map to study national-level crime, nor would we use a globe to map a crime series in a single apartment complex. The same holds true for time. Before we can meaningfully analyze the timing of events, we must establish a temporal study area. Just as a map will require two dimensions (X and Y), we must make a one-dimensional

Temporal Analysis

timeline where the starting and ending points of the line are fitted to the time we wish to use.

What is the correct length for a timeline? The timeline must be long enough to include all of our data. So, if we are studying a five-year long crime problem we must have a timeline no less than five years in length. But is even that enough? No, because we have to include a little buffer space at both ends of the timeline to avoid mathematical problems that crop up when studying points near the edge of a study area, called "edge effects" or "boundary errors." The question is how much of a boundary do we need?

Although the analyst might exercise her judgment in order to change the timeline for any given series, a good rule of thumb is to buffer each end of the timeline by the mean nearest interval between events plus two standard deviations.

The mean nearest interval is the temporal equivalent of the mean nearest neighbor, a statistic often seen in mapping. To calculate the mean nearest interval, the analyst first derives the interval in chosen time units, such as hours or days from each event to the event closest to it in time—in either direction, before or after. These scores are totaled and then divided by the number of events to find the mean. The standard deviation is as it would be for any mean score. By adding two standard deviations onto the mean nearest interval, the analyst arrives at a score that makes an effective temporal buffer to subtract from the time of the first case, and add onto the time of the last case, to use as endpoints of a timeline. The timeline between these points is the temporal study area and the time period we will use in subsequent analytical steps.

Why do we use the mean nearest interval plus two standard deviations? Given a normal distribution (in other words, if we were studying the interval between temporally random events), this method would give us a 95% confidence interval. So, if we want to be sure that we have a timeline long enough to catch any important temporal events before the first case or anything after the last case, this would enable us to feel about 95% confident that we have done so.

Temporal Distribution

In both spatial and temporal analyses, the word distribution is a technical term that describes how a set of points fills its study area. When we study distribution, we first need to know the size of the study area. For spatial analysis, this is the scale of our map—the area that it takes up in map units (square feet, square meters, square miles, acres, etc.). For temporal analysis, it is the length of our one-dimensional timeline in time units (hours, minutes, days, years, or whatever the analyst chooses).

Distribution describes how events are situated throughout the study area in relation to one another. There are three types of distributions: *clustered*, *random*, and *uniform*.

- *Clustered* events tend to occur in close proximity to one another.
- *Uniform* events tend to occur far apart from one another.
- *Random* events are neither clustered nor uniform.

On a map, these distributions are relatively easy to perceive. Less commonly considered is the fact that the timing of events can also be measured in term of distribution along a timeline, and can still be classified as Clustered, Random, or Uniform.

In spatial analysis, we use tests like the *Nearest Neighbor Test*, *Ripley's K*, *Cramer-von Mises test for Complete Spatial Randomness* (CSR), or others to measure distribution. All of these techniques also work on a timeline to determine temporal distribution; instead of comparing distances in feet or miles, we compare intervals in hours or days.

We call it a clustered distribution when events are closer together on the timeline than we would expect them to be if they were randomly distributed. This type of distribution looks clumped when viewed on a timeline.

Uniform distributions tend to fill in the length of the timeline more fully. Sometimes these can be very regular, but not always. There is usually some slight clumping of events, and few long gaps between cases in a uniform timeline.

Random distributions are neither clustered nor uniform. The term random is a technical term that describes this type of distribution, but it is a somewhat unfortunate choice of words, because it implies unpredictability and chaos. In fact, random distributions are often perfectly predictable. In the context of distributions, remember that random simply means a distribution that is neither clustered nor uniform.

Remember that these distributions can be combined—for instance, events might be clustered, but the clusters could be uniform.

The temptation to rely on one's eyes to see how events are distributed should be resisted. The human eye seems to do a very good job of picking out clusters, but a poor job of detecting uniformity. Most uniform distributions look random to the naked eye. Even if the distribution appears obvious, use a reliable mathematic technique. If the results confirm your initial guess, you will have recovered a useful measurement when you quantify a distribution, and you will therefore be able to meaningfully compare it to the distribution of other crimes and see how it changes over time. If not, you have learned something new and surprising about your data.

One of the best techniques to identify a distribution is the Nearest Neighbor Test. This test is usually performed against spatial data in two

Temporal Analysis

dimensions, but it applies perfectly to temporal data in one dimension with only a slight modification.

The formula for the Nearest Neighbor Statistic in two dimensions (e.g., for dots on a map) is:

$$R_n = \frac{\bar{D}}{.5 \cdot \sqrt{\frac{A}{N}}}$$

- In this formula, R_n is the result of the nearest neighbor statistic, a number between 0 and 2.15. Zero indicates perfect clustering (every point located on another point), 2.15 indicates perfect uniformity (each point as far apart as possible from every other point), and 1 indicates randomness (not unpredictability, but neither a clustered nor random distribution).
- $\bar{D}$ is the mean distance between each point and the point closest to it. To derive this score, record the distance from each point to the one closest to it; sum these scores, then divide by the number of points.
- A is the area in which the points have been distributed, measured in the same units as the D score (but square, e.g., square meters versus meters).
- N is the number of events.

This formula works pretty well in two dimensions, but when we analyze events in time alone, we are using only one dimension. Therefore, we need to change our formula slightly to adapt it:

$$R_n = \frac{\bar{I}}{.5 \cdot \frac{L}{N}}$$

- In this formula, $\bar{I}$ stands for the mean nearest neighbor interval; that is, the shortest time interval between each event and the event closest to it on the timeline (which will either be the event immediately before or after it).
- L stands for the length of the timeline (measured in the same temporal units as $\bar{I}$, e.g., hours, minutes, days).

Analysts should test the distribution of events on their timeline very early in their analysis. Identifying the distribution of events on the timeline, using the Nearest Neighbor Test or some other valid and impartial metric (not just your eyes), is an important part of the temporal analysis process.

Tempo

The distribution of events does not always stay the same. As the series progresses, the interval between cases might become shorter, longer, or stay the same. The variation in intervals might become more regular, less regular, or stay the same. In addition to analyzing the distribution for all events altogether, the analyst should also determine how the distribution changes over time. This change in pace is called the tempo of a series.

There are three types of tempo; these are *accelerating, decelerating*, and *stable*.

- *Acceleration* occurs when the interval between events decreases as the number of events increases (negative correlation between interval and number of events).
- *Deceleration* occurs when the interval between events increases as the number of events increases (positive correlation between interval and number of events).
- *Stabilization* occurs when the interval between events neither increases nor decreases as the number of events increases (no correlation between interval and number of events).

Like distribution, tempo can be measured easily as a function of the change in interval over the change in number of events; in other words, the change in X over the change in Y, the same simple calculation for the slope of any line.

One very easy technique for measuring tempo is Pearson's Correlation Coefficient (also called the product-moment coefficient). This statistic is used to compare two variables to determine whether they are correlated, and, if so, whether the correlation is positive or negative. Use the following formula to calculate the correlation coefficient for a series of events to determine whether they are accelerating, decelerating, or stable:

$$\rho = \frac{\sum Z_x Z_y}{N-1}$$

Although ρ looks like the Latin letter p, it is actually the Greek letter *rho*, which stands for the resulting coefficient score when it is used against a population; that is, every measurement, not just a sample. This will be a number between −1 and 1. Negative numbers indicate a negative correlation; that is, as one value increases, the other decreases, while positive values indicate a positive correlation. Values near zero indicate no meaningful correlation; changes in one number do not seem to affect the other one. When used to

Temporal Analysis

calculate tempo, ρ scores less than −.25 indicate an accelerating tempo, while those greater than .25 indicate a decelerating tempo.

The Z_x score for each measurement is the Z-score of the T-coordinate for each case.

The Z_y score for each measurement is the Z-score of the interval between each case and the case closest to it in time (the nearest neighbor interval).

A simple and effective tool for visualizing tempo is a *tempogram*. A tempogram is a specially formatted scattergram chart that shows change in time along the X (horizontal) axis (in this case the number of events), and change in interval on the Y (vertical) axis. Notice that we cannot plot the interval (Y mark) for the last known event—because, of course, we do not know how long it will be until the next (future) event.

Sometimes a series does not seem to either accelerate or decelerate; these are categorized as *Stable*.

One useful feature of a tempogram is that it can be used to calculate a trend line using a method such as the Linear Trend Estimation (q.v.) method or one of its many variants. By extrapolating this line through the last case, we can then project the intervals of future events, enabling us to predict future crimes.

Velocity

The tempo of a series lets us project the rate of acceleration of events, but this cannot go on forever, especially when we consider accelerating tempos. Look at the illustration showing the trend in an accelerating series of cases. This linear trend is accelerating rapidly—perhaps too rapidly. The predicted interval between cases will eventually reach zero, meaning an infinite number of cases will occur instantaneously with one another.

In the real world, events have some minimum interval between them. In other words, there is a sort of speed limit, which we call the *terminal velocity*. This is the fastest rate at which events can occur. Instead of a linear acceleration, it is often better to use a logarithmic trend line which approaches, but never exceeds, this terminal velocity. The terminal velocity is the maximum sustainable frequency of a series of events.

Terminal velocities differ among offenders and offenses; finding out what it is remains part of the challenge of serious temporal crime analysis which can be at least partly resolved using statistical calibration.

Temporal Cycles

The two primary tools for measuring time—clocks and calendars—operate on a cyclical basis; that is, as time progresses, the units being measured move away from the starting point for awhile, then come back around to it again in a neverending loop. The hours of the day repeat. The days of the week repeat. The weeks of the month repeat. The months of the year repeat.

Two time cycles dominate all human activity. The first is the circadian rhythm—the 24-hour day. Wired into the very cells of every human being during hundreds of thousands of years of biological shaping, this rhythm follows the sun. Analyze any human behavior, and you will almost invariably discover a 24-hour repeating pattern within it.

The second is the seven-day week. The importance of the seven-day week might be obvious from a Western perspective; the Julian and Gregorian calendars that we inherited from the Roman Empire and the Catholic Church both rely on the repeating seven-day cycle to mark time. But is the seven-day cycle important to other cultures as well?

Yes, it is. The seven-day cycle, like the circadian rhythm, is programmed into human beings at a very basic level. Even in societies with no calendar, seven-day repeating behavioral cycles are seen. Why is this? Does not the seven day cycle come from our historical calendars and our mythology or Judeo-Christian background? It is obvious that the 24-hour cycle is built into us by a natural rhythm; the rising and setting of the sun. But what about the seven-day cycle?

The answer is that the seven-day cycle is a harmonic; that is, an evenly divisible sub-cycle of a larger, natural rhythm—the 28-day lunar cycle. Not only women but also men are biologically attuned to the phases of the moon and its patterns, like those of the sun, shape human behavior.

These two cyclical patterns are closely intertwined. When we combine the two, we can create a matrix of time-of-day by day-of-week that greatly helps to visualize and explain human activity.

Time Series Analysis

Time series analyses are a set of methods for analyzing and forecasting measurements based on points of data measurements in time. Although at first glance, these might sound like a perfect match for our tactical needs, these are actually more strategic and administrative functions. Time series methods attempt to analyze and forecast numeric values, rather than discrete events (forecasting, rather than predicting). Because they fall largely outside the purview of this book, we will treat them only briefly, to explain the fundamentals of how time series work.

Moving Average: This technique is a smoothing technique used against time series data. Instead of plotting measurements for each datum point, the average (mean) measurement for a rolling group of data points is plotted. This tends to visibly smooth a line in the same way that any mean calculation does; by reducing the influence of "outliers," data that are unusually high or low. This simple process can be modified by weighting, using exponential rather than mean values, and so forth.

Extrapolation/Interpolation: Extrapolation is the process of inferring an unobserved measurement that lies outside a series of observed measurements. Interpolation is the process of inferring an unobserved measurement that lies between two or more observed measurements. There are many types of extrapolation and interpolation; most involve regression statistics. Regression is the process of examining a series of measurements to discover a function or formula that best describes a rule that governs the series. Specialized functions such as growth curves, learning curves, ARIMA, and others can be applied to specific time series problems.

Spectral Density: Any repeating pattern has a frequency; that is, the number of times the pattern repeats over a given period of time (e.g., ten/day, 1500 per second, etc.). The frequency of sound waves is usually measured, for example, in Hertz—the number of times a sound vibrates each second. Sounds that vibrate at a faster rate have a higher frequency, and sound like a higher tone to the ear. But any repeating pattern can be analyzed in terms of its amplitude at various frequencies—even crime series. When the frequency is a routine cycle—such as the 24-hour day or the seven-day week—we are usually better off examining the pattern in terms of an activity schedule.

But sometimes the frequency strengths of a time pattern are unusual. For example, criminals who have unusual schedules may deviate from the seven-day week and might display an unusual frequency distribution. How can these be detected?

A family of methods called "Fourier Transformations" can convert any sequence of data in time into a spectral density graph. Spectral density is a display of how strong a signal is at many different frequencies. This technique is exactly the way radio and television signals work. By tuning to different frequencies, the analyst can look for spikes in the amplitude of the signal. This indicates a repeating pattern in the offender's activity at the specified frequency. By comparing these high frequencies to the activity patterns of suspects, it might be possible to determine who is committing crimes (based, for example, on their work or travel schedules). These high frequencies can also be useful when attempting to forecast or predict future activity, too.

Statistical Trend Estimation: One of the most commonly-used methods for time series analysis is statistical trend estimation. This can also take many forms, but the most common in crime analysis is *percent change* calculation. To calculate the percent change between two measurements, simply subtract the old number from the new number, then divide by the old number; multiply the result by 100 and you have a percentage change from one measurement to the other. Another, more powerful method is *linear trend estimation* (q.v.).

Geographic Profiling   7

Introduction

Geographic profiling is a term that means different things to different people. It can be applied very specifically to a particular set of techniques to help prioritize suspect investigations based on the geographic distribution of serial crimes, or more broadly to any such technique or method. Few other analytical systemologies can claim to be so controversial or divisive, even among practitioners. While many claims of success have been touted for various methods of geographic profiling, few have been documented. In this chapter, we will thoroughly explore the various schools of geographic profiling, their histories and claims, and most importantly their methods.

Background of Geographic Profiling

Although police agencies have used maps and simple geographic analyses techniques to assist in serial crime investigations for many years, it was not until the early 1990s that true geographic profiling systems were developed. The underlying rationale of geographic profiling is influenced by several different criminological theories, including the routine activities and rationale choice theories as well as research into mental maps, awareness space and journey-to-crime. Possibly the biggest influence on geographic profiling comes from crime pattern theory and research conducted by Paul and Patricia Brantingham (Rossmo, 1995a). In their research, the Brantinghams used an understanding of a criminal's activity space to predict where the offender will commit crimes. They found that, generally, offenders commit crimes where there is an overlap between suitable targets and their personal awareness space (Brantingham and Brantingham, 1991). Offender search patterns usually follow a distance decay function in which there is an inverse relationship between the number of crimes committed and the distance from the offender's awareness space (Rossmo, 1995a). Journey-to-crime research supports these ideas, indicating that most criminals travel relatively short distances from home to commit a majority of crimes (Phillips, 1980). Geographic profiling essentially inverts these ideas in an attempt to reduce the search area for an offender based on where he has committed crimes (Rossmo, 1995a).

Using information about where an offender has chosen to commit crimes, geographic profiling attempts to determine an offender's most likely anchor points. While the media and others often interpret anchor points as meaning only an offender's home, offender anchor points can include work, shopping, former residence, a friend's residence, and other locations where an offender has a close association (see Chapter 4). While both crime pattern theory and geographic profiling have different purposes and inputs, the underlying concepts and ideas are fairly similar.

Using crime site location information and distance-decay analysis, geographic profiling seeks to help narrow the search area through the creation of a geographic profile region. While the form, shape, size, and type of profile region varies greatly by the type of geographic profiling method, all methods attempt to provide a graphical representation of the areas within the offense domain where the offender is most likely to reside. This information is then used by law enforcement officials to develop new investigative strategies, leads, and responses. Thus, geographic profiling can best be thought of as a strategic information management system designed to support investigations into serial crimes, with the purpose of helping to narrow the search area for an offender (Rossmo, 2000).

Geographic Profiling Schools of Thought

Within geographic profiling there are five important "schools" or methods for profiling, all of which are closely associated with the individuals who developed the methods. These five schools are criminal geographic targeting (CGT), also known as the Rigel or Rossmo school; investigative psychology (I-Psy), also known as the Dragnet, Canter, or Liverpool school; journey-to-crime (JTC), also known as the CrimeStat or Levine school; wedge theory, also known as the predator or Godwin school; and geoforensics, or the Newton-Swoope school.

In addition to these fairly well-known and established schools, there are also several emerging systems that merit discussion: missed-opportunity profiling (MOP), or the Bodnar method for the originator; line-of-bearing (LOB), or movement-based profiling; offender travel-demand modeling (TDM); and inverse time-weighted density analysis (ITWD). Finally, some extremely simplistic—but possibly useful—methods have also been used and deserve discussion. These are centroid profiling; first-point proximity; and the marauder circle hypothesis.

These schools and methods have the common aim of assisting the police apprehend serial criminals by helping to identify possible suspects for investigation based on the spatial location of his crimes. They can differ radically as to precisely how they accomplish this aim.

Criminal Geographic Targeting (CGT)

AKA: The Canadian School, the Rigel Method, the Rossmo School.

Personalities and History

CGT was developed by Darcy Kim Rossmo, PhD, formerly a constable in the Vancouver, BC, Canada, Police Service. In 1995, Constable Rossmo was a student of Paul and Patricia Brantingham, two well-known criminologists who theorized about the implications of place in criminal behavior at Simon Frasier University. The Brantinghams introduced Rossmo to the work of environmental criminologists such as George Rengert, David Canter, Jim LeBeau, Robert Keppel, and many others. Rossmo attempted to synthesize some of their ideas into a usable tool for law enforcement.

Rossmo's name and work is probably the best known and most widely associated with Geographic Profiling among the major players in the field.

Application

CGT is expressed as a four-step algorithm:

1. Establish a Study Area (Consists of the Minimum Bounding Rectangle buffered by half the mean interpoint distance); divide this into 40,000 analytical cells.
2. For each cell, calculate the Manhattan distance to each crime scene.
3. Identify whether the cell falls within the "Buffer Zone," a distance equal to half the mean nearest neighbor distance.
4. Sum the values using the following function. If the cell is within or on the edge of the buffer zone, then:

$$P_{ij} = k \sum_{N=1}^{C} \left[\frac{(1-\phi)(B^{g-f})}{(2B-d)^g} \right]$$

but if the cell is outside, then:

$$P_{ij} = k \sum_{N=1}^{C} \frac{\phi}{d^f}$$

In these equations:

- P_{ij} is the probability of an anchor point at the cell in row i, column j;
- Φ is a weighting factor – 1 if the crime is outside the buffer, 0 if inside or on the edge;

k is an empirically determined constant used as a normalizing factor;
B is the radius of the buffer zone (half the mean nearest neighbor distance);
C is the number of crime sites;
f is an empirically determined exponent (1.2 in Rossmo's dissertation);
g is an empirically determined exponent (1.2 in Rossmo's dissertation);
d is the Manhattan distance to each crime.

This formula is presented in Rossmo's book, *Geographic Profiling*; which states that it is based on the results of his unpublished doctoral dissertation, *Geographic Profiling: Targeting Patterns of Serial Murderers*.

In his book and his considerable number of other publications, Rossmo addresses a plethora of additional factors with respect to identifying an offender's anchor point(s); however, there is no explanation as to how any of these ideas (including local permeability, boundary effects, offender hunting patterns, and psychological profiling) can be effectively used. In the end, the only quantifiable part of the process is the formula.

Many points have been raised regarding peculiar aspects of this formula, which appears in different forms in different publications (Rossmo originally suggested that cell values should be multiplied, rather than summed, until the mathematic defects of this method were publicly challenged). Most of the contention has surrounded three factors: Manhattan distance metrics, Buffer Zones, and his "empirically derived exponents."

The *Manhattan distance* between points is calculated by summing the difference in their X and Y coordinates:

$$d = |(x - x_i)| + |(y - y_i)|$$

This results in much larger distances than the more common *Euclidean* distance, which is equal to the square root of the sum of the squares of the difference in coordinates:

$$d = \sqrt{(x - x_i)(y - y_i)^2}$$

So, why use the Manhattan distance rather than Euclidean? Rossmo explains that of the three main methods for calculating distance (Euclidean, Manhattan, and Network—where the shortest path along a transportation network is used), the Manhattan distance tends to fall between the Euclidean measurement, which will always be the shortest, and the Network, which tends to be the longest. Why this makes the Manhattan measurement better is not clear. Other research into mental perception of distance finds that the Euclidean distance is, overall, the most representative of how people see distances in their personal environment.

A *buffer zone* is an area surrounding an offender's anchor point in which he prefers not to strike because the crime will be "too close for comfort." The concept of a buffer zone is widely accepted in environmental criminology, and seems reasonable. After all, it seems to be common sense that a criminal can't often repeat attacks right in his own immediate neighborhood without being spotted very quickly.

Unfortunately, as we have seen, many criminologists find no evidence of buffer zones. Richard Block's research into robberies in Chicago indicates that many repeat robbers routinely attack their victims literally outside the robber's front door. Even if we accept the premise that a buffer zone might exist, how big is it? Rossmo settles on half the mean nearest neighbor distance as the solution. Unfortunately, this is not justified in his published work.

Investigative Psychology (I-Ψ)

AKA: The British School, the Liverpool School, the Canter School, the Dragnet School.

Personalities and History

As an environmental psychologist, Prof. David Canter of the University of Liverpool was an expert in the interaction of people and their geographic surroundings. In 1985, he was approached by the Surrey Police Service to assist in the investigation of a murder series, dubbed the Railway Rapist, in the United Kingdom. Canter was asked to help create an "FBI-style psychological profile." Unfortunately, he had no idea how the FBI managed to perform their celebrated and highly successful profiling magic. Starting with the premise that it *could* be done, and that it must use sound scientific and psychological principles, Canter set about reconstructing the process of criminal profiling. The end result barely resembled the FBI methods. Canter had developed new techniques and quickly focused on geography and environmental criminology as quantifiable, powerful investigative areas. Out of touch with American criminology, Canter relied upon methods and research conducted in Europe and the Middle East for much of his background material.

He developed an entire school of thought regarding criminal behavior, and formed the Centre for Investigative Psychology at the University of Liverpool. Along with a number of other experts, he began to develop new research methods and technologies for investigating crime. He and his school have also frequently dropped or de-emphasized some of their own work when their own research has shown it to be unreliable.

The Centre for Investigative Psychology has turned out a large number of students, mostly British, but including Canadians, Americans, Europeans, Indians, and others. Geographic profiling is only one aspect of the centre's curriculum and several methods are presented, ranging from complicated to simplistic. Great effort is expended toward understanding how and why geographic profiling methods work—and, most importantly, whether they work at all.

Application

Like Rossmo, Canter originated an algorithm based around a distance decay function. This has been incorporated into a software program called "Dragnet;" it is therefore referred to as the Dragnet Algorithm. The five-step Dragnet process is as follows:

1. Identify a Study Area by buffering the minimum bounding rectangle by 10% of its dimensions. Superimpose a grid of 13,300 cells.
2. Select a decay coefficient (β – usually between .1 to 10)
3. Normalize Euclidean distances (by mean interpoint distance or Q-range)
4. Sum the values using the following function:

$$Y = \alpha e^{\left(-B\frac{D_{ij}}{P}\right)}$$

In this function:

Y is the probability of the offender's home location being within the target cell;
α is an arbitrary constant;
β is the coefficient of the distance (thus an exponent of e);
P is the normalization constant;
e is the base of the natural logarithm.

5. Finally, calculate the Search Area as the fraction of the study area needed to be searched to find the anchor point.

Dragnet is a stand-alone software application that can read only limited types of files. It is difficult to work with and does not interoperate well in a GIS environment. The newest variants of Dragnet, however, have been reformulated as extensions for ArcGIS under a project called iOPS, a program of

Geographic Profiling

the UK Home Office. Previous versions of Dragnet have often been criticized as immature from a software standpoint and lack the interesting visuals of Rigel. The application's output has always been fairly restricted, although it has undergone many improvements over time.

CrimeStat

AKA: Journey-to-Crime, the Levine Method.

Personalities and History

CrimeStat is a software program funded by the National Institute of Justice (NIJ), developed by Dr. Ned Levine for the purpose of performing fast spatial statistics on crime data. A fraction of its functionality involves geographic profiling, but this fraction has received more attention than the rest. The module within CrimeStat built to perform geographic profiling is called "journey-to-crime," or JTC. This term was used by environmental criminologists for years to describe the movements of the criminal from his base of operations to the scenes of his offenses, until the more sound bite-friendly "geographic profile" was introduced by Rossmo.

CrimeStat has received lavish amounts of federal funding since it was awarded its initial grant in 1997 Justice (grants 1997-IJ-CX-0040, 1999-IJ-CX-0044, and 2002-IJ-CX-0007). It is available for free download from the Inter-university Consortium for Political and Social Research (IPCSR) at the University of Michigan, on the internet at http://www.icpsr.umich.edu/CRIMESTAT.

Application

The JTC module in CrimeStat is unique among the major geographic profiling software packages in that it does not rely on any one pre-selected mathematical function. While Rigel and Dragnet use "hard-coded" functions that claim to be based on research, CrimeStat allows users to calibrate the JTC module themselves by training CrimeStat with solved crime data. Users can use datasets containing actual crime scene locations and the home locations (or base sites) of the offenders responsible, and the JTC algorithm will "reverse-engineer" the data to determine what kind of distance-decay curve actually exists. This can vastly improve the accuracy of the resulting profiles, but takes additional time and the process is not well documented, so it is seldom used.

CrimeStat offers no visualization opportunities whatsoever—instead, the output is in the form of raw coordinates and statistics. These, however, can be packaged into common file formats such as ESRI shapefiles and then viewed using ArcGIS or another GIS program.

The journey-to-crime module within CrimeStat functions in five steps:

1. A grid is superimposed upon the user-defined Study Area (either generated by CrimeStat or imported from another format);
2. Distances between each cell and each crime are calculated (using either Euclidean or Manhattan distances as specified by the user);
3. A Distance Decay function is applied to each cell-incident pair; CrimeStat offers five different distance decay functions, or the user may alternatively use a pre-calibrated empirical decay function;
4. All cell values are summed;
5. The cell having the highest value is returned as a point (of maximum likelihood), and the resultant cellular grid is exported in a GIS-compliant format.

The five theoretical decay functions available in CrimeStat are:

1. Linear Decay (the simplest):

$$f(d_{ij}) = A + B(d_{ij})$$

In this function:

$f(d_{ij})$ is the likelihood that the offender will commit a crime at a given location;
d_{ij} is the distance between the offender's residence and location i;
A is the slope coefficient (default is 1.9);
B is a constant (default is -.06).

2. Negative Exponential:

$$f(d_{ij}) = A\left(e^{Bd_{ij}}\right)$$

In this function:

$f(d_{ij})$ is the likelihood that the offender will commit a crime at a given location;
d_{ij} is the distance between the offender's residence and location i;
e is base of the natural logarithm;
A is a theoretically-derived coefficient (default is 1.89);
B is a theoretically-derived exponent (default is -.06).

3. Normal:

$$f(d_{ij}) = A\left(\frac{1}{S_d(\sqrt{2\pi})}\right)e^{-.5Z_{ij}^2}$$

Where:

$$Z_{ij} = \frac{d_{ij} - MeanD}{S_d}$$

In these formulae:

$f(d_{ij})$ is the likelihood that the offender will commit a crime at a given location;
d_{ij} is the distance between the reference location and the crime location;
e is base of the natural logarithm;
A is a theoretically-derived coefficient (default is 29.5);
MeanD is a theoretically-derived mean distance (default is 4.2);
S_d is the standard deviation of distances (default is 4.6);
π is the ratio of the radius of a circle to it's perimeter ($\approx$3.14159).

4. Lognormal:

$$f(d_{ij}) = A\left(\frac{1}{(d_{ij}^2)(S_d)\sqrt{2\pi}}\right)e^{-\frac{[\ln(d_{ij}^2)-MeanD]^2}{2S_d^2}}$$

In this equation:

$f(d_{ij})$ is the likelihood that the offender will commit a crime at a given location;
d_{ij} is the distance between the reference location and the crime location;
e is base of the natural logarithm;
A is a theoretically-derived coefficient (default is 8.6);
MeanD is a theoretically-derived mean distance (default is 4.2);
S_d is the standard deviation of distances (default is 4.6);
π is the ratio of the radius of a circle to its perimeter ($\approx$3.14159).

5. This method consists of two functions, a linear (used for crimes near the home location to simulate a buffer zone) and a negative exponential (for outside the buffer zone).

The *linear* function is used fo distances less than or equal to the buffer zone:

$$f(d_{ij}) = Bd_{ij}$$

The *Negative Exponential* function is used for distances greater than the buffer zone:

$$f(d_{ij}) = A\left(e^{-Cd_{ij}}\right)$$

In these functions:

$f(d_{ij})$ is the likelihood that the offender will commit a crime at a given location;

d_{ij} is the distance between the reference location and the crime location;

e is base of the natural logarithm;
A is a the transposed y-intercept;
B is the slope of the linear function;
C is a theoretically-derived Exponent (default is -.2).

The buffer zone default is .4.

Empirically Calibrated Decay Functions

The major mathematical difference between CrimeStat's journey-to-crime algorithm and the Rigel or Dragnet algorithms is not just flexibility, but also the ability to use an empirically-calibrated decay function. This means that the user can "train" CrimeStat using real, local data rather than rely on research results from distance cities or countries, or some other researcher's pet theories about criminal behavior—the user can see what criminals in his area actually do, then use this as the statistical basis for trying to model a new crime series problem.

The analyst "plugs in" solved crime data, and attempts to model it with variations of the five types of functions that CrimeStat allows. Using visual approximation and goodness-of-fit tests, the analyst can fine-tune a decay function that best describes actual criminal behavior in the local area.

Wedge Theory

AKA: The Godsin School, the Predator Method, Psycho-Geographic Profiling.

Personalities and History

Grover Maurice Godwin, PhD is a former police officer with the Oxford, North Carolina, Police Department. He obtained his doctorate from the University of Liverpool and began teaching and consulting on geographic and psychological profiling on his own in Alaska and North Carolina. He currently teaches unaccredited online classes on these topics. He has been a frequent guest on talk shows such as *Geraldo*, and is a flamboyant media contributor and prolific writer.

Godwin's methodologies to some degree seem to resemble both Canter and Newton-Swoope, with the addition of taking into account directional movement within the series. Godwin professes that serial criminals (whom he categorizes with typologies including "vipers" and "cobras" to differentiate their hunting patterns) typically generate a wedgelike shape around their home bases; his software program, Predator, which does not appear to be used anyone other than Godwin, generates jeopardy surfaces very similar to those produced by Rigel or Dragnet. Godwin offers many examples of accurate profiles which he offers to the police and press; however, independent verification of the authenticity or reliability of these profiles has weighed against him with the academic community.

Application

No details or practical instructions concerning the Wedge Theory Method are available.

Geoforensic Analysis

AKA: Newton-Swoope School; Baton Rouge School; Louisiana School; LSU Method.

Personalities and History

Dr. Milton Newton taught at Louisiana State University at Baton Rouge. He and his colleague, E. A. Swoope, published in 1987 a treatise on "Geoforensic Analysis of Localized Serial Murder." This document described an early form of Geographic Profiling which still has adherents today, including Prof. Michael Leitner. The team of Newton-Swoope is relatively unknown in mainstream crime mapping and analysis circles, but is well known and respected among academics and experts in the field of Geographic Profiling.

Application

Newton and Swoope advocated a four-step algorithm for prioritizing suspect lead lists based on the location of the offenders' homes in relation to existing cases. Unlike many other researchers and practitioners, they did not develop any specialized software application to perform their method, nor did they use a modern GIS. Their four-step algorithm is as follows:

1. Define a Study Area using the Minimum Bounding Rectangle;
2. Identify the Arithmetic Mean coordinates for each lag of sequential cases in the series (i.e., the first case is collocated with the arithmetic centroid at lag-1; the centroid at lag-2 will be the mean of the first two cases coordinates; etc.);
3. A search radius of decreasing size is buffered around each lagged centroid, the radius being defined by the following equation, where R is the radius, A_{xy} is the distance between the farthest cases, and N is the total number of cases;

$$R = \frac{\sqrt{\frac{A_{xy}}{\pi}}}{N-1}$$

4. Finally, these circles are superimposed upon one another to produce a Venn diagram, or summed over a cellular grid to create a jeopardy surface.

Philosophical Foundations

Underpinning all geographic profiling techniques are a set of philosophical assumptions that serve as the foundation on which geographic profiling methods are built. Although these assumptions are sometimes restated in different manners by their proponents, the most common are the Least Effort Principle, the Distance Decay Hypothesis, and Routine Activity Theory.

The Least Effort Principle was conceptualized in 1949 by linguist George Zipf and has been applied to a number of human activities. The basic principle is that when faced with two equivalent behavioral choices, humans will generally opt for the one that requires the least effort. While this principle undoubtedly applies to much human behavior, it is highly suspect, however, in the area of crime.

The Distance Decay Hypothesis is that the probable relationship between events diminishes with distance. This was epitomized by geographer Waldo

Tobler's "First Law of Geography," which states, "Everything is related to everything else, but near things are more related than distant things." While this principle, also, is prima facie persuasive, it fails under scrutiny. For example, it suggests that one is more related to one's next door neighbor than to one's mother, provided she lives more than one house away.

Routine Activity Theory is a viewpoint on criminality advanced by Cohen and Felson, in which crime is essentially a normal behavior that occurs when opportunity presents itself. Therefore, it is the occurrence of opportunities in an environment that makes it criminogenic.

While each of these philosophical concepts has contributed to the development of the current view of geographic profiling, it is fair to say that their underlying assumptions and weaknesses are not often considered closely by practicing crime analysts, who may be more inclined to take such assumptions on faith in the expertise of those who present GP rather than question them.

One of the greatest fundamental weaknesses of GP is its reliance on extrapolating from aggregate data to specific cases—a defect known as the *Ecological Fallacy*.

Individual Methods

Some GP techniques do not adhere to a particular school, have yet to be implemented into a methodology, or stand alone due to their simplicity. These include Arithmetric Centroid prioritization, Marauder Circles, and Line-of-Bearing extrapolation. Others represent emergent technologies which are not fully matured yet. These include the Offender Travel-Demand Model and the Missed Opportunity Profiling methods.

Arithmetic Centroid Prioritization: One of the simplest methods for geographic profiling is to start looking for the suspect in the middle of the series and work outward. The middle of the series is usually defined by the arithmetic centroid, the mean of both x and y coordinates for all events in the series. Simply prioritize leads based on their proximity to the centroid and work outward. Under post-hoc effectiveness analysis by Eastern Kentucky University's Prof. Derek Paulsen, this easy method frequently outperformed elaborate software on real crime series.

Marauder Circles: The Marauder/Commuter dichotomy was developed by Prof. David Canter at the University of Liverpool based on his early experiences with environmental criminology and it is one of the concepts for which he is best known. Briefly, Canter defines a marauder as an offender who lives in the immediate area of his crimes, as defined by a circle having the two farthest cases as endpoints of its diameter. Offenders living outside this area are called commuters. Canter himself has moved past this dichotomy in favor of more complicated and flexible spatial typologies, but it remains highly popular and the basic split between a "local" versus "visiting" offender remains one of the most significant concepts in geographic profiling, and is in fact one of Rossmo's prerequisites for a geoprofile.

Line-of-Bearing Extrapolation: Often, in addition to the scene of the crime, other crime sites are available. These include evidence recovery sites, observation points where the subject was spotted, or other locations where the offender was known to be after the primary offense. The Brantinghams and others note that many criminals return to their bases of operation immediately after a successful crime. This means that they may have been heading toward home from the crime scene when they were spotted or left behind their evidence. A line-of-bearing is a line that connects the crime scene, through the post-crime site, and then extrapolates beyond it. Many of these lines eventually intersect. The analyst can mark each intersection with a point, then analyze the distribution of points for clusters; these clusters mark places toward which the offender was probably moving, making it possible to identify anchor points including transportation corridors.

Missed Opportunity Profiling: This method does not depend on the physical distance between cases, but rather the actual distribution of available targets. The analyst must calculate how many potential targets were bypassed from each potential anchor point (e.g., grid cell in a jeopardy raster) when the offender struck. Based on the Least Effort principle, which also drives the more simplistic but similar distance decay methods, this method assumes that the offender will attack easy (nearby) targets first; this more explicitly incorporates shopping behavior—the way in which people choose where they shop based on where they live, work, and play. This is the only method to explicitly incorporate local geography in the form of target distributions, although it is implicit in other schools of profiling, such as those advocated by Canter, Rossmo, and Levine. This method has recently been advocated by Paul Bodnar, who may be developing it into a tool for law enforcement analysis. He now refers to this method as *retrogeographic analysis*, or RGA.

Offender Travel-Demand Models: Like everyone else, criminals must move around their environment using available transportation. Levine hypothesizes that offender travel decisions are governed by the same principles as other types of travel decisions, such as where to shop, where to buy gas, where to park, and so forth. He has incorporated transportation planning travel-demand models into the newest versions of CrimeStat.

Although not intended for tactical analysis against individual serial offenders, this method may be applicable to specific tactical problems.

Research on the Accuracy of Geographic Profiling Systems

Since 2003 there has been an increasing interest in evaluating the accuracy of the various different geographic profiling systems. While an evaluation of the different systems may at first seem like a fairly straight forward process, most of the studies that have been conducted involved differing methodologies resulting in more controversy than answers. The first evaluation of a geographic profiling system was conducted by Rossmo (2000), and involved only the CGT or RIGEL system. In assessing the accuracy of the CGT software system, Rossmo (2000) employed a data set consisting of 13 serial murder cases comprising 15 serial killers, 178 victims and 347 crime locations. Methodologically, Rossmo (2000) quantified the accuracy of his system using hit percentage values, which is the percentage of the software designated offense domain that needs to be searched to locate the offender's home base. In his findings Rossmo (2000) found that all else being equal, a geoprofile using CGT would find the offenders' residence in 12% of the time it would take a random search. Importantly, the accuracy of the model was found to improve as the number of crime sites in a series increased, with 6 crime sites producing a geoprofile that would narrow the search area to only 10% of the original offense domain.

The second major study on geographic profiling accuracy was conducted by Canter of the dragnet method. In assessing the accuracy of dragnet, Canter et al. (2000) used a sample of 79 serial murderers and employed an accuracy measure called the search cost. The search cost accuracy measure, while functionally similar to Rossmo's hit score, is slightly different in that it is the percentage of overlaid grid cells, rather than a software determined offense domain, that needs to be searched to locate the cell with the offender's home base (Snook, Zito, Bennell, and Taylor, 2005). In terms of the accuracy of dragnet, Canter et al. (2000) found that their model was able to accurately predict 51% of all offender residences within the top 5% of the offense domain and 87% of the offender residences with the top 25% of the offense domain. Overall the model was able to reduce the original rectangular offense domain to 11% of the total size (Canter et al., 2000).

Snook, Canter and Bennell (2002) undertook to analyze the accuracy of dragnet in comparison to human predictions. Using a small group student volunteers, Snook et al. (2002) sought to determine if students that were given two simple rules about offender spatial behavior were as accurate in geographic profiling as the Dragnet software system. In contrast to earlier studies, Snook et al. (2002) determined accuracy of the profiles through an "error distance" measure, in which error is recorded as the distance between the predicted home location and the actual home location of the offender. The final results revealed that the error distance of those students that used the two simple rules were not significantly different from those of Dragnet. Importantly, while Snook, Taylor, and Bennell (2004) later replicated and broadened this study with a larger sample of volunteers their results were consistent to the pervious study. Specifically, humans using simple heuristics performed as well or better than complex profiling systems.

Snook et al. (2005) later did another analysis of geographic profiling systems, this time comparing the accuracy of 11 different profiling strategies using a data set of 16 residential burglars who had committed at least 10 crimes. Functionally, the analysis conducted by Snook et al. (2005) was very similar to that conducted by Levine (2002) in that they both analyzed the five JTC routines within CrimeStat in comparison to a set of spatial distribution strategies. Moreover, both analyses employed error distance as the only accuracy measure. The main difference between the two analyses appears to center around the spatial distribution measures used, data sets, and the overall goal of the analyses. Importantly, the goal for Snook et al. (2005) focused more on the relationship between the complexity *and* accuracy of the different strategies rather than just simply looking at accuracy. Overall, Snook et al. (2005) found that strategy complexity was not positively related to accuracy, in that the profiling routines did not perform significantly better than the simple spatial distribution strategies.

While some of the previous assessments involved multiple profiling systems, or at least multiple methods, none of the previous studies had actually compared all of the different methods against each other with the same data and the same analysis methods. The only study to directly compare several of the different profiling models was conducted by Paulsen (2006b) in which RIGEL, Dragnet, and the 5 different profiling methods of Crimestat were all tested along with three spatial distribution methods (CMD, Median Center, and mean center). The data used in this analysis was a complete set of all offenders arrested for three or more of the same crimes in Baltimore County, Maryland between 1994 and 1997. In total, 247 separate serial crime series were analyzed, representing a full range of crimes both against person and against property as well as a range of the number of crimes committed within a series. The analysis methods included a simple dichotomous determination of accuracy (correct or not), error distance, profile error distance, and a search cost measure. The results indicated that the spatial distribution measures were more accurate than the traditional profiling methods across a range of different accuracy measures. Paulsen (2006c) later expanded this research to include comparing human subjects against RIGEL, Dragnet, Crimestat and the three spatial distribution methods. While, the research involved a random sample of only 25 crime series in which there were 6 or more crimes, the results were similar to the previous study. As with the previous study, the results indicate that traditional geographic profiling methods were not substantially better than spatial distribution methods or even human subjects using simple heuristics.

Glossary of Terms

Activity Schedule: The temporal extent of a human being's routine activities (Golledge).
Activity Space: The geographic extent of a human being's routine activities (Golledge).
Ambusher: An attacker who offends a victim after enticing her to a controlled crime scene (Rossmo); also, an offender whose attack pattern is to attack the victim from a hiding place (Helms).
Anchor Point: A geographic feature which acts as an anchor to the offender's actions (Golledge).
Buffer Zone: An area near the offender's home where he does not commit crimes (Brantingham).
Coal Sack: An area near the offender's home where he does not commit crimes, analogous to the buffer zone (Newton).
Commuter: An offender who lives outside the vicinity of his crimes and visits to attack (Canter).
Distance Decay: A function in which intensity decreases over distance (such as gravity).
Hunter: An offender who sets out specifically to find a victim, using his residence as a base (Rossmo).
Marauder: An offender who lives in the vicinity of his crimes and strikes out from a central base (Canter).
Modus Operandi (MO): The methods and actions used by the offender to commit the crime.
Poacher: An offender who sets out specifically to find a victim, using something other than his residence as a base, or who commutes to another city to search (Rossmo).
Raptor: An offender who attacks the victim upon encounter (Rossmo).
Routine Activity Theory: The criminological theory that routine activities by the offender and victim result in interactions, which can result in crime opportunities when the offender and victim are at the same place, at the same time, in the absence of a guardian (Felson).
Signature: Distinctive methods or actions used by the offender that are extraneous to the actual commission of the crime (Keppel).
Stalker: An offender who first follows a victim upon encounter, then attacks (Rossmo).

Trapper: An offender whose routine activities results in victim encounters, or who entices victims into a controlled crime scene (Rossmo).

Troller: An offender who opportunistically encounters victims while engaged in other activities (Rossmo).

Forecasting and Prediction

8

Overview

Once we have analyzed the information available about our crime problem, we usually want to foresee how the problem will evolve in the future. In everyday conversation, the words "forecast" and "prediction" are usually interchangeable; however, in the arena of crime and intelligence analysis, they are technical terms, and therefore have reserved, specific meanings. In this chapter, we will use these terms in their technical sense, giving them operational definitions that distinguish them. *Prognostication* is a good word to describe both—so when we use that word, we can refer to either forecasting or prediction, or both.

The terms forecasting and prediction have similar meanings, but they do not convey precisely the same idea. Webster defines forecasting as "to plan in advance, foresee. To estimate or calculate in advance" (Webster's New World Dictionary of the English Language, 2nd College Edition; New World Publishing, New York, 1978). The same source defines prediction as "a statement of what will happen; to foretell a future event or events." The distinction is subtle, but important. The key to understanding the difference lies in that critical word "event." As we have already learned, an event is a discrete incident having unique coordinates in time and space. The difference is that predictions attempt to foretell events, while forecasts perform estimations and calculations. In crime analysis terms, forecasting is a strategic and administrative discipline while prediction is tactical and operational.

Although the distinction may seem purely semantic, it is much more. Forecasting and prediction share many attributes, and some specific techniques apply to both; others are unique to one or the other. The primary difference, however, is in the goal. As always, the crime analyst should begin the process of forecasting or predicting with the question, "What do I want to do?" The answer dictates which set of techniques should apply. If the analyst is facing a strategic or administrative question (Where should we put our new substation? How many cops will we need to hire next year? What will happen to our response times when the new shopping mall opens up?), then forecasting methods can be effectively used to inform decision making. On the other hand, tactical and operational problems cannot be effectively tackled with forecasting; predictive methods will work better when you are facing these tasks (Where will the Serial Predator strike next? How will Gang A react to the recent drive-by shootings by Gang B?).

In this chapter, we will discuss both forecasting and prediction. We will explore methods for prognosticating both temporal and spatial variables. We will also discuss the strengths and weaknesses of these methods, from both a research and a practical standpoint. Perhaps most importantly, we will explore the level of expectations that are reasonable for success using these techniques in the world of serial crime.

Why Forecasts Work

Like predictions, forecasts are extrapolations based on previous observations—a fundamental scientific process. By observing what is already happened, we can reasonably hope to foresee what will happen in the future. Observation of the apparent movements of sun, moon, and stars led to the science of astronomy and the development of accurate calendars. Forecasting works because the world really does make sense (mostly, at least). When it rains in the mountains, we can forecast that rivers will rise, because these measurements are causally linked. Although forecasting has long been the province of physical sciences, social phenomena are also susceptible to forecasts. Population growth, for example, can be forecast with great precision. Population movements from place to place are also amenable to forecasting. Because the world does not behave in a completely random and unpredictable way, forecasting can be a useful process that can tell us what to expect—and therefore, perhaps, lead us to plan for it effectively.

Why Forecasts Don't Work

Unfortunately, foretelling the future is never as easy as it sounds. While it is true that the world and the people in it usually behave in explicable and therefore expectable ways, it is also an extremely complicated place. In order to forecast any kind of phenomenon, we need sufficient observations of how the phenomenon occurred before. Also, we must be aware of the factors that influence that phenomenon and have observations of those factors, too.

Often, however, we lack sufficiently numerous and accurate observations of past behavior to enable good forecasts. For example, we may count the number of crimes that happen in a jurisdiction day by day for several months and determine that they have a predictable average. On the basis of these observations, we might then forecast that the daily crime level next month would be similar to what has happened before—only to discover that the crime rate actually rises dramatically. Why? Perhaps a seasonal variation such as the transition from winter to spring is occurring and making it easier for criminal activity to occur. To account for this type of seasonal variation, we would need years of observational data, not just months.

Also, we can easily fail to include all the relevant information. We simply might not know what factors are important, or new factors may arise that greatly change the outcome. For example, forecasts of the number of letters mailed in any given month have traditionally been thoroughly explored, enabling the U.S. Postal Service to accurately estimate the amount of effort needed to transport mail in advance—until the advent and increasing prevalence of email. Factors that had previously been the most important—population, holidays, weather, and the economy—were suddenly overshadowed by a completely novel influence.

The Utility of Forecasts

As a primarily statistical function, forecasting (which attempts to estimate how much of something will occur in a given area over a given time period) can be very useful to police and public safety planners. If we can forecast where crime will increase and decrease over time, we can reconfigure our police mechanisms to optimize their usefulness. For example, if we know that a given beat is likely to generate more calls for service next year, we can allocate sufficient resources in advance to avoid suffering any slowdown in response times due to the increased demand.

Because forecasts usually inform strategic and administrative analyses and these types of questions seldom demand rapid results, the analyst often has the liberty to take a considerable amount of time to carefully obtain and prepare data, construct research plans, craft a forecasting system, and calibrate results. Many criminologists, particularly those in the academic sector, conduct very advanced forecasting which, when properly applied, can be remarkably accurate.

Temporal Forecasting

Since forecasting is the estimation of a future measurement, temporal crime forecasting can be defined as the estimation of how many crimes will occur over a given time period. There are many methods for performing temporal crime forecasting, ranging from simple to complex, and effective to nearly useless.

As we have already discussed (see Chapter 6 on Temporal Analysis), the analysis and forecasting of the timing and frequency of events can be challenging. Even though it seems it should be a simple task to determine when a crime or other event has occurred, there are in fact many obstacles, which we have enumerated to some degree. These difficulties multiply the challenges facing the forecaster. Small inaccuracies in date and time measurements can quickly balloon into mammoth errors when extrapolated by forecasting techniques.

Spatial Forecasting

Attempting to predict how much activity will occur in a given area is the province of spatial forecasting. There are numerous methods for performing spatial forecasting; most of them are methodologically very similar to the simpler problem of temporal analysis and involve similar processes, such as autocorrelation, density estimation, etc.

Spatial forecasting requires valid spatial data which, in itself, can be quite difficult to obtain. Trying to determine exactly where a crime occurred can be even more difficult than determining when it occurred. Even if we have access to good information, idiosyncrasies in coordinate systems, projection, and mapping software can throw numerous technical and mathematical obstacles in our path.

Fundamental errors in logic also often overtake the spatial forecaster. For example, an analyst might analyze spatial trends in residential burglaries, and detect a progression—for example, from east to west. Based on this progression, the analyst might forecast that the trend will continue and residential burglaries will continue to push toward the western part of town. However, if a lake or mountain occupies that space, or if it is filled with commercial properties, this forecast really can not come true. If a barrier— such as a river or freeway—hems in the progression, it may not be able to break through. While these considerations may seem simplistic, there are thousands of subtler influences that may escape the analyst's notice for a variety of reasons.

Why Predictions Work

Good predictions are the outcome of a Decision Model. Decision models come in a variety of styles, the most common being the Discrete Choice Model. Basically, a discrete choice model works by posing a series of questions that can be used to prioritize a set of choices. It is conceptually similar to a Decision Tree.

Decision models in general, and discrete choice models in particular, are a fundamental concept that crime analysts must absolutely master before any attempt at prediction can succeed reliably, so we'll spend several pages making sure this idea is thoroughly understood.

Every human action is the result of a decision—nothing is really random. Nobody ever "accidentally" buys groceries or gas, or "randomly" buys a house. Every action is the result of a decision. That is good news for crime analysts, because it means that these decisions might be modeled and if they can be modeled, they might be predicted.

A discrete choice model attempts to explain how a criminal makes his decisions about where and when to strike. It does this by breaking down each crime into a series of small decisions. When these decisions are added together, they produce a comprehensive model that can be used to explain past actions and predict future ones.

Decision Models

The easiest way to mirror the decision process in a discrete choice model is probably by illustration, so let us imagine an example based on a simple choice: Where should you sit in a movie theater.

Let us begin with a simple situation: a couple walks into a movie theater, and has to choose where to sit. Like any decision, this will actually be quite a complicated choice. There may be hundreds of seats in the theater. Which should they choose?

The first consideration is the layout of the theater itself (the terrain). How many seats are there? How are they arranged? How big is the screen? How many entrances and exits are there? Where are the aisles? Are some seats reserved for handicapped patrons, and therefore off limits?

The second consideration is the position of people who have already arrived. Already taken seats are off limits and must be excluded. Moreover, the position of other patrons might influence the desirability of seats near to them.

The third consideration is which entrance the couple used to get in. This entrance will be closer to some seats than others, which will arbitrarily bias the couple's choice in favor of close seats.

These three factors, taken together, are considered the "starting position," the situation on the ground at the instant that the couple begins the decision-making process that will result in their choosing a particular pair of seats. These factors are essentially outside their immediate control, and cannot readily be altered or overlooked by the couple.

At this point, the couple walks into the theater and looks around. They see the layout of the theater, notice which seats are taken, and get their bearings.

ILLUSTRATION: MOVIE THEATER-1
Then, they quickly consider a number of other factors which cumulatively determine the desirability of every seat in the theater, culminating in a prioritization that leads to a decision (see Figure 8.1). Many of these factors will be based on personal preference and individual idiosyncrasy.

For example, eyesight and vision will be a factor. If either partner has poor eyesight, he or she may not be able to see the screen from some seats.

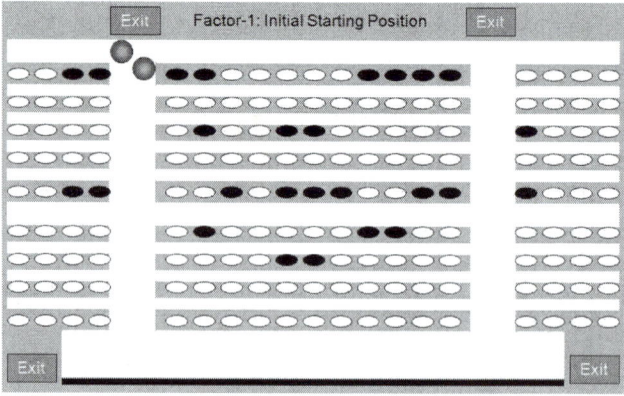

Figure 8.1 Making a spatial decision: starting out.

Therefore, seats with a good view of the screen will be scored favorably compared to those that are bad. Notice that different people will start making different decisions right away: A nearsighted moviegoer would not prefer to the same seat as a farsighted patron and, of course, whether or not the individual wore glasses (and remembered them) would affect the choice.

Another factor might be proximity to an aisle. If one partner likes to be able to leave quickly, she will prefer a seat on an aisle. Therefore, those seats will get a higher priority to seats that are far from aisles.

ILLUSTRATION: MOVIE THEATER-2
A romantic couple will certainly want to sit together; so single seats will not be attractive (see Figure 8.2). Only side by side seats will be desirable.

Many people don't like to sit immediately adjacent to a stranger. Therefore, seats at least one seat away from the nearest other patron will be given a higher score than those next to someone else.

ILLUSTRATION: MOVIE THEATER-3
Other factors might involve special situations that can not be predicted in advance (see Figure 8.3). A crying baby in one part of the theater will make that entire section much less desirable to most moviegoers. A crowd of surly teenagers with their feet on the seats in front of them are not likely to inspire a sense of welcome. On the other hand, the chance glimpse of a good friend in the theater might present a powerful attraction to sit near to the friend, even if the nearby seats are not intrinsically desirable.

Every seat in the theater is compared to each step in the decision-making process. These steps are called "layers" in the discrete choice model. In the end, some seats are consistently desirable, while others are undesirable. The couple will identify and choose the pair of seats with the highest relative desirability.

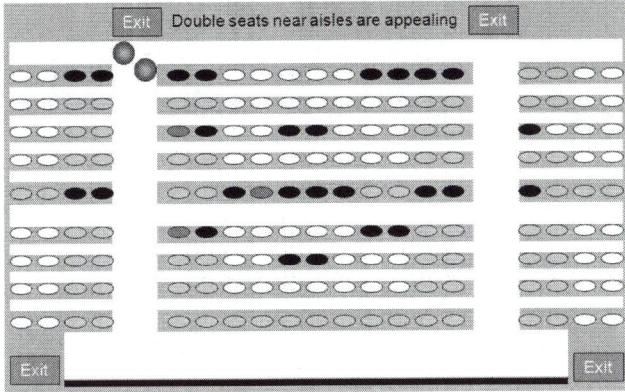

Figure 8.2 Making a spatial decision: additional considerations.

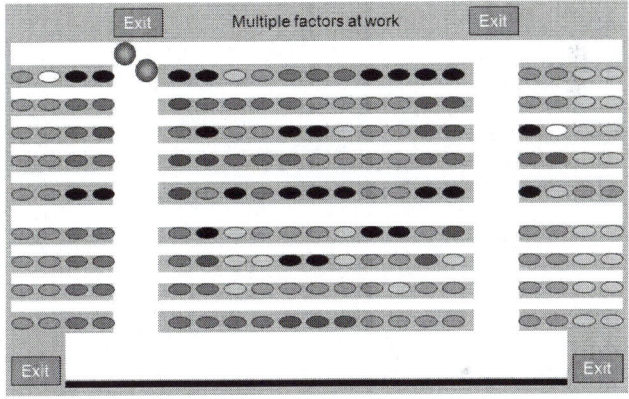

Figure 8.3 Making a spatial decision: multiple factors at work.

ILLUSTRATION: MOVIE THEATER-4
This entire process will only take a moment in the real world; perhaps only a few seconds (see Figure 8.4). Few, if any, of the layers in the model will be consciously considered as part of a rational, intentional choice. But intuitively, the moviegoers will perceive some seats as being good and others as bad.

This same process can be applied to any sort of decision, including when or where to commit a crime. When a burglar breaks into a house, he is making a series of choices. Which house should he hit?

This decision consists of numerous layers, too. Does the burglar like houses in cul-de-sacs (so nobody will see him break in), or on corners (so he can get away quickly)? Does he like one-story houses (where he will not get trapped and will not have to negotiate any stairs), or two-story (where any residents might be upstairs, buying him precious time in case they hear

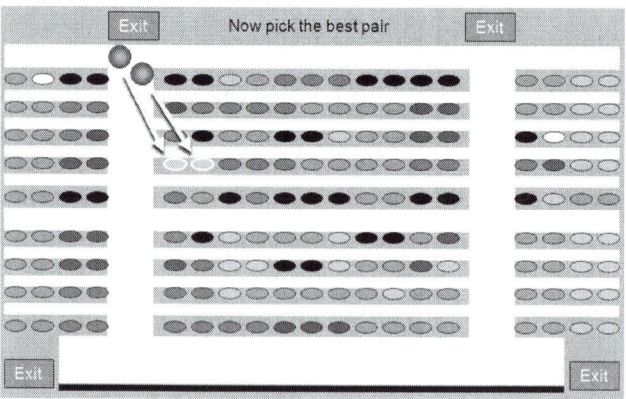

Figure 8.4 Making a spatial decision: final choice.

him)? Does he like fenced yards? Is he afraid of dogs? Does he target suburban single family homes, where people are usually absent during the workday? Or perhaps instead he likes apartments in urban neighborhoods, where strangers are unlikely to be noticed?

These distinctions typify some important elements of a hypothetical residential burglar's decision-making process. This burglar is a cat burglar: he strikes at night, while the victims are asleep (not a common MO, but something most jurisdictions come across now and then). Therefore, his targets must fit his specific needs. He prefers two-story houses. With the household asleep upstairs, he can enter through the ground floor with less chance of being heard; also, if the victims stir, he has more time to get away. He likes to hit several houses in one night, so targets should be close together. He does not want his car to be seen, so he parks someplace nearby so there must be an inconspicuous parking lot close at hand, preferably a lot without security guards or cameras. He then walks to his crimes. Therefore, there must be paths for him to follow safely on foot, but they should screen him from sight.

Discrete choice models like this can be used to explain and predict any kind of criminal activity. But how do the analysts determine which factors to use? How can we tell what kinds of decisions the criminal will make?

We always begin by examining what the offender has done in the past. Where has he struck before? What are the geographic features of the locations of previous crimes? What are the characteristics of previous victims? When has he struck? How has he struck?

When the offender repeats his choices, it is usually easy to spot the pattern, and determine what factors are important to him and predict how he will choose in the future. A "second-story man" will not attack a ranch-style (single-floor) house, so those can be excluded from our prediction. An offender who always strikes near freeway on-ramps will probably continue to do so, so we can prioritize our search for future events in similar areas.

Sometimes, however, the offender does not repeat his choices. Some offenders may intentionally avoid patterns by choosing to change their targeting preferences. However, that in itself is still a pattern. If the offender consistently changes the type of targets he hits, we can exclude the sort of places he has struck previously in our prediction.

Why Predictions Don't Work

The critical weakness of this process is that the choices being made must always be performed by the same decision-maker. In other words, discrete choice models are only effective against serial criminals.

This is a huge problem and a major defect of many methods used to predict crimes that are not restricted to serial crimes. To understand why this assumption is critical, let us imagine what would happen if we tried to analyze the movie theater example.

The right way is to attempt to predict what a single individual (or group that shares the decision) will do. To develop our model, we would keep a record of where that individual sat in movie theaters several times before trying to predict his next choice. We would write down how close he sat to the nearest neighbor; how many people he came with; how near he was to the aisles and the exits; how far from the screen, etc. We would then examine these choices to see which factors seemed the most stable. Then, we could create a discrete choice model that described his decision-making process. This would give us a powerful tool to predict where he might sit in any given future situation.

The wrong way to predict is to attempt to predict what more than a single individual will do. If we examined the seating choices of many people, recording their preferences, our model would be horribly flawed. Some people like to sit near exits, others far from them so these factors would tend to cancel each other out in our model. Some sit near aisles, others in the middle; these, too, would cancel one another. In the end, by trying to understand everyone, we wind up with a model that predicts nothing at all.

An equally fundamental error is the misuse of math, confusing statistics with prediction. This is one of several crippling flaws in a once widely-used prediction method, the Gottlieb Rectangle (named for Steve Gottlieb, the crime analyst author who originally promulgated this method in his seminal work, *Crime Analysis: From First Report to Final Arrest*) or distribution rectangle method. Unquestionably one of the poorest prognosticative methods ever devised, it has the excuse of being among the first ever developed specifically for the prediction of serial crime events. For many years, it stood nearly alone because no superior methods were presented for consideration.

Bryan Hill, a longtime proponent of the method, includes it in his more complicated Probability Grid Method (PGM) approach, and describes the technique thus:

> "The basic process requires you to know the X and Y Coordinates of the crimes in your series. Once you have obtained them through a hand-drawn method, or using a computer mapping application to 'geocode' the events, you must then find the mean, and standard deviation of the X and Y coordinate sets. Once you have the mean and standard deviation, you should [calculate] the corners for the 68th (1 standard deviation) and 95th (2 standard deviations) percentile areas...
>
> "Once you have obtained these numbers, you then place points on your map and connect the corner points to make the rectangles. This can be easily done in a computer mapping program."
>
> (Narrowing the Search: Using a Probability Grid in Tactical Analysis, Bryan Hill, 2001. http://www.iaca.net/Articles/probgrid.pdf, accessed on January 15th, 2008)

A more thorough critique of the distribution rectangle method is found in the publications of the Crime Mapping & Analysis Program:

> "In order for the distribution rectangle method to work correctly, a great many unspoken assumptions must hold true.... The biggest... is that the points being examined must adhere to a so-called Normal Distribution [bell-curve].... This is almost never the case in serial crime....
>
> "The biggest fallacy, however... is the basic error of attempting to estimate an individual case from a statistical sample. This is a fundamental fallacy...."
>
> Dan Helms, Tactical and Operational Crime Analysis Using ArcGIS 9x Manual, NLECTC-RM, University of Denver, Denver, 2001.

This great error—the Ecological Fallacy—overshadows the several other defects of the distribution rectangle that have been described elsewhere. The Gottlieb Rectangle method is sufficiently exploded that it need not be further demolished here. But almost all purely statistical approaches to forecasting suffer from the Ecological Fallacy, and analysts should be on guard against it.

Forecasting and Prediction

Another error that often traps crime analysts attempting to model behavior is multicolinearity. Multicolinearity occurs when the analyst includes the same element in the decision model several times, thinking that each element is different when actually each measures the same thing. We can use our Movie Theater model example to explain this. Imagine that you want to model the behavior of a patron and you must decide which variables to include in your model. Which factors should you consider? You might try to look at how far each seat was from the nearest entrance—maybe that is something the moviegoer uses in his decision. You might also look at the number of people who pass by the seat; that could be another factor (perhaps the moviegoer does not like having lots of other people passing by). Another factor might be the amount of outside noise that can be heard from each seat. You might consider the distance from the screen as an important variable. Finally, you might consider how long it will take the moviegoer to walk to each seat as a factor.

Unfortunately, while these factors might seem like good choices, they are fraught with multicolinearity. They are really all measuring the same thing—distance to the entrances. Think about it: the number of people passing will always be greater, the closer you are to the entrances. The amount of noise from outside will always be greater the closer one is to the entrances, too. Distance from the screen? That also is directly proportional to the distance from the entrances. And, of course, how long it will take to walk to the seat depends on how far it is from the entrance.

This example demonstrates that instead of having one good model with five good decision layers factored into it, we have created one terrible model that includes one factor five times and does not include anything else!

Crime analysts violate this rule with all sorts of predictive methods, such as the Probability Grid Method, which gained some notoriety in the early 2000s (Narrowing the Search: Using a Probability Grid in Tactical Analysis, Bryan Hill, 2001. http://www.iaca.net/Articles/probgrid.pdf, accessed on January 15th, 2008). This method appears at first glance to use a discrete choice model approach to create a grid; the values for each layer in the grid are summed to calculate an overall probability for future behavior. This method was adopted because analysts at the time were aware of a handful of basic spatial forecasting methods, but did not have any quantifiable way to choose which among them to use in any particular car. In addition, the results of these methods were usually overly vague and many analysts were aggressively seeking ways to reduce the areas of the forecasts they produced. Bryan Hill suggested that by combining these different forecasts as layers in a model, a more refined and accurate result would emerge.

The basic idea sounds like a decision model—not a bad method at all. Unfortunately, the Probability Grid Method (PGM) incorporates rampant multicolinearity by including spider distance, standard deviation ellipses, and statistical confidence rectangles—all of which are actually measuring the same thing (distance from the center).

Instead of a well-formed discrete choice decision model in which different factors are weighed and compared resulting in a prioritized decision strategy, the PGM technique simply squishes together half a dozen, old-fashioned, poor-performing, overly simplistic forecasting methods in the expectation that they will somehow perform better together than separately. This logic is somewhat akin to the idea that we can make a better cake by adding more ingredients to the mixing bowl: flour, sugar, laundry soap, lint, gasoline, etc. On closer inspection, it is not an inspired approach.

There is another problem with prediction.

The world usually makes sense, but in a larger sense, every part of it is highly unpredictable. Any number of inexplicable factors might change the pattern of a series, making it unpredictable without our knowing it.

For example, a serial offender may strike as regularly as a metronome—only to unexpectedly skip an attack right when the analyst has predicted one. Why? Who knows? Perhaps he got a flat tire. Perhaps he fell ill. Perhaps a relative came to visit for several weeks. Maybe he saw a helicopter and thought he was being watched. We may never know. But no matter how accurate and reliable our predictions are, some of them will always be wrong. Always.

Therefore, the analyst must temper expectations. Prediction of serial crime is perfectly possible. Many crime analysts have successfully predicted events, and criminals have been arrested and crimes interrupted because of predictions. But no prediction method is perfect, so the wise analyst will avoid making extravagant claims that might mislead commanders and officers into thinking that a prediction is foolproof.

Methods

Both forecasting and prediction are based on extrapolation from past observations. This is not quite the same as saying that what has happened before is what will happen next; it would be more accurate to say that what has happened before points the way toward what will happen next. In order to perform any type of prognostication, therefore, we must extrapolate from data.

There are innumerable methods for extrapolating and estimating how observations will evolve over time; many are very complicated. In this chapter we will focus on fairly simple, straightforward methods that can be applied to both forecasting and predictive problems, without specialized software. We will concentrate on Percent Change, Correlation, Autocorrelation, and Linear Regression.

Forecasting and Prediction

Percent Change

Probably the most common type of temporal forecasting is simple growth estimation, usually based on calculation of percent change. Percent change is the amount of increase or decrease in activity between two time periods, normalized into a percentage. To calculate percent change, the analyst uses the following simple formula:

$$\left(\frac{Y-X}{X}\right) \times 100$$

In this formula, X is the older of the two measurements, and Y is the newer. This can be remembered using the expression, "New minus old, divided by old." Multiplying the result by 100 converts the score into a percentage.

For example, if we had 200 robberies in 2007, and 250 in 2008, the result would be:

$$\left(\frac{250-200}{200}\right) \times 100 = \left(\frac{50}{200}\right) \times 100 = .25 \times 100 = 25\%$$

thus, a 25% increase.

The simplest change-based forecasting method is basic growth estimation, which assumes that the rate of increase, as described using percent change, will continue into the future. The analyst simply multiplies the last measurement by the percent change, and adds it onto the last measurement to forecast the future value. Therefore, if we wanted to forecast the number of robberies we would have in 2009 using the same example, we would multiple 250 x 25% and add that number to 250. In other words, we would add 62.5 (which is 25% of 250) onto 250; our result is 312.5, which we could round up to 313. So, a simple growth estimate based on percent change suggests we should expect 313 robberies in 2009.

Unfortunately, this pleasingly simple method is not very useful. Because it is only based on two measurements, it really can not take into account any anomalies such as special events, holidays, etc. that might have influenced either measurement. Like most statistical methods, it becomes increasingly unreliable as the size of the numbers involved decrease—in other words, it does not work with small numbers. Yet crime remains a relatively rare phenomenon, especially serial crime. Even a very prolific serial criminal is unlikely to commit more than a few dozen offenses per month; a more typical offender will usually commit far fewer. These low numbers make percent change comparisons and forecasts very chancy.

For example, imagine a serial killer commits one murder in 2007, and two in 2008. Using the formula described above, this would amount to a 100% increase in murders, which certainly sounds like a lot. Using the simple growth estimate method described previously, we would therefore expect his murders to double again in 2009—to four. This might be a reasonable estimate for some serial murders, but certainly not for all, or even most. But the method performs even more poorly when we continue to extrapolate from it into the future: in 2010, this method predicts 8 murders by the same offender; in 2011, 16, and in 2012, 32. In other words, based on three killings over a two-year period, the growth estimate by percent change forecasting method winds up predicting a whopping 57 victims over a six-year period!

Better methods for temporal forecasting might involve using more measurements than just two. By measuring the amount of crime over shorter periods, we can identify smaller trends and cycles in behavior that might allow our forecasts to be more precise. Unfortunately, again because crime remains a somewhat rare phenomenon, measuring crime over shorter periods, such as hourly, daily, or weekly, will result in much smaller individual measurements, which in turn reduces the statistical validity of the analyses.

Many methods for forecasting that are based on sequential measurements over time are collectively known as Time Series Forecasts. There are many types of time series forecasting methods. The majority rely on regression or analysis of variation in one form or another.

At best, forecasting will only tell us how many events to expect over a given time period. While this might be informative and highly useful for strategic analysis purposes, tactical problems such as serial crime are difficult to address with such results. Even if we can make a meaningful forecast and expect a given number of crimes over a given period, what can we do about it? Problem-solving police methods might be of use. But rather than forecasts, attempts to actually *predict* future crimes—to make a scientific guess as to when a crime will actually occur—can be much more useful. Armed with a valid prediction, a police agency might be able to intercept a serial criminal, deter or deny the offender the opportunity to attack, or otherwise intervene in the series itself.

Growth estimation can also be used to predict events by predicting individual attributes of serial events such as interval between crimes or spatial coordinates.

To create a temporal prediction based on percent change, calculate the average percent change in interval between events, and then add that interval onto the date and time of the last event.

To create a spatial prediction based on percent change, calculate the average percent change in both X and Y coordinates between events and then add that value onto the coordinates of the last event.

Unfortunately, percent change is typically an even weaker tool for prediction than it is for forecasting.

Correlation

Sometimes one measurement might be determined by another. For example, the length of the day influences the temperature (the longer the sun shines, the warmer the day gets); the distance between points influences the time it takes to travel between them (the farther apart they are, the longer it will take to walk, drive, or fly from one to the other). This is sometimes true in criminal behavior as well. For example, the amount of money a robber gets in a crime may influence the interval until he robs someone else (if he makes a lot of money, he may not need to attack again soon). Or the frequency of police street patrols might influence the likelihood of a neighborhood being selected by a burglar. The mathematical comparison of the influence of one measurement upon another is called *correlation*. There are many techniques for performing correlation analysis; one of the best known is the Pearson Product-Moment technique, and that is what we will demonstrate in this section.

To use this technique, the analyst must have two sets of measurements, one for the dependent variable, and one for the independent variable. The following formula explains the process:

$$r_{xy} = \frac{\sum x_i y_i - n\bar{x}\bar{y}}{(n-1)S_x S_y}$$

Here, r is the resulting normalized score, which will be between -1 and 1. X is the independent variable at measurement i, and Y is the dependent variable at measurement i. Bar-X and Bar-Y are the sample means of the two series; S_x is the sample standard deviation of the X series, and S_y is the sample standard deviation of the Y series, and n is the number of events in the series.

The result, r, will fall between -1 and 1. A score of -1 indicates a perfect negative correlation: As the independent variable goes up, the dependent variable goes down, and vice versa. A score of 1 indicates a perfect positive correlation: As the independent variable goes up, the dependent variable also goes up, and vice versa. Scores near 0 indicate no correlation: changing the independent variable does not seem to change the dependent variable at all.

The analyst can calculate the correlation coefficient between any two series of measurements to see if one predicts the other. Take careful note that correlation does not imply causality; in other words, even if two variables are clearly correlated, it does not mean that one actually makes the other one happen.

Autocorrelation

Autocorrelation is a set of techniques to look for patterns in time series data. These data can be any set of sequential numeric measurements.

Autocorrelation looks at the relationship between the amount of events and the time between them. It does not include any external factors. The basic idea is the same as with correlation, except that correlation is based on explaining one factor based on another, while autocorrelation is based on explaining one factor based on itself alone.

Discrete autocorrelation for a time series can be calculated using the following formula:

$$R_{xx}(j) = \sum_n x_n \overline{x_n - j}$$

In this equation, R is the autocorrelation at lag j for a discrete signal measured at X_n. To use it, the analyst converts her data into a series of numeric observations.

For temporal forecasting, autocorrelation can be used to predict how many events will occur in a given time period by analyzing a series of the same periods and autocorrelating the number of events to each period.

For spatial forecasting, autocorrelation can be used to predict how many events will happen in a given area (usually defined as a polygon). Simply count the number of events within each polygon and then treat them as a signal. However, the formula used to calculate autocorrelation spatially differs. There are several spatial autocorrelation functions to choose among. Moran's I statistic is one of the oldest, simplest, and best known.

$$I = \frac{N \sum_i \sum_j W_{ij} \left(X_i - \overline{X}\right)\left(X_j - \overline{X}\right)^2}{\left(\sum_i \sum_j W_{ij}\right) \sum_i \left(X_i - \overline{X}\right)}$$

In this formula, N is the number of polygons being studied. X_i is the amount of crime in one polygon; X_j is the variable at each other polygon to be compared to i. Bar-X is the mean number of crimes per polygon. W_{ij} is a weight score applied to the relationship between polygons i and j; the score is 1 if the polygons are adjacent, 0 if they are not (alternatively, a sliding normalized distance index can be used, but that method is more complicated) and probably requires a Geographic Information System (GIS) to implement correctly.

The result of Moran's I statistic is a number between 1 and -1. A score of 1 indicates perfect positive correlation (high scores tend to group together spatially; low scores tend to group together spatially). A score of -1 indicates perfect negative correlation (high scores tend to be next to low scores, and vice versa). A score of 0 indicates spatial randomness.

Forecasting and Prediction

Autocorrelation can be used for temporal prediction by calculating the autocorrelation score against the interval between events in a series. The analyst simply uses the interval between each event and the next (in hours, days, or some other convenient unit of measurement) instead of the number of events. By adding the predicted value onto the date and time of the last event, the next event can be predicted.

Autocorrelation can be used for spatial prediction by calculating the autocorrelation score against the changes in X and Y coordinates between events in a series. The analyst simply uses the change in coordinate rather than the number of events. The analyst then adds the predicted values onto the coordinates of the last known event to arrive at the expected location for the next event in a series.

Linear Trend Estimation (Regression)

Linear trend estimation is a method for predicting how measurements grow over time.

$$\hat{Y}(n) = -\sum_{i=1}^{p} a_i x(n-i)$$

Here, $\hat{Y}(n)$ is the expected signal value; $x(n-i)$ are the previously observed values, and a_i are the predictor coefficients. The root mean square is often used as the predictor coefficient, which reduces the squared error. This number can be calculated using:

$$x = \sqrt{\frac{1}{n}\sum_{i=1}^{n} x_i^2}$$

In other words, add up the squares of all values; divide by the number of values, then find the square root of that number. The result is the *root mean square*, which can be used as a term in the calculation for linear trend.

Linear trends estimation is a good temporal forecasting method; use the number of events in each time bin as the basis for the linear trend.

In addition, linear trend estimation can also be used to predict the timing of future events by calculating the trend against the interval between cases. The predicted interval value may then be added to the date and time of the last event to arrive at a predicted time for the next one in a series.

Linear trend estimation can also be used to predict the location of events by calculating the trend against the change in X and Y coordinates between cases. The predicted change values are added to the coordinates of the last event to arrive at an expected location for the next one in a series.

Linear trend estimation has the advantage of being able to cope with change. If events are accelerating or decelerating in tempo, expanding or contracting in space, or staying steady, this method can be used both to forecast and predict with relative ease.

Unfortunately, it has a few significant weaknesses. For one thing, it does not work well with clustered or random distributions of events in either space or time, so save it for uniformly distributed series when possible. Another weakness is that the "straight line" resulting from the prediction can in some cases result in absurd predictions, such as events that happen infinitely fast in time or infinitely far apart in space.

Intervention 9

Introduction

Before we begin seriously discussing the specifics of serial crime intervention, it is critical that we thoroughly understand the following key concepts, some of which come from outside the traditional law enforcement organization. We also need to develop some operational definitions that will allow us to share ideas exactly, without misunderstanding one another or misinterpreting a critical concept.

Crime Analysis is the systematic study of crime and disorder problems as well as other police-related issues to assist the police in criminal apprehension, crime and disorder reduction, crime prevention, and evaluation (Boba, 2005).

Problem is a qualitative unit of police work (Goldstein, 1990). A tactical crime problem is a specific pattern of criminal activity that can be resolved through tactical disposition and deployment (Helms, 2004).

Strategy vs. Tactics: These terms are often confused, and need to be put into a law enforcement context. Strategy has been defined as the art and science of employing assets in a synchronized and integrated fashion to achieve objectives; tactics have been defined as the orderly deployment of specific resources to achieve strategic objectives. These terms obviously come from a military perspective; as police are often described as a paramilitary organization, it is appropriate that these concepts be adjusted to reflect the slight differences between the police and military cultures.

Police Strategy is the art and science of developing and employing police assets in a synchronized and integrated fashion to achieve organizational objectives.

Police Tactics are the orderly deployments of specific police resources to achieve strategic objectives.

Tactics, therefore, are the means by which strategies are accomplished; strategies being the means by which public safety can be achieved.

Crime series, patterns, and trends are, themselves, tactical problems for law enforcement because they represent specific rather than general problems that can be addressed individually. However, as we attempt to deal with these tactical problems, we shall choose a strategy to defeat each problem, and then adopt specific tactics to implement our strategy (Liddell-Hart, 1967; Fast, 2005).

Operations: Also often confused with strategy and tactics, an operation is a specific action or set of actions which tactically implements a given strategy.

Action vs. Reaction: Police agencies are overwhelmingly reactive in nature. That is, rather than aggressively attacking crime problems, most efforts are directed toward responding to the actions of criminals. Increasing numbers of forward-thinking agencies have begun experimenting with reducing the percentage of officers who respond to calls for service, instead increasing the availability of officers to work as they think best. Many of these efforts have been concentrated in special squads such as Community Oriented Policing or COP units, Problem-Solving Units or PSU teams, etc.

Initiative: Discussion of action and reaction leads to another critical, fundamental concept, that of *initiative*. Initiative is defined by Webster as "an introductory step or movement; an act which originates or begins." It has the further connotation of "the right or power to introduce a new measure or course of action."

In any adversarial process—such as a police intervention—the side with initiative can *act*, forcing the other side to *react* (Clavell, 1983).

Crime Decision Equation: We can model the process that goes into a criminal's decision to commit a crime using a "decision equation" (Helms, 2002).

$$D = \frac{(S_p) \cdot (G_p)}{(R_p) \cdot (P_p)}$$

In this equation, the Decision (D) is equal to the perceived chance of success (S_p) times the perceived gain (G_p), divided by the perceived risk (R_p) of being punished multiplied by the perceived unpleasantness of the punishment (P_p). When the score D is greater than 1, the offender perceives the benefits as outweighing the costs of committing a crime, and is likely to offend. This equation is important because, if he can sustain the initiative, we can use active measures to alter the values in the equation, and change the offender's behavior.

Objectives

The analyst and police staff must first identify the objectives they hope to accomplish when creating an Action Plan. The choice of objective should be based on the reasonable expectation of success for an optimal desired out-

Intervention

come with the tools and techniques immediately available. This choice will greatly influence the subsequent choice of intervention strategies.

There are five basic objectives to crime pattern interventions (Helms, 2002):

1. Disruption
2. Displacement
3. Development
4. Disintegration
5. Detention

Disruption: Disruption of a series means forcing the offender to change his behavior. The primary benefit of successfully disrupting a crime series is the regaining of initiative by forcing the offender to react defensively. The idea is to force the offender to move away from a winning MO to one that might be less effective. This can include changing victim behaviors to degrade the criminal's MO, forcing him to wear a disguise by publishing his description, change the vehicle he uses by informing the public as to its known features, etc. Care must be taken to avoid forcing the criminal to evolve to a better MO, which is an unfortunately unintended consequence of police disruption that has not been carefully planned.

Example: A neighborhood has been plagued by daytime burglaries in which objects and tools are taken from open garages. With no other leads, other prospects having failed, the police go door to door to cite homeowners who leave garage doors open and unattended in violation of city ordinances. The public quickly grows accustomed to closing their garage doors, forcing the burglars to completely change their methods to continue to steal.

Displacement: Displacement is the practice of forcing the offender to change his activity space and schedule. This means moving his crimes to different neighborhoods, environments, or times and dates. Most often, displacement is an unintended consequence of poor police work. By pouncing on a "hotspot," law enforcement professionals can usually suppress activity in one confined geographic area, but seldom actually solve the problem. Sometimes, it causes the problem to shift to another location. This might actually make matters worse for the public than if the police had done nothing. This effect was noted by observers in a major southwestern city, when an aggressive sheriff launched a massive anti-prostitution "street cleanup" campaign on a notorious red-light street. After a couple weeks, prostitution had all but vanished from the targeted area; unfortunately, despite the claims of success by proponents of the cleanup, the prostitutes, drug dealers, and other street criminals had merely relocated to adjacent streets, seriously blighting previously tolerable neighborhoods. When the "surge" ended, the criminals returned to their previous haunts—but also maintained their new presence on the neighboring streets. One local police sergeant described the operation as "like trying to get rid of a pile of dung by stomping on it. [The sheriff] just spread it everywhere."

However, displacement need not always be unintentional. Sometimes a good plan can aim to displace the offender, possibly moving him into an area where he can be more readily targeted, prying him away from hiding places, bolt-holes, safe houses, and friends. Even though he might continue to commit crimes, the new crimes might be someplace more amenable to police response, giving law enforcement the edge it needs to detain the offender in a subsequent operation.

Example: A serial burglar is targeting three neighborhoods, but the police do not have sufficient resources to enact surveillance on all three. They decide to attempt to intentionally displace the burglar from two neighborhoods by making an ostentatious display in those areas—high-visibility patrols, helicopter overflights, and "Crime Watch" flyers left on doorknobs (not so much for the public as for the offender to see). The police then concentrate surveillance and response assets on the one target neighborhood intentionally neglected, with an increased certainty that the offender will strike there next.

Development: Development is the act of increasing the number of available leads, clues, and analytical information. This may seem to be a weak police effort, since it is indirect and unlikely to result in any quick change in the crime series. On the surface, it may appear to the public and press as though the police are not responding at all. Despite this appearance, however, developing additional information may be a necessary precursor to effective action, and will probably be time and money better spent than some high-profile "knee-jerk" reaction, such as saturating a "hotspot" with cops without a clearly-defined plan of operations.

Example: Faced with a serial rapist, the police might suspect that some victims have not come forward to report their crimes. By using the media to their advantage, the police might attempt to persuade previously unknown victims to step forward and give evidence. Perhaps they will be able to provide missing pieces to the puzzle—descriptions, vehicle information, places, dates and times, etc. There could possibly be remaining physical evidence to recover, even if the crime has gone unreported for a long time.

Another example: Unable to identify a serial offender because crime scenes have not been thoroughly processed, a police department might elect to concentrate crime scene technicians and equipment near the affected neighborhoods and retrain officers in those beats to protect the scenes more effectively. Although this action alone will likely be invisible to the serial criminal and will not lead to a flashy arrest, it might be a necessary first step toward gathering the information needed to identify the culprit and put him away.

Disintegration: Disintegration is the objective of breaking up a criminal team or offender network, or of detaching an offender from his social group. Disintegration often targets those close to an offender—perhaps a family member or friend who is shielding the criminal; possibly an accomplice who shares the responsibility for the crimes. The first can sometimes be persuaded to come forward by playing on the sense of shame, outrage, or justice. Possibly a girlfriend has suspicions that her brutal boyfriend may be involved in some serious crimes, but is afraid of him. If she sees other victims on the evening news, her sense of outrage at what other people are suffering might overcome her fear of retaliation enough to make her approach the police with information. The second category—accomplices and fellow criminals—can sometimes be persuaded to "rat out" a fellow on the "there is no honor among thieves" precept. By offering immunity from prosecution, reduced sentencing, or even rewards, co-conspirators can frequently be induced to work with law enforcement.

Like development, this objective may sometimes appear rather ineffectual to the public. When properly applied, however, it has been proven to be a particularly effective technique, particularly in long-term problems.

Example: Faced with a child molestation series with few leads, the police use the media to release sketches of the offender, and offer a $2,000 reward for information leading to a conviction.

Another example: When a series of brutal rapes can not be tackled quickly using forensic analysis and standard investigation techniques, a police department may highlight the vicious nature of the crimes on network television, showcasing the crimes in such a way as to emphasize the cruelty and depravity of the attacks. This might cause a suspicious relative, friend, or accomplice to feel sufficiently guilty to make an anonymous tip.

Detention: Detention prevents the offender from committing further crimes by taking him into custody and supervising him directly. This is the first objective most analysts and police professionals think of when faced with any tactical problem. It is also usually the last. Arresting the suspect is the only objective many police professionals are interested in. To most cops and certainly to the public in general, arrest is the one and only solution for a crime problem. However, detaining the offender might not always be a realistic goal, at least at first. For detention to be effective, prosecution must follow. Even if a suspect is arrested, tried, and convicted, few offenders stay in prison forever, and upon release may pick up their crimes where they left off. So, while detention is certainly a desirable outcome, it is not a perfect solution in many cases. Simply arresting suspicious characters ("Round up the usual suspects!") is unlikely to affect a crime series unless the arrests are well informed and substantiated by effective prosecutions. Even if a prosecution could be successful, the local District Attorney may decline to prosecute given a limited budget that can only support a limited number of trials each year—causing low-priority offenders to be released even when guilt can be proven. Limited jail and prison space may also be a factor resulting in ineffectual detentions. These "revolving door" problems at the interface between police, courts, and corrections agencies can result in "catch-and-release" police work, which seldom helps the public.

Although it can sometimes feel as though detaining the offender is futile, it is not. Even if the offender is released, at least he wasn't committing new crimes for the period of his detention. Moreover, he may be more cautious about his future behavior; certainly some offenders are rehabilitated by incarceration, although what percentage of the offender population abandons the life of crime upon release remains a hotly debated question.

Intervention Strategies

There are four families of intervention strategies available to law enforcement strategists: *Deterrence*, *Denial*, *Investigation*, and *Interception* (Helms, 2002). Once the police agency has chosen the objective (or objectives) they hope to accomplish, they must determine which strategy or combination of strategies to use to enact it. The choices they make will determine what specific tactics will be available to them when crafting their final result, an Action Plan.

Deterrence: Deterrence is the strategy of changing the offender's behavior by changing his perception of risk and cost. There are four main elements to deterrence:

1. *Success* is the aspect of the benefit part of the crime decision equation which describes how likely it is that the offender will succeed with the crime.
2. *Risk* is the aspect of the cost part of the crime decision which describes how likely it is that the offender will be apprehended.
3. *Punishment* is the aspect of the cost part of the crime decision equation which describes how adversely being caught will affect the offender.
4. *Gain* is the aspect of the benefit part of the crime decision which describes how beneficially a successful crime will affect the offender.

In order to be effective as a deterrent, the tactics employed during a deterrence intervention must affect the offender's perceptions of the crime decision equation; therefore, the police must make their efforts perceptible and credible to the offender.

Deterrence can also be an unintended consequence of knee-jerk, reactive police action. The reflex of some police agencies to pelt a neighborhood with police units when they detect a hotspot or possible crime series can sometimes influence criminals to cease attacking in that vicinity. When this inhibits criminal activity and improves public safety, it is a good thing; however, when it results in unintentional displacement (improving the quality of life in one neighborhood at the expense of another), or spoils an investigation, or causes the offender to improve his tactics, it is bad. Analysts should carefully consider the potential consequences of deterrence strategies, not only on the particular serial offender they are targeting, but on others as well. Will the public be glad to see numerous patrol cars in their neighborhood, or will that actually make them feel less safe? Will other criminals in the neighborhood disperse to other locations?

Denial: Denial is the strategy of rendering the offender unable to commit his crimes by denying him the opportunity to attack. This intervention method works by removing the environmental, social, and other factors which the offender exploits to succeed with his crimes. There are two main branches of denial strategies: *Target-Based* and *Method-Based*.

Target-Based Denial interventions seek to remove or diminish the list of potential targets available to the offender. Target-based denial is sometimes called *target hardening*.

Example: A serial rapist targets exotic dancers and escorts by arranging "dates," but then attacking his victims, robbing them, assaulting them, and escaping. The police respond by working with the city council to outlaw exotic dancers and escort services within the jurisdiction. Now there are no targets, so this crime series can not continue using its present MO: the offender is denied victims. Instead, he will have to target some other pool of victims; perhaps they will be less vulnerable.

Method-Based Denial interventions seek to foil the offender by denying him the opportunity to use the methods that have proven successful in the past.

Example: Drug dealers use pay phones to contact one another and their customers without fear of interception or tracing; the community removes old payphones from many slum neighborhoods where they no longer serve a legitimate purpose, and places video cameras near others to make them unserviceable to drug dealers.

Denial strategies often directly affect the community in which they occur. They are likely to be noticed by citizens and may be intrusive on their quality of life. They are often incorporated into "problem-oriented policing" strategies or police "problem solving." They can be very effective when applied carefully, but as always the analyst should carefully consider the potential unintended consequences of implementing denial strategies. By suppressing one problem, another may be created, which is even worse.

Investigation: Investigation is the strategy of identifying the cause of a tactical crime problem and eliminating it, thereby abating the problem at the source. This usually takes the form of identifying the offender or group of offenders, and arresting them.

Investigation is a proven, tried-and-true success. It has been the mainstay of modern police effectiveness for many years. Detectives, also called investigators, have the primary responsibility for performing this function in law enforcement agencies, although many line officers and even support staff such as crime analysts and crime scene technicians also play prominent roles in this effort. Investigation is responsible for most arrests and convictions used to close cases across the United States and around the world.

Unfortunately, investigation also requires a substantial investment in resources; a typical detective can only effectively investigate a few cases at a time, and it may take days, weeks, months, or sometimes years to complete an investigation. Often, teams of detectives are required to untangle the twisted skein of clues, leads, tips, and hints related to a single crime. The plain truth is that the overwhelming majority of crimes are never actually investigated. The volume is simply too great for the number of professionals available. Instead, minor crimes are usually set aside, allowing detectives to prioritize on violent and high-profile crimes. Unfortunately, crimes that are difficult to investigate are also often set aside, although this usually does not happen if the crime involves homicide or rape.

Interception: Interception is the strategy of interdicting the offender, usually while engaged in some aspect of criminal behavior, such as targeting, attacking, escaping, or consolidating. This usually takes the form of forecasting the offender's behavior and attempting to catch him in the act of committing another offense, or preparing to do so.

Interception has a strong appeal for tactical crime analysts, and is for many police officers, detectives, and analysts the "holy grail" of good police work. Unlike other police functions, seldom is any specifically-defined unit tasked with planning and preparing interception within the law enforcement community. Investigation is performed by detectives; deterrence is performed by patrol units; denial is performed by public information officers, neighborhood liaisons, and spokespersons. Interception, which requires prediction to be successful, is performed on an ad hoc basis by any interested and authorized part of the police organization. However, tactical crime analysts typically are best suited to perform this role—they usually have the right tools, training, and data to make a scientific prediction and learn over time how to do it better.

Interceptions, however, have their drawbacks. Catching the criminal red-handed sounds like a great victory, but it might not be. A prediction might come true, but the bad guy could still elude capture—criminals escape pursuits more often than people like to think. Even worse, confronting a criminal during the commission of the crime could lead to tragedy: a hostage or barricade situation, exchanges of gunfire, high-speed pursuits, crashed vehicles.... There are many ways for an interception to end badly.

Even when an interception goes smoothly and works well, the criminal often succeeds with his crime just before the interception succeeds in nabbing him. If his crime was larceny or burglary, the risk may be acceptable to police. If the crime is child molestation, sexual assault, kidnapping, aggravated assault, or murder, the risk of the operation may be too great. One more victim might be too high a price to pay, even to catch the bad guy. In these circumstances, it might be better to make the crime series go away using some other method, even if it does not provide the same satisfaction and sense of closure usually derived from a successful interception.

Opportunity Cost

Opportunity cost expresses how choosing one course of action may "cost" the chance to try something else. Concentrating on a "Deterrence" strategy, for example, might make it impossible to simultaneously or later attempt an "Interception."

Because limiting the extent of a tactical problem is a key requirement, requestors will want to resolve the series using the quickest means. Therefore, when creating recommendations and formulating an Action Plan, the analytical team must calculate the opportunity cost of each available alternative. By choosing the alternative (or combination of alternatives) with the least opportunity cost, the best plans will be tried first, and will least interfere with later efforts (Fast, 2005; Helms, 2001).

Calculating opportunity cost for intervention alternatives is difficult, largely because it is hard to quantify crime. It is easy to add up the monetary cost of how much a police response program will probably entail, but it is impossible to set a valid dollar figure for the price of a rape, child molestation, or a murder. Therefore, these imponderables need not be quantified; simply leave them out of the opportunity cost calculation altogether. Address them instead in the Caveats section of the Action Plan Operations section.

Tactics

Tactics are the specific actions taken at the level of individual police resources (officers, teams, and units) to enact the strategy or strategies that have been selected. Tactics are infinitely variable and depend on local circumstances to a high degree. A tactic that is successful for one agency is likely to produce failure elsewhere. Copying strategies from other, successful police departments is usually a good idea; copying tactics, however, is seldom beneficial. Tactical ideas must always be adapted to fit the idiosyncrasies of each particular police agency, the jurisdiction in which it operates, and the nature of the crime problem to be addressed.

A strategic plan involving deterrence, for example, might call for police to display a visible presence in a particular area in the hope that the offender will see the police presence and decide not to strike there. But how can this be accomplished? Should we just send cops blindly driving around a particular neighborhood, possibly alarming citizens and certainly squandering one of our agency's most valuable resources—the on-duty time of sworn officers? Perhaps a better idea would be to kill two birds with one stone. We might identify the biggest day-to-day police or public safety issue in the target community, and assign officers tasks there that will help amend it. For example, if the target neighborhood has a problem with traffic accidents, we can easily assign a swarm of officers to tackle traffic violations. This will keep them highly visible, thereby accomplishing our primary objective (deterring a serial criminal from striking in that area), while also accomplishing a valuable secondary objective (making the streets safer and reminding drivers to exercise caution), and even to some degree a tertiary objective (generating revenue from citations that will help pay for this kind of operation).

If the biggest problem in the target neighborhood was something completely different—say, noise complaints at apartment complexes—then the pretext of traffic enforcement would be neither sensible nor efficient. But that problem, too, could be to some degree addressed by an increased presence of uniformed patrol. A good tactician, therefore, fulfills the strategic objectives of the serial crime intervention plan by using sound tactics that deploy the resources to be used in the most efficient way.

The Action Plan—A Combined Approach

The best police responses to serial crime problems seldom consist of a single objective or a single strategy. Instead, the best methods often interweave a variety of these elements together to create a comprehensive action plan that attacks the problem from several angles. Even if one part of the plan fails, the others might succeed. In a well-designed plan, each strategic and tactical element reinforces the others, so the likelihood of any given part of the plan working is increased by the activities of the other parts.

For example, let us imagine a crime series: a serial rapist is stalking illegal immigrant women in a southwestern city by impersonating a U.S. Immigration Agent. The offender targets Hispanic women at bus stops, convinces them of his official status as an immigration officer, implies or explicitly warns of deportation consequences for the victims or their families unless they cooperate with his demands, and eventually rapes them in his vehicle. He strikes during daytime or early evening hours and has recently begun displaying a gun. What can be done? More to the point, what should be done?

This is precisely the scenario confronting the Austin, Texas Police Department in 2000, when they detected a distinctive pattern of behaviors being reported by victims. Investigation by Violent Crimes Analyst Tess Sherman, revealed cases stretching back to 1994, and finally 12 events were identified and linked to the same offender.

Tess and her colleagues applied excellent spatial and temporal skills to the problem and quickly identified important patterns in the offender's behavior; they were able to identify the specific bus routes targeted, and also mapped out the driving routes where the offender kidnapped his victims, identifying movement patterns and common streets that painted a picture of the offender's activity space. On the basis of these findings, they were able to craft a prediction and began to set about designing a bait/decoy operation using an undercover police woman to intercept the suspect.

However, while this was happening, the police still had to protect the community. They decided on a denial campaign to warn potential victims of the serial rapist's MO and description. This would have a two-fold benefit: first, it would improve the safety of the public by denying the offender targets of opportunity; second, it would improve the chances for the bait/decoy operation by reducing the pool of vulnerable victims, making the bait officer more attractive to the offender. Tess described her agency's actions to the author in 2001:

> "Once the series had been solidly identified press releases and news stories in English and Spanish informed Austin residents of the series and how to respond. A suspect composite and information about the suspect posing as an INS official was publicized not only in an effort to alert residents but to encourage further reporting of additional cases. The last mapped case in the series was not a rape but a suspicious person report. The intended victim was approached by the offender but since she had been warned by her husband not to get into any car with a man claiming to be an INS agent she fled in time. Her husband had seen the story on a recent news broadcast. In this instance more information became available about the offender's time and space patterns which we included in our data set but without the traumatic consequence of another rape."

Tess Sherman in Advanced Crime Mapping Topics, Crime Mapping & Analysis Program, University of Denver, Denver, 2001.

But it was not the bait operation that eventually caught the Austin serial rapist—the interception effort never actually happened. Because while the other parts of the intervention effort—denial and interception—were underway, the investigative effort was attaining fruition.

Originally confronted by four cases, the crime analysis unit had been able to identify eight others, stretching back to 1994, making a total of 12. These cases were not linked by DNA or other physical evidence—just behavior (emphasizing the critical importance of behavioral data pattern detection methods, such as the IZE method). But it was actually the earliest case in the series that led to the arrest of the offender more than six years later. In that first case, the offender had given the victim a false name; but he had not chosen randomly. He used his middle name as a pseudonym. To investigators at the time, the name meant nothing and the lead could not be exploited. Years later, in a completely unrelated domestic violence call, the offender's real name and personal information were entered into the police databases. In 2000, crime analysts rediscovered that old, blind lead, and used simple database mechanics to compare it to other combinations of names in the system. When persons with similar physical descriptions with partially matched names had been selected by the computer, the analysts compared their home and work addresses to the location of the crime series. They discovered only a few that lived or worked within the offender's predicted activity space, and a few others that had at one time, but had since moved away. With this smaller list, detectives constructed a photo-lineup and showed it to the victims, new and old, resulting in a positive match.

The offender was arrested before he had a chance to strike again, without need to deploy the bait/decoy officer, or endanger the public further.

This combined, simultaneous approach to serial crime intervention exemplifies many of the best features of a good police action plan. The Austin PD used several approaches simultaneously; some strategies were mutually assisting. For example, by reducing the number of potential victims using a public awareness (denial) campaign, the probability that the bait/decoy officer would have been attacked was drastically improved. They fulfilled their most important objective—protecting the public—while continuing lines of attack that would also lead to arrest and prosecution.

Good action planning is a recursive process. As the analyst learns more about one factor in the series, the new information will probably cause her to change her previous thinking about other factors. Those in turn will lead to more re-evaluation, *ad infinitum*. The analyst can be an important supporting element to detectives, uniformed officers, special units, and police command staff, on whom the bulk of responsibility for the action plan will fall. By providing effective operational analysis, the analyst can help make each part of the overall plan of attack better, more effective, less expensive, and less detrimental to the community.

Section II

Getting Started 10

Goals of This Section:

1. Access the textbook Web page.
2. Download and install ATAC. Request evaluation CD of ArcGIS.
3. Open and evaluate different data formats using ATAC and Excel.

Introduction

In this section we will introduce students to the textbook Web page and online resources, and explain how to obtain and begin using ATAC and ArcGIS software. Both of these software applications are vital to subsequent exercises: ATAC is the most widely used tactical crime analysis application while ArcGIS continues to dominate the GIS market. Both applications are the focus of this workbook because of their analytical functionality for the purposes of crime analysis. Whenever possible, widely available and lower cost applications such as Microsoft Excel and Google Earth will also be used to demonstrate a lesson.

Students will learn how to open various data structures in ATAC and become familiar with some of ATAC's more useful features. Subsequent lessons will explore ArcGIS and its spatial analysis features. Students who desire a more in-depth instruction of either ATAC or ArcGIS should review the "Further Readings" list at the end of each chapter as well as consult the online resources for each chapter on the textbook Web page.

Accessing the Textbook Web page

Online Resources

In addition to the sample data and accompanying codebooks there are also extensive online resources available to students and professors. In order to access these online resources simply click on the appropriate buttons on the Web page (Links, Further Readings, and Lab Resources) and follow the onscreen instructions.

Included in the online resources are links to:

- Related Web pages
- Article downloads
- A PDF lab manual that provides step-by-step instructions with screen captures
- Online movies which provide step-by-step instruction for the labs

Obtaining the Software

In order for the student to use the workbook they must first access the Bair Software Web site to download ATAC; this specialized software application is used by tactical crime analysis professionals and is a vital tool for subsequent exercises. The ATAC installation includes the ATAC application and all sample data used throughout this workbook. In addition, there are other links on the Bair Software Web site including a link to SPACE (Spatial Predictive Analysis of Crime Extension), a free extension to ArcGIS that will perform many of the functions found in this workbook.

ATAC: From the Bair Software Web site at www.bairsoftware.com, follow the links to download an evaluation copy of ATAC.

ArcMap: Visit the ESRI Web site at www.esri.com and follow links to request an evaluation CD for ArcGIS. The ArcView version of ArcGIS is the most applicable to the lessons in this workbook.

Open and Evaluate Data Using ATAC

As described in Chapter 5, data is the life force for an analyst. The following lessons introduce students to the various types of data they may encounter in a public safety agency.

Lesson 1: Open the Sample Database in ATAC

1. In ATAC, select **Open Data** from the **File** menu or click the Open Database button located on the toolbar.
2. Select "**Sample.atx**".
3. Click the **Open** button.

Practice on Your Own: Evaluate Crime Data using ATAC
Navigate horizontally and vertically through ATAC's Matrix to discover the various variables available in this data set. Are there categories of data that

Getting Started

are not present? Do the available categories appear to contain valid and useful data?

ATAC and Microsoft Access

Microsoft Access is a relational database management system that combines the relational Microsoft Jet Database Engine with a graphical user interface. It provides a robust data storage medium superior than those of Microsoft Excel, dBASE or other file-based formats. Because of its portability and ease of use, many public safety agencies use it to store data.

Lesson 2: Open a Microsoft Access Database in ATAC

To open non-ATAC databases use the Open Database Wizard. The Open Database Wizard provides the interface to establish those variables essential to ATAC's operations. ATAC can open a single table in an Access database or connect to a stored query. (See Figure 10.1)

1. In ATAC, select **Open Data** from the **File** menu or click the Open Database button located on the toolbar.
2. Change the **"Files of Type"** to **Microsoft Access 2002**.
3. Select "**Examples.mdb**" from the ATAC installation directory.

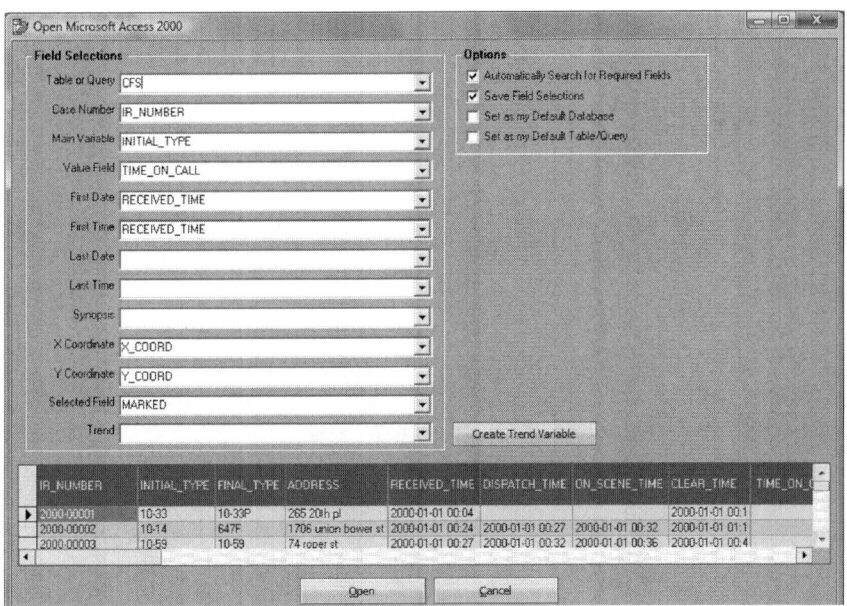

Figure 10.1 Select Save Field Selections in ATAC.

4. Click the **Open** button. The Database Wizard will display and select the first table in the database. Select the CFS table under the Table or Query dropdown menu. The fields contained in the current table will display in the data grid. Use the data grid to verify key fields and the values contained therein.
5. Click the "**Automatically Search for Required Fields**" checkbox to automatically search and populate ATAC's required fields. If key fields were not identified by ATAC, manually select a field by selecting it from the drop down combo box.
6. Specify the "INITIAL_TYPE" field as the main variable, the "RECEIVED_TIME" field as the first date as well as the first time. Notice how ATAC can extract the necessary date and time information from the one field.
7. Click "**Save Field Selections**" to automatically save the current field configuration for the next time this database is opened.
8. Click the **Open** button to open the database. If the "Save Field Selections" button was checked, the database's field schema and connection properties will be stored in the Schema.ini file located in the root of where ATAC is installed. The next time this database is opened in ATAC, all the required fields will automatically be populated. The number of records contained in the CFS table in Examples.mdb will be displayed on the status bar at the bottom of the main form.

Practice on Your Own: Evaluate Call for Service Data

Navigate horizontally and vertically through the Matrix to learn about the available categories of data. How might the call data be useful? When would you want to use the call data instead of the crime data?

ATAC and Microsoft Excel

Microsoft Excel is the most popular spreadsheet program in the world. Many public safety agencies use Excel to store their tabular data, perform statistics, calculate time series, and even perform Geographic Profiling.

Microsoft Excel was originally developed to perform spreadsheet operations; specifically, financial analysis. Recently, it has become a comfortable storage medium for many analysts. However, its storage and data formatting capabilities should be understood. For example, version 2008 allows for the storage of up to 1,000,000 rows. Earlier versions of Excel (including Excel 2003) were limited to only 65,536 rows—a critical weakness. Because of Excel's popularity, the authors of this workbook have included numerous lessons to demonstrate crime analysis techniques using Excel.

Getting Started

Lesson 3: Open a Microsoft Excel Spreadsheet in ATAC

1. Select **Open Data** from the **File** menu.
2. Change the "**Files of Type**" to **Microsoft Excel 97/2003**.
3. Select **CAD.xls** from the ATAC installation directory.
4. Click the **Open** button. Depending upon the structure of the Excel file, a sheet may not automatically populate the "Table or Query" combo box. In this case, manually select the CAD worksheet from the drop down list.
5. Click the "**Automatically Search for Required Fields**" checkbox to automatically search and populate ATAC's required fields. If key fields were not identified by ATAC, manually select a field by selecting it from the drop down combo box.
6. Click "**Save Field Selections**" to automatically save the current field configuration for the next time this database is opened in ATAC.
7. Click the **Finish** button to open the database. If the "Save Field Selections" button was checked, the file's field schema and connection properties will be stored in the Schema.ini file located in the root of where ATAC is installed. The next time this database is opened in ATAC, all the required fields will automatically be populated. The number of records contained in the spreadsheet will be displayed on the status bar at the bottom of the main form.

Lesson 4: Open the Sample Database in Excel

1. **Launch Microsoft's Excel 2003**. Note: Microsoft Excel 2007 is substantially different in appearance than version 2003 and earlier. If the analyst is using version 2007, use the Help documentation to find related menu or button commands. (See Figure 10.2)
2. Select **Open** from the **File** menu.
3. Navigate to the sample data directory and open "**Sample.xls**".

Practice on Your Own: Evaluate Data Using Microsoft Excel

Scroll vertically through the Sample.xls spreadsheet from the first record to the last. How many records are there in this spreadsheet? Scroll horizontally through the columns. Note the various categories of data available as well as the formats they are stored. Assess the data for its completeness and note any categories you might want that are not available in these data.

Lesson 5: Import Data from Access into Excel

In this lesson we will import data from an Access database into a worksheet in Excel. (See Figure 10.3)

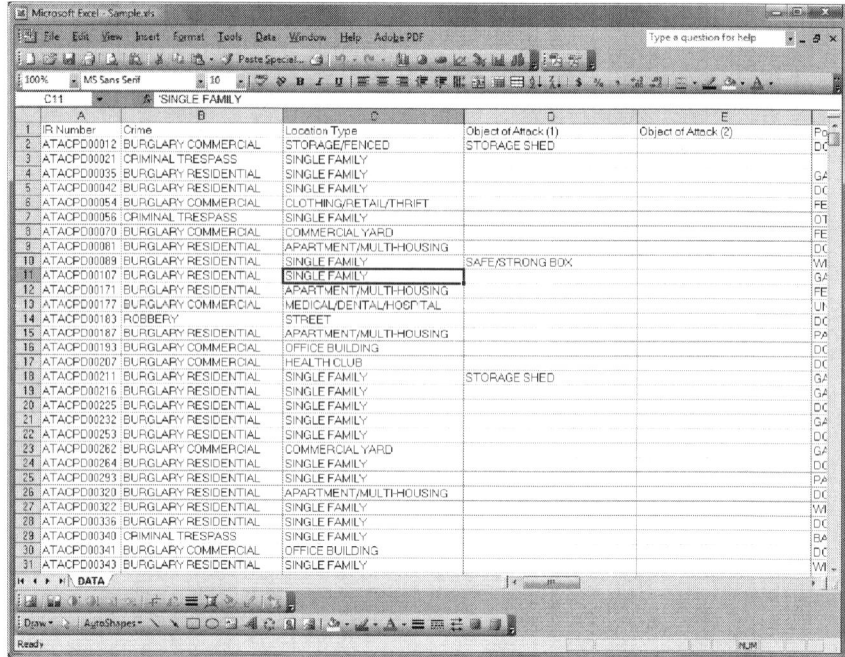

Figure 10.2 Sample Database opened in Excel.

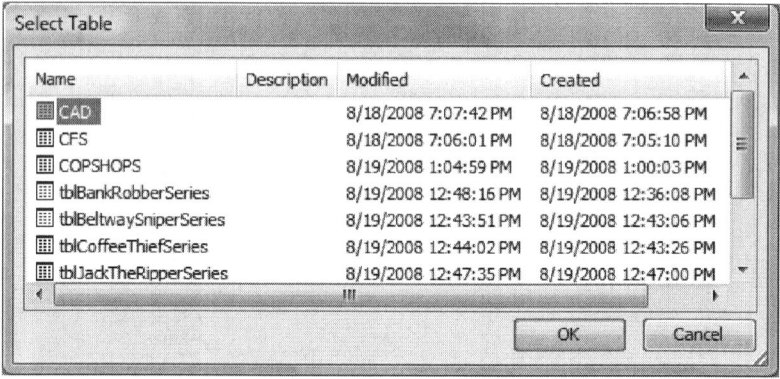

Figure 10.3 Select CAD Table in Excel.

Getting Started

1. In Excel, go to the **Data** menu, click **Import External Data** and select **Import Data**.
2. Navigate to the database that you would like to import, in this case **Examples.mdb**, and click **Open**.
3. Select the table that you would like to import, in this case the **CAD** table.
4. In the **Import Data** dialogue box, select **New Worksheet** and click **OK**. This will import all of the data that was in the access database into a new Excel spreadsheet.

Practice On Your Own: Import Data into Excel

Import the CFS.mdb database located in the root of ATAC into Excel. Verify all the records imported by scrolling to the bottom of the matrix. Try importing other data into Excel such as dBase tables and text files.

Review Exercise: Open Other Data

Expanding on previous lessons, try opening other data formats in ATAC and Excel. Open your own agency's data and see how it performs. Or, search the Web for free data. Identify the variables that seem important, such as dates, times, and locations in each of the data files. Note any deficiencies or potential issues with the data. For example, are the date and time fields properly formatted? Does the data only provide codified values that will need to be translated or are there literal values stored in each variable?

Review Questions

1. What are the various data types used in a Public Safety Agency and how do they differ?
2. Why would an agency maintain separate databases for calls for service and crime data?
3. What are the strengths and weaknesses of each data as they relate to pattern identification?

Identify Patterns Using the IZE Method (Process Models)   11

Goals of This Section:

1. Review the IZE method for pattern identification.
2. Evaluate the categories of example data.
3. Understand the purpose and function of creating layouts.
4. Understand the need for sorting data to further the organize phase.

Introduction

The IZE Method is an organized, formal process for identifying patterns in data. Traditional methods for identifying crime series include reading all the police reports and playing a mental matching game of finding like cases. Using IZE, analysts have a standardized methodology that, when used, can enable the analyst to identify more crime series than before. Using the IZE Method, analysts Categorize, Generalize, Organize, Minimize and Maximize your data in such a way that patterns begin to emerge. The general steps are outlined below:

- **Categorize**—Create variables conducive to finding crime trends (Hair, Race, Sex, Point of Entry, Weapon Type, Vehicle Make, etc.)
- **Generalize**—Create general values for your categories (Handgun, Rifle, Male, Female, Brown, Black, Blonde, etc.)
- **Organize**—Group certain MO variables and person categories together; sort data.
- **Minimize**—Query for clusters in the data by selecting increasingly exclusive subsets.
- **Maximize**—Query features salient to the identified crime series.

Various software applications can assist us in creating layouts of variables organized such that we can more efficiently find patterns. In the following lessons we will use several software applications to organize crime data for more rapid comparison of categories.

Layouts in ATAC

Layouts are displayed on the Layouts tab located on the left side of the ATAC Hub. Once an organization of categories is created, it is a good practice to save the configuration for future use. Analysts often find themselves viewing one type of data organized the same way each and every time.

Lesson 6: Organizing a Layout Using ATAC

In this lesson we will create a layout that will help identify sexual assault patterns.

1. Click the Layout Organizer button at the bottom of the Hub's toolbar. (See Figure 11.1)
2. Click the Remove all Variables button from the Layout Organizer's toolbar.
3. Double-click a variable from the "Available Variables" list to move it to the Matrix Variable list. You can also select multiple variables from the left and drag and drop them to the right. The variables in the Matrix Variable list will be those displayed in the matrix in the order they appear in the list. This step is where you as the analyst begin to determine those categories significant to the identification of a particular type of pattern.
4. Continue selecting the variables you believe are important for identifying patterns in sexual assaults. Pay particular attention to those

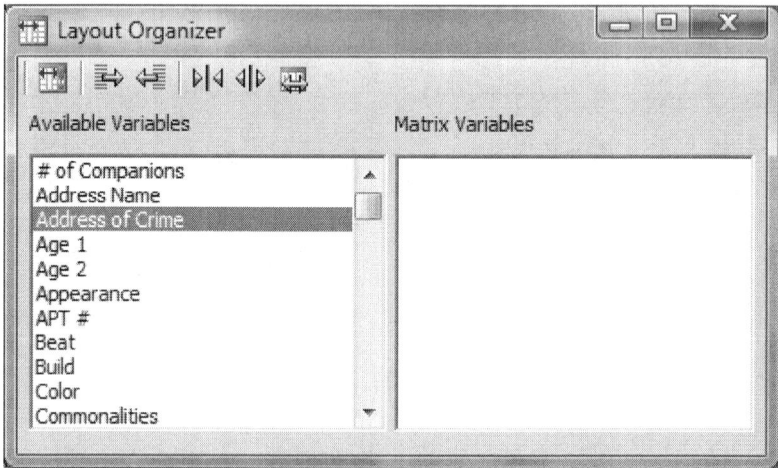

Figure 11.1 Available variables in Layout Organizer in ATAC.

Identify Patterns Using the IZE Method (Process Models)

variables that contain data as well as how the variables that best describe how the crime was committed. For instance, variables such as: location type, offender's race, sex, hair, and suspect's actions are usually variables that provide detail about a sexual assault.

5. **Click** and **drag** column headers to a new location in the Matrix Variables list to organize your data horizontally.
6. Once you have designated all the variables you want available in the Matrix, **click** the **Apply** button from the toolbar.

Lesson 7: Saving a Layout in ATAC

In this lesson we will save a layout in ATAC for future use. (See Figure 11.2)

1. Click the right mouse button while over the Hub's layout window. A popup menu will appear.
2. Click the Save Layout menu.

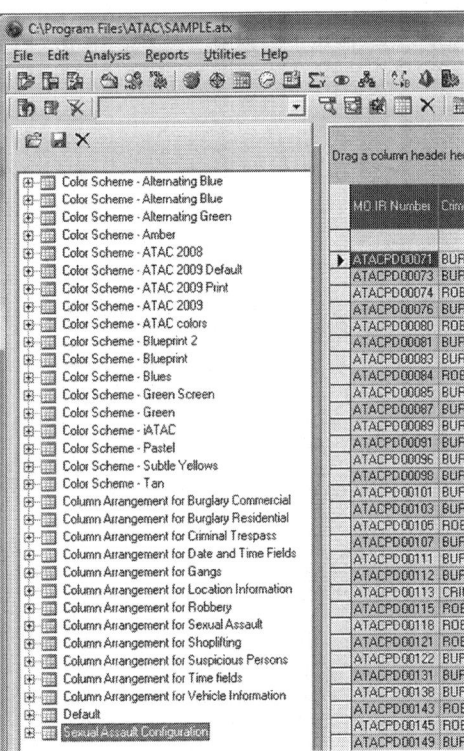

Figure 11.2 Sexual Assault added to layouts in ATAC.

3. Enter a Windows compliant file name in the File name text box. For this example enter "Sexual Assault Configuration."
4. Click Save. Notice that the "Sexual Assault Configuration" has automatically been added to the layouts window. The icon representing this layout indicates that it was created using the current database as its structure.

Tip: The Refresh Database's Original Variable Configuration button will restore the current database's variable order as stored in the database. All layout configurations will be removed and hidden variables will be restored.

Layouts in Excel

While users can not save predefined layouts in Excel, users can still create a layout by grouping variables together in a worksheet. Unfortunately, there is no easy way to reapply a layout once a workbook is closed.

Lesson 8: Organizing a Layout Using Excel

In this lesson we will create a layout in Excel. Layout files store and display the position of each column or variable in a Matrix to expedite the comparison across categories of data.

1. Open the **Sample.xls** workbook in Excel.
2. To move a column from one position to another, right click on the column's header. For this lesson, click **AH** and select **Cut**.
3. Right click on column **D** and select **Insert Cut Cells**. Column **AH** will be inserted in front of column **D**.
4. Now select columns **G, H,** and **I** and select **Cut**.
5. Right click on column **C** and select **Insert Cut Cells**. All three columns will be inserted in front of column **C**.

Practice On Your Own: Create a Robbery Layout Using Microsoft Excel

Using the steps in the last lesson, organize the columns in a way that simplifies the comparison and analysis of robbery data. As described in Chapter 5, categories such as location type, weapon, and suspect's race are all useful when analyzing robberies. Likewise, categories like point of entry and method of entry are less useful. If necessary, delete columns you find completely unnecessary for the comparison of robbery categories. One such variable may be X coordinate. Although easy for a computer, comparing X coordinates of

Identify Patterns Using the IZE Method (Process Models)

robberies is not the most effective or efficient means to identify patterns of robberies.

Sorting Data

Lesson 9: Organizing Data by Sorting in ATAC

Using the IZE method, we have just horizontally organized our data. Now to complete the IZE phase, we must organize our data vertically. To do so, we simply use ATAC's various sorting capabilities. (See Figure 11.3)

1. Select the **Burglary Residential** layout.
2. Click the **Sort** tab located on the lower left of the Hub.
3. Select the **Sort Descending** radio button.
4. **Double click** on the **Point of Entry (1)** variable from the **Available Fields** list. Use the vertical scroll bars to locate the Point of Entry (1) variable from within the list of available fields. Notice that the variable was removed from the list and added to the "Sort Order" list in the order selected.
5. Click the **Execute SQL Statement** button.

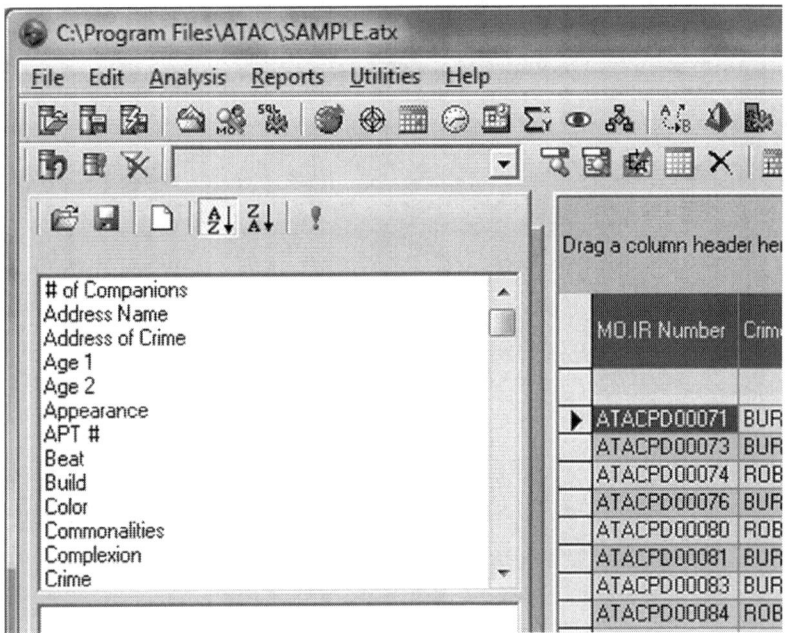

Figure 11.3 Double-click on Point of Entry in ATAC.

Lesson 10: Organizing Data by Sorting in Excel

1. Using the **sample.xls** workbook, click the **Location Type** column to select it.
2. Click the **Sort A to Z** button located on the **Sort & Filter** area if using Microsoft Excel 2007. If using earlier versions, simple click the **Sort A to Z** button located on the main toolbar, then choose **Expand the Selection** when the **Sort Warning** box appears.

Tip: To expand sorts to contain multiple fields in differing orders using Excel, use the Sort dialog box. In Excel 2007, users may specify numerous sort "levels." Earlier versions were limited to only a handful of sorting orders. In ATAC, analysts can perform multi-order sorts using the Sort tab located on the Hub. ATAC, like Excel 2007, permits dozens of sorting orders and variables; however, practically the data becomes too subdivided after the 3rd or 4th combined variable sort.

Review Exercise: Create Sorts for Three Crime Types
Using Excel, ATAC or another Matrix-based application, construct sorts against different layouts to group relevant data together. Using ATAC, save the sort orders for future retrieval and use.

Review Questions:
1. How did organizing the data both horizontally and vertically improve your ability to see similarly related events?
2. What other software applications might be useful for creating layouts and sorting data?

Minimize and Maximize—IZE method 12

Goals of This Section:

1. Use ATAC and Excel's various query capabilities to perform Deductive Analysis.
2. Use Regular Expressions to identify meaningful information in data.
3. Create and use a Concept against various data sources to find incidents of graffiti and copper theft.

Introduction

As described in Chapter 5, using deductive approach, the analyst starts with all the data and begins to organize the data such that specific cases having like values emerge. We can use the organization of categories to group like values and then leverage Structured Query Language (SQL) to minimize the data or expand our queries further.

With an inductive approach, it is usually a lone case or anomalous case that prompts the analyst to inquire as to other like cases. SQL can assist us with this inquiry of our data. However, Regular Expressions can expand on those capabilities even further.

Structured Query Language

SQL can be difficult to write. Luckily, several tools exist that provide a graphical user interface upon which to build one's queries. Programs like Access, Excel, Crystal Reports, ArcGIS and ATAC all provide query interfaces that take some of the burden out of writing raw SQL. In the following lesson, we will use ATAC's Visual Query Module to develop a query. Behind the scenes, ATAC is creating the SQL statement. We can use programs like ATAC to develop a query and then "peek" at the underlying syntax to better understand and learn the language.

Lesson 11: Minimize Using the Visual Query Module in ATAC

1. From the Hub, click the Visual Query tab. It is located at the bottom-left of the form.
2. Click the ellipse button located next to the checkbox and select Add a New Elementary Condition from the popup menu.
3. Click the first asterisk and select the Crime variable from the drop list of variables.
4. Click the blue, underlined Equals To operator and select Starts With from the drop list.
5. Click the last asterisk and type "BURG" in the box. (See Figure 12.1)
6. Click Execute Query button from the toolbar. The Execute Query button is the exclamation point.
7. From the Analysis menu, select SQL Viewer. Study the SQL to determine how the query is constructed.

In ATAC, the Filter Bar allows you to query the database by simply typing in a query value above the variable you wish to query. (See Figure 12.2) Depending on the type of database being examined and queried, the selection values may be case sensitive (e.g., dBase IV). The Filter Bar provides a quick way to query data and see the parameters of a query as they relate to each variable. Excel provides a similar filtering function but does not allow for partial word searches or multi-value searches. In the next lesson we will use the Filter Bar functions in both Excel and ATAC to minimize data.

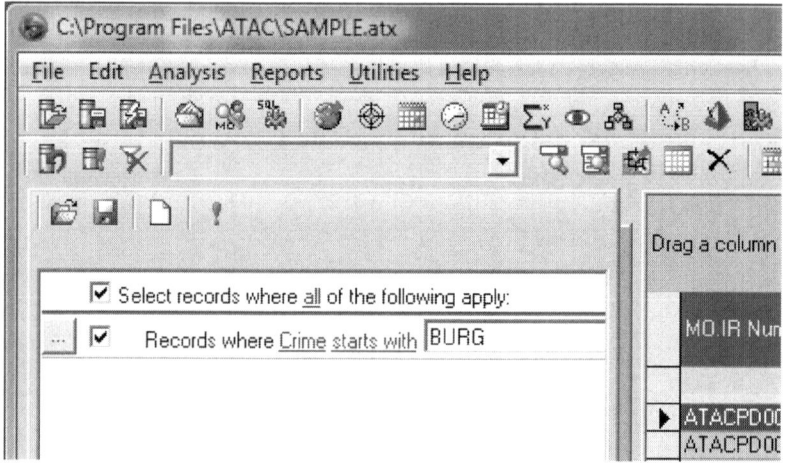

Figure 12.1 Crime starts with Burg in ATAC.

Minimize and Maximize—IZE method

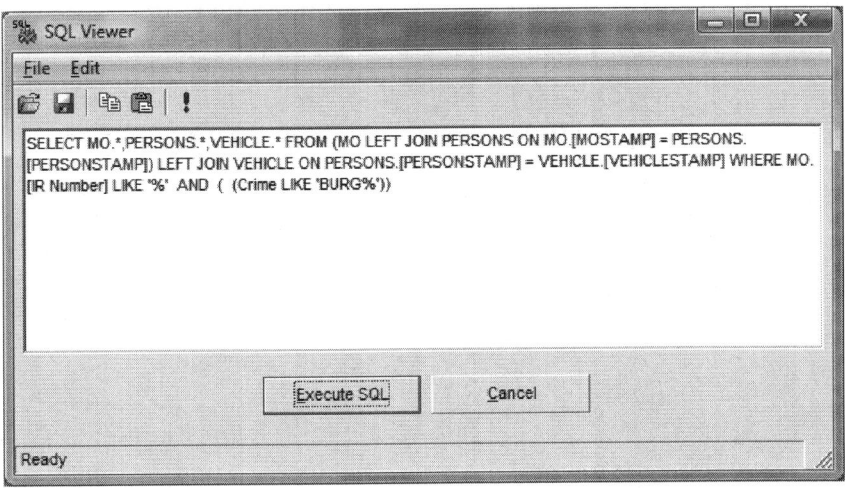

Figure 12.2 SQL Viewer in ATAC.

Lesson 12: Minimize Using the Filter Bar in ATAC

1. In ATAC, verify that the Show Filter Bar menu is checked from the Preferences menu.
2. To improve the readability of our returned data, double-click the Robbery layout from the layout list.
3. Click in the empty row below the Crime variable's header. The filter bar dropdown arrow will appear.
4. Click the dropdown arrow for Crime. A list of the possible crime values will appear.
5. Click ROBBERY from the drop list and press the Enter key. If ROBBERY is not visible, scroll through the list of values until Robbery appears. Only those records that are robberies should appear in the matrix. From the matrix, several different location types should be visible. One such Location Type is STREET.
6. Click on any of the Location Type cells that contain the word STREET. That cell should become highlighted. (See Figure 12.3)
7. Right click on the highlighted cell and select Add Cell Text to Filter Bar from the popup menu.
8. Click the Enter key or click the Execute Filter Bar Search from the toolbar. To clear the filter, click the Clear Filter button from the toolbar.

Tip: ATAC's filter function permits partial or multiple value searches within each category of data. For example, typing "%burg%" in the Crime category will return all those records that contain "burg" somewhere in their

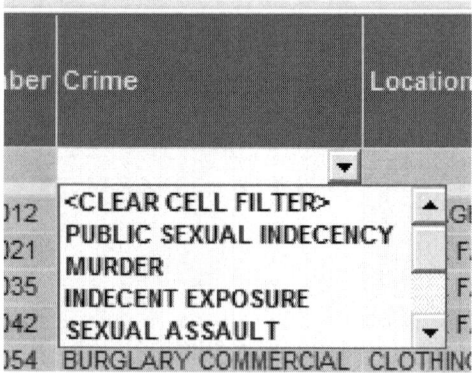

Figure 12.3 Filter bar dropdown under Crime in ATAC.

title (e.g., residential burglary, commercial burglary, burglary from vehicle). Multiple filter values can be achieved by separating the values with a comma (e.g., "ROBBERY,%BURG%:). This filter will return only those records whose exact title is ROBBERY and those that contain the word BURG.

Lesson 13: Minimize Using the Filter Bar in Excel

Using Excel 2007 (See Figure 12.4):

1. Using the sample.xls workbook, click the Filter button located on the Sort & Filter area if using Microsoft Excel 2007.
2. Click the Down Arrow at the right-hand side of the Crime column and deselect (Select All). All values in the Crime field should become unchecked.
3. Click the checkbox next to "ROBBERY" and click the OK button. Only those records where the Crime was a ROBBERY will display.
4. From the Location Type filter, deselect (Select All) and click the checkbox next to BANK/ATM and CONVENIENCE STORE. The results should be only robberies that occurred at either banks/atms or convenience stores.
5. To retrieve all the records, simply click the Clear button from the Sort & Filter area.

Using Excel 2003:

1. Using the sample.xls workbook, click Data, then Filter and then select Auto Filter.
2. Click the Down Arrow at the right hand side of the Crime column and select (Custom…).

Minimize and Maximize—IZE method

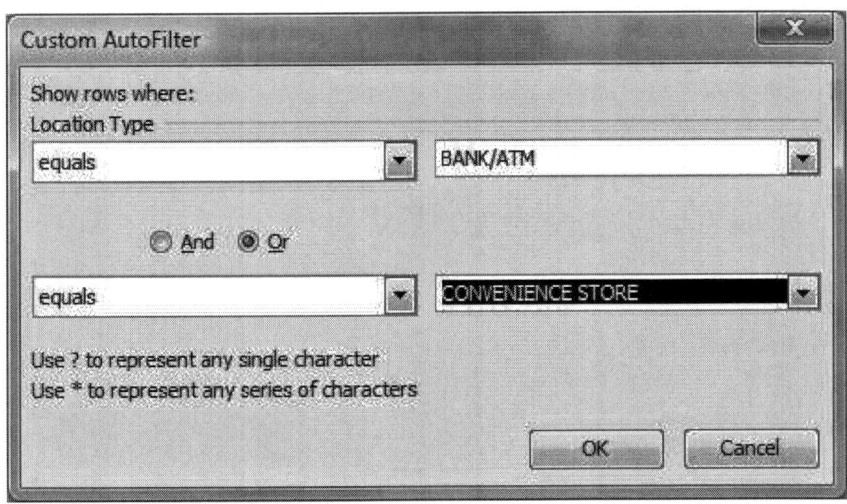

Figure 12.4 Convenience Store in custom auto filter in Excel.

3. Select ROBBERY. Only those records where the Crime was a Robbery will display.
4. From the Location Type filter, select (Custom…).
5. In the Custom AutoFilter box, select equals from the first dropdown list and BANK/ATM from the adjoining dropdown.
6. Click Or.
7. Select equals from the third dropdown, and select CONVENIENCE STORE and click the OK button. The results should be only robberies that occurred at either banks/ATMs or convenience stores.
8. To retrieve all the records, click Data and select Show All.

Practice on Your Own: Minimize Data Using Excel
Drawing upon the previous for the version of Excel you have installed, filter on Burglary Residential. Then, select only those crimes that are Burglary Commercial. Practice filtering against several of the variables both individually and combined.

Practice on Your Own: Find the Twins
Using the Sample.atx ATAC database and the various organization and querying capabilities previously covered, find the twins. Open the Sample.xls database in Excel and use its functions to identify the set of twins in the spreadsheet. Organize the various Excel columns to enhance the comparison across important categories and use Excel's sorting functions to organize the values vertically for quick identification of similar data and groups.

Practice on Your Own: Identify a Crime Series

Expanding on the Find the Twins exercise, continue honing these skills by finding a crime series located in the Sample.atx database using either Excel, ATAC or any other matrix-based application that you have available.

Regular Expressions

In the lessons to follow, we will use Regular Expressions language to perform the inductive method in an attempt to identify information in our data. That is, we take one idea or item and expand our search to uncover similar items.

Lesson 14: Create and Run a Regular Expression

1. From the Hub in ATAC, select the Quick Expression option from the Analysis menu.
2. In the Expression text area at the top, enter COPPER.
3. Click the OK button. The proximity search results area will display a gray sphere for unfound items and a green sphere for found items. (See Figure 12.5)
4. Close the Quick Expression dialog and select the "Concepts" tab from the Hub. If any data contained the word COPPER the number of the case it was found within will be displayed in the list.
5. Double-click the row with IR Number ATACPD00262. ATAC will immediately activate that record in the grid. The selected row is identified by the black arrow at the left of the row.

Tip: Separate multiple values with the pipe character |. The pipe character acts as the Boolean OR operator (e.g., COPPER|METAL|TIN). This search would return any records containing COPPER, METAL or TIN.

As with many queries, users may get more than they bargained for with a single word search like in our previous example. Consider the need for searching for a "black truck." Using SQL, one might either search for the combined phrase or for each word individually resulting in a multitude of false positives. What is needed when doing inductive queries against multiple words is to search for those words within proximity of one another. The word "black" in a record is not significant unless it is near "truck." When those two words are near each other "black Chevy truck", "black truck," "black F-150 truck," etc. then they become desirable. What is not desirable is searching through all records found that contained both "black" and/or "truck."

Minimize and Maximize—IZE method

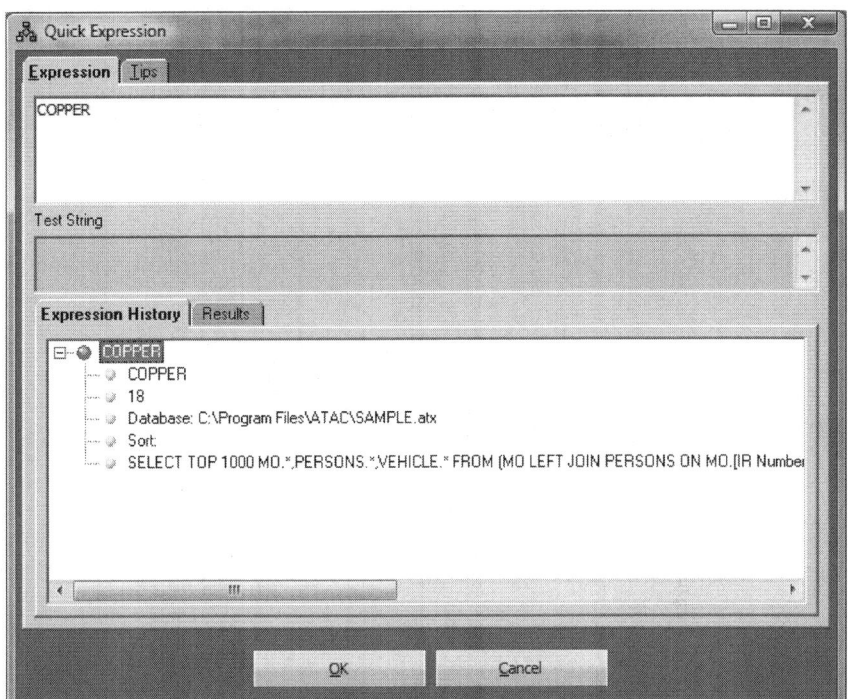

Figure 12.5 Quick expression Copper Results in ATAC.

Let us perform a proximity search expanding upon the previous COPPER search. We do not want all those records that contain the word COPPER, what we want in this inductive search is to return only those records where the word COPPER is near WIRING.

Lesson 15: Create and Run a Proximity Search Regular Expression

1. From the Hub, select the Quick Expression option from the Analysis menu.
2. In the Expression text area at the top, enter "COPPER within 5 words of TUBING." If "and separated by X words" is not specified, ATAC assumes you do not want any words separating these two items.
3. Press the Enter key or click the OK button to execute the search. The proximity search should return true.
4. Click the plus sign next to the green ball to see some details regarding the search, expression, and number of records found. Close the Quick Expression window and navigate to the "Concepts" tab on the Hub.

5. Note the list of found items in the Found Items list. Double-click anywhere on a row to move to that row in the Matrix.

A query such as the Copper Tubing example might need to be written such that it can be re-run tomorrow, against other data sources, or be complete enough to account for variations in spelling and different taxonomy for the items. For example, an officer may have investigated a burglary where copper tubing was taken from a home under construction; however, in her narrative referred to it as tubes, wire or wiring. What is needed is a concept to describe the types of copper that is taken to allow for the various ways it's found in data.

Lesson 16: Create a Concept

In this lesson we will create a Concept to find the various type of copper item routinely stolen. (See Figure 12.6)

1. While on the Hub's Concept tab, click the Create Concept button. The Concept Module form will appear.
2. Click the Add button to begin creating a Concept.
3. In the Concept Name box, type WIRING.
4. Click the "Concept Development" tab to begin constructing the actual regular expression. Users can select from one of the Standard Expressions and then edit it to construct your Concept. When

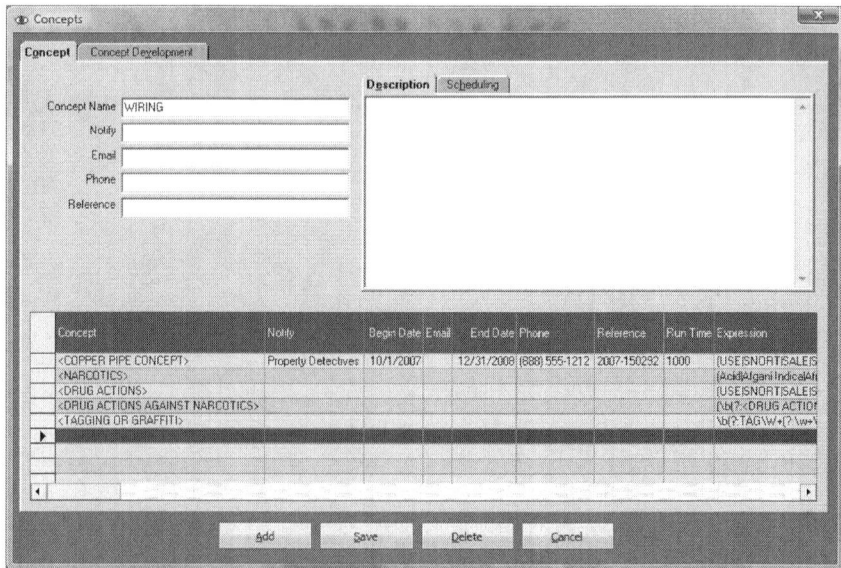

Figure 12.6 Copper Thefts Concept results in ATAC.

Minimize and Maximize—IZE method

selecting from one of the samples, the text at the right of the form will change to describe what type of pattern the search expression will search. We'll first build a concept to describe all the various types of material that are taken during Copper theft.

5. In the "Word, Phrase or Concept" box at the top, of the form, begin typing the various material types that are found "near" the word copper. Separate values with the pipe character "|". The pipe character acts as the Boolean "OR" operator. For example, "tubing" is often found near copper in a sentence. "Wiring" is also a material found in proximity of "copper." We do not want copper colored vehicles (e.g., COPPER MAZDA) but we do want (COPPER COLORED WIRE TAKEN).
6. Type "WIRE|WIRING|TUBE|TUBING|PIPE|PIPING."
7. Click the Build Concept button.
8. Click the Save button to save this newly created "WIRING" Concept.

A Proximity Search queries for words, phrases or concepts within a distance of other words, phrases or concepts. Both forward and bi-directional searches can be specified. To construct a Proximity Search, simply type in the "word, phrase or concept" box the values to be searched, or select from one of the existing Concepts. Next, specify a "within" parameter. This is the number of words the other word, phrase or concept must be within to make a match. Because ATAC can search across all variables combined, this means that users can specify a "within" distance that would include the number of words in other variables. Knowing that ATAC will combine all variables, it is good practice to set the "within" distance large in order to account for all possible words within a combined row. The "And Separated By" function specifies how many words must be between the two parameters. The Concepts module enables analysts to perform a proximity search in any combination of Concepts, Words or Phrases. In the next lesson we will use our existing WIRING Concept along with Copper to refine our inductive search.

Lesson 17: Create and Run a Proximity Search Concept

1. While on the Hub's Concept tab, click the Create Concept button. The Concept Module form will appear. (See Figure 12.6)
2. Click the Add button to begin creating a Concept.
3. In the Concept Name box, type "COPPER THEFTS."
4. Click the "Concept Development" tab.
5. From the Proximity Search area, type COPPER in the first "Word, Phrase or Concept" box.

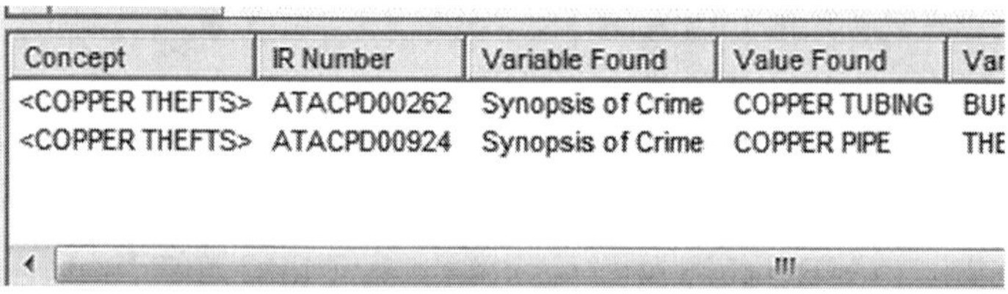

Concept	IR Number	Variable Found	Value Found	Var
<COPPER THEFTS>	ATACPD00262	Synopsis of Crime	COPPER TUBING	BUI
<COPPER THEFTS>	ATACPD00924	Synopsis of Crime	COPPER PIPE	THE

Figure 12.7 Concept result from ATAC.

6. From the second Word, Phrase or Concept drop list, select the "WIRING" Concept. We will leave the default "within" and "and separated by" values alone for now.
7. Click the Build Concept button. The Regular Expression is built using an existing Concept as well as the word copper.
8. Click the Save button to save this newly created "COPPER THEFTS" Concept.
9. Click the Cancel button or close the Concept window to return to the Concepts tab on the Hub.
10. Click the Selected checkbox next to the COPPER THEFTS row in the Concepts grid.
11. From the toolbar, click the Search each Variable Individually button. ATAC will perform an inductive search against the selected COPPER THEFTS concepts.
12. Once complete, review the found records in the Concept list area. Click column headers to sort a column in alternating ascending and descending orders. Double-click a row to jump to that record in the Matrix. Notice the various ways that the data are entered in the database as well as the different variables the information is found.

Review Exercise: Using RegEx to Perform the Inductive Method

Create a Concept to identify Graffiti incidents. Consider all the variations to the spelling of graffiti as well as synonyms that might exist. For example, "tag" might be a word often used to describe graffiti. However, one probably would not want the search to return records referring to Tag Hauer watches, vehicle tags, or tag in "heritage rd". Once created, test it against the ATAC sample.atx database. Then test the Concept against other data including other data. If necessary, invent data to test a Concept.

Review Questions

1. Compare and contrast the strengths and weaknesses of SQL and RegEx in performing inductive and deductive analysis.
2. Which language allows for the ability to perform a proximity search in data?
3. Both ATAC and Microsoft Excel provide for a "filter" function. Which language does the filter function use to construct a query?

The Behavioral Dimension
Describing the Problem

13

Goals of This Section:

1. Review definition and purpose of an archetype.
2. Create an archetype from a crime series.
3. Understand purpose and uses of a Movement Log.
4. Develop a Movement Log based on your actions.

Introduction

The first stage of attacking a tactical problem is to describe it. This begins with clearly identifying relationships between cases to ensure we are studying a related group. Once we have identified a reliable core group of cases that are clearly related, we can then look outside for other, related cases. A good process for looking for groupings within data is the IZE or "Eyes" method, which should be used to determine the similarities between all cases and develop archetypes. Once the core cases have been identified, and all relevant data absorbed, the facets of each dataset must be described.

Archetypes are simply a summary of the crimes in a series. They embody a set of crimes into one crime called an Archetype. You can use the Archetype record to identify future cases in the trend. Since the Archetype summarizes all the crimes in series, it is an excellent case to use when performing the maximize phase in the IZE method. Archetypes are also useful for disseminating a "summary" of the crime series in a single record format. They would not be as useful when performing inductive analysis as they, by definition, summarize the most frequent actions in each event thus removing individual items or actions.

Archetypes

Archetypes can be created for a collection of MOs to study actions in a series, to study a summary of an offender's characteristics provided by witnesses, or to summarize the descriptions of all the victims in a series. For example, Archetype might review that the Dog Door was the most prevalent point of entry in a burglary series even though it was not the only point of entry. It might also review that, generally, witnesses described a robbery suspect as Hispanic and Heavy in build even though some of the witnesses described him as Indian and Average build. Finally, an Archetype might reveal that a suspect was targeting free-standing banks even though his targets included in-store bank locations.

Lesson 18: Creating an Archetype from ATAC

1. From the Hub, select a set of cases to archetype. All Archetypes are created from a current selection of cases. For our example, select Sexual Assault Series from the Sample.atx database.
2. Click the Create Archetype from the Selected Records button.
3. From the Archetype form, type "Sexual Assault Series." This will be stored in the "Trend" variable in the Archetype record. It is named the same as the series so that we can compare the archetype to the rest of the records in the series by simply selecting the Sexual Assault Series trend. (See Figure 13.1)
4. Click the Save button. The results of the Archetype analysis will be displayed in the Archetype Summary list and the Archetype record will be added to the current database.

Movement Logs

A movement log is a matrix of spatial and temporal events for one's activity. They are similar to activity schedules in that they log the actions of a victim or offender throughout a week, but differ in that they provide more detail and can be used to correlate other events spatially and temporally.

Detectives and analysts might use a movement log to scribe all of a victim's actions 24 hours prior to being victimized. Doing so for all victims in a series might uncover significant time and space relationships or similarities across the victims. For example, several female victims might have shopped at the same grocery store just 30–60 minutes prior to being robbed of their diamond rings while unloading groceries back at their residence.

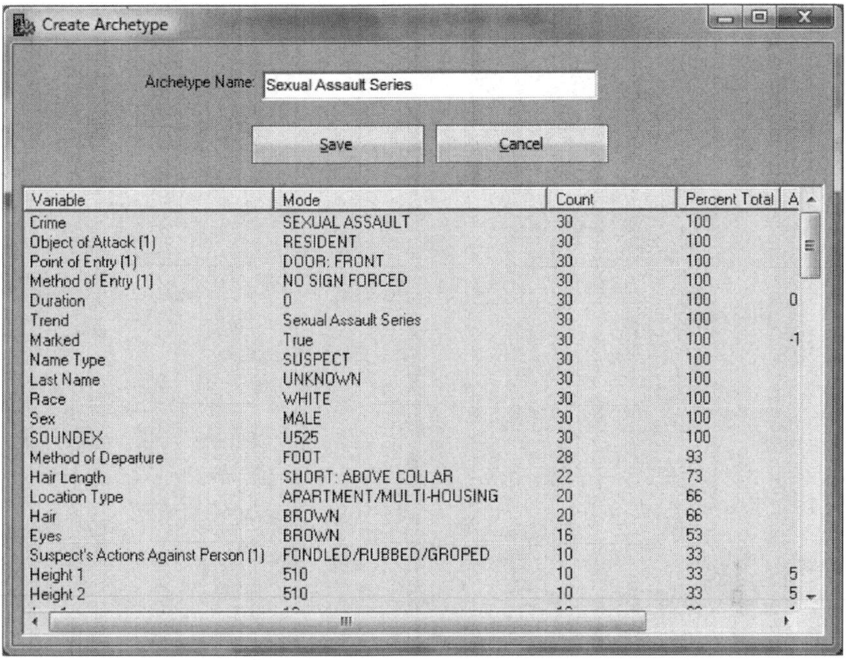

The Behavioral Dimension

Variable	Mode	Count	Percent Total	A
Crime	SEXUAL ASSAULT	30	100	
Object of Attack (1)	RESIDENT	30	100	
Point of Entry (1)	DOOR: FRONT	30	100	
Method of Entry (1)	NO SIGN FORCED	30	100	
Duration	0	30	100	0
Trend	Sexual Assault Series	30	100	
Marked	True	30	100	-1
Name Type	SUSPECT	30	100	
Last Name	UNKNOWN	30	100	
Race	WHITE	30	100	
Sex	MALE	30	100	
SOUNDEX	U525	30	100	
Method of Departure	FOOT	28	93	
Hair Length	SHORT: ABOVE COLLAR	22	73	
Location Type	APARTMENT/MULTI-HOUSING	20	66	
Hair	BROWN	20	66	
Eyes	BROWN	16	53	
Suspect's Actions Against Person (1)	FONDLED/RUBBED/GROPED	10	33	
Height 1	510	10	33	5
Height 2	510	10	33	5

Figure 13.1 Sexual Assault Series Archetype in ATAC.

These spatial and temporal overlaps are uncovered by creating and capturing victims, offenders and other's movements using a movement log.

Lesson 19: Develop a Movement Log

Develop a movement log for a week of your travels. Write down significant locations you stop and visit; such as grocery stores, gas stations, work, the gym, the bank, your morning coffee house, etc. Do not list stops at your home. We will use your movement log in future lessons to see if we can predict your home location from your movements. (See Figure 13.2)

1. Open Temporal Examples.xls using Excel and navigate to the Movement Log sheet.
2. Study the example movement log. Using the example as a template, let us create a new sheet for your activities. First, copy the row header in the Movement Log sheet by highlighting cell A1 through G1 and press CTRL + C on your keyboard to copy the contents into the Windows Clipboard.
3. Right click on the Movement Log tab and select Insert from the popup menu.
4. Click the Worksheet option and select OK.

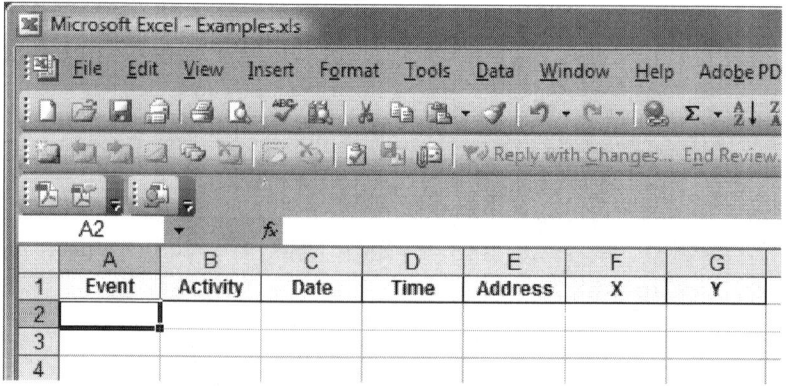

Figure 13.2 Create a Movement Log in Excel.

5. While in cell A1 on the new worksheet, press CTRL + V to paste the Movement Log column headers into this new sheet.
6. Enter the events for your week using the Movement Log as an example.

Review Exercise: Creating an Archetype

Select the Weekend Cat Burglar series from the Sample.atx database and create an archetype off of it. Name the Archetype "Weekend Cat Burglar" so it becomes linked with the series. Study the archetype's values. Does the archetype do a good job of describing the series?

Review Questions

1. What is an archetype?
2. What statistical technique is typically used to calculate an archetype?
3. Did keeping a Movement Log enable you to see what other data might be useful to capture in a victim's interview?
4. Could a Movement Log be a useful post-arrest technique to learn about how your offender moved throughout his or her activity spaces?

The Temporal Dimension 14

Goals of This Section:

1. Learn various static and dynamic temporal analysis methods to identify, analyze, and forecast patterns in temporal behavior.
2. Understand the strengths and weaknesses of the different time analysis methods.
3. Use Excel and ATAC to create Temporal Topologies, Tempograms, and Variograms.
4. Incorporate previous lessons learned to enhance your ability to query and analyze information.

Introduction

The temporal (timing) aspect of a tactical problem should be examined very closely in conjunction with the spatial aspect. Spreadsheets, analytical software, and statistical packages can be useful tools.

The following descriptive factors should be considered when analyzing events temporally:

Aoristic: Find probable times of occurrence when dealing with time ranges. Assess the overall temporal "make-up" of a collection of cases.
Tempo: Is the offender's timing of events accelerating, decelerating or remaining stable?
Correlation: Does the timing of crimes correlate to the timing of other events objects, such as the amount of money obtained during a crime, holidays, or other schedules?
Activity Schedule: Identify the overall times when the offender acts. The activities of the victim can also play an important role in uncovering motives or timing corollaries.

Activity Schedules

Like any other person, the criminal has only so many hours in the day. Crime takes time and effort, and the criminal must allocate his finite resources of both in order to carry out his attacks. Obviously this is true of any behavior; it takes a certain amount of time to go to school, to eat, to sleep, to earn a living, to commit a robbery. Like any other person, the offender must allocate his 24 hours each day among the many tasks he is driven to pursue. When we study the temporal allocation of time by any person, how we view the rational process of this allocation varies greatly with our unit of analysis. (See Figure 14.1)

Lesson 20: Creating an Activity Schedule

1. Open the **Temporal Examples.xls** Excel Spreadsheet located in the sample data folder.
2. Activate the **Activity Schedule – Blank** sheet. (See Figure 14.2)
3. Consider your own activities for the week and enter generalized values in the various days of the week and times of day as seen in the previous example.

Hour (0-23)	Monday Activity	Tuesday Activity	Wednesday Activity	Thursday Activity	Friday Activity	Saturday Activity	Sunday Activity	Modal
0	Sleep	Sleep	Sleep	Sleep	Sleep	Sleep	Sleep	Sleep
1	Sleep	Sleep	Sleep	Sleep	Sleep	Sleep	Sleep	Sleep
2	Sleep	Sleep	Sleep	Sleep	Sleep	Sleep	Sleep	Sleep
3	Sleep	Sleep	Sleep	Sleep	Sleep	Sleep	Sleep	Sleep
4	Sleep	Sleep	Sleep	Sleep	Sleep	Sleep	Sleep	Sleep
5	Sleep	Sleep	Sleep	Sleep	Sleep	Sleep	Sleep	Sleep
6	Sleep	Sleep	Sleep	Sleep	Sleep	Sleep	Sleep	Sleep
7	Eat	Eat	Eat	Eat	Eat	Sleep	Sleep	Eat
8	Drive	Drive	Drive	Drive	Drive	Sleep	Sleep	Drive
9	Work	Work	Work	Work	Work	Eat	Eat	Work
10	Work	Work	Work	Work	Work	Drive	TV	Work
11	Work	Work	Work	Work	Work	Outdoors	TV	Work
12	Eat	Eat	Eat	Eat	Eat	Outdoors	TV	Eat
13	Work	Work	Work	Work	Work	Outdoors	Eat	Work
14	Work	Work	Work	Work	Work	Eat	Drive	Work
15	Work	Work	Work	Work	Work	Outdoors	Outdoors	Work
16	Work	Work	Work	Work	Work	Outdoors	Outdoors	Work
17	Work	Work	Work	Work	Work	Outdoors	Outdoors	Work
18	Drive	Drive	Drive	Drive	Drive	Drive	Drive	Drive
19	Work Out	Work Out	Work Out	Work Out	Work Out	Eat	Eat	Workout
20	Eat	Eat	Eat	Eat	Drive	Eat	TV	Eat
21	TV	TV	TV	Movie	Eat	Movie	TV	TV
22	TV	TV	TV	Movie	Eat	Movie	Sleep	TV
23	Sleep	Sleep	Sleep	Sleep	Drive	Sleep	Sleep	Sleep
Modal	Sleep & Work	Sleep & Work	Sleep & Work	Sleep & Work	Work	Sleep	Sleep	

Figure 14.1 Activity schedule example in Excel.

The Temporal Dimension 173

	Monday	Tuesday	Wednesday	Thursday	Friday	Saturday	Sunday	
Hour (0-23)	Activity	Activity	Activity	Activity	Activity	Activity	Activity	Modal
0								
1								
2								
3								
4								
5								
6								
7								
8								
9								
10								
11								
12								
13								
14								
15								
16								
17								
18								
19								
20								
21								
22								
23								
Modal								

Figure 14.2 Activity schedule blank in Excel.

4. Calculate the modal values (most frequent value) for each day of week and time of day and enter them in the appropriate cells. If there is a tie, combine them to show both values as in the example found on Thursday.

Lesson 21: Create a Temporal Topology Using Excel

As explained in Chapter 7, a Temporal Topology is a useful way to visualize the combination of time and weekday in one graph.

1. Open the **Temporal Examples.xls** Excel Workbook and click the **Temporal Topology** sheet. Notice how the times of day and days of week have already been aggregated. If your data were still in raw form, you would need to use either Excel's Pivot Table function or Access Crosstabulation query to prepare your data. This process is beyond the scope of this workbook but readers are encouraged to use either application's help file for a step-by-step instruction on aggregating the data. In ATAC, the crosstabulation of the data is handled on the fly against any raw data.

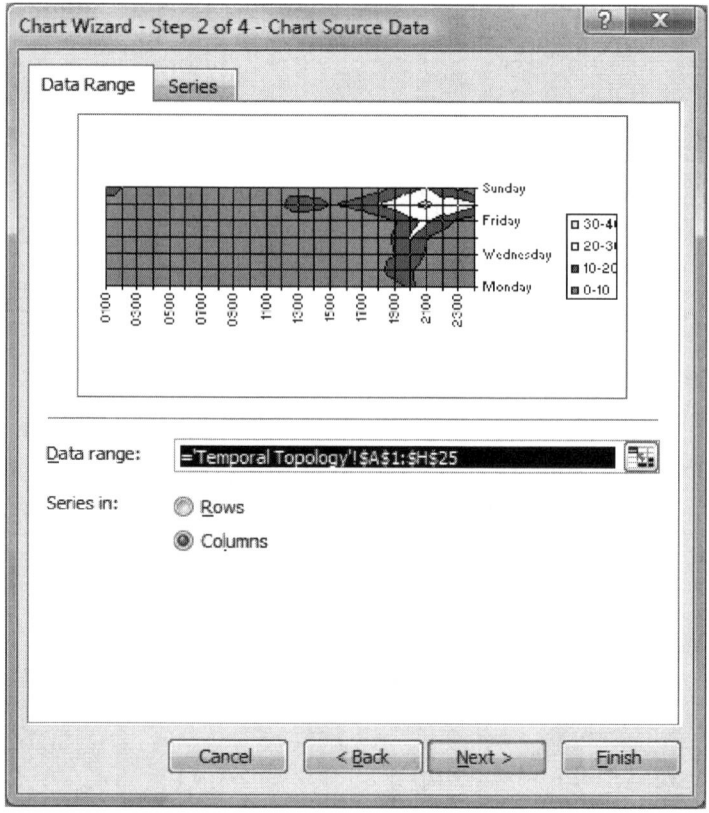

Figure 14.3 Chart Wizard Step Two in Excel.

2. Select the data from cell **A1** to cell **H25**.
3. Using Excel 2007, click on the **Insert** menu and select the **Other Charts** drop button. From the list of available graphs, click the **Contour** graph. If using Excel 2003 or earlier, click the graph button from the toolbar and select **Surface** graph.
4. From the list of **Standard Types** select the **Contour** graph.
5. Click the **Next** button to continue through each of the graph's options until the graph is complete. (See Figure 14.3)
6. To modify the graph's colors, titles, fonts, etc. using either version of Excel, simply right-click on the graph and begin editing. (See Figure 14.4)

Lesson 22: Create a Temporal Topology Using ATAC

In this lesson, we will use a Trend already identified and contained in the Sample.atx database–the Sexual Assault Series. We will first select the series from the Sample.atx database.

The Temporal Dimension

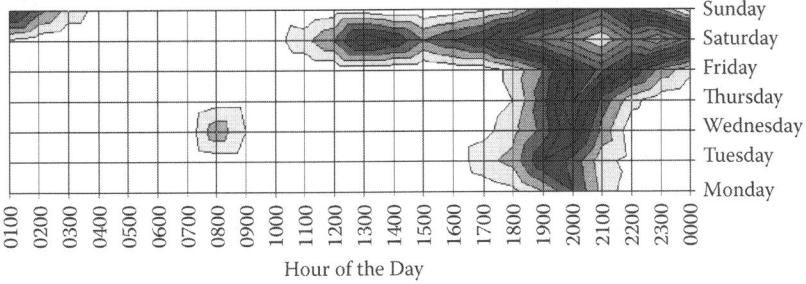

Figure 14.4 Temporal Topology in Excel.

1. Load ATAC and ensure the **Sample.atx** database is the active database.
2. From the Hub's Matrix, scroll to the **Trend** variable. Make certain that the Filter Bar is enabled and type in the Trend variable's Filter bar "**Sex%**". From previous lessons we have learned that adding the percent character after a series of characters will return all those values that begin with search parameter. In this example, the Sexual Assault Series is the only Trend that begins with "Sex."
3. Press the **Enter** key on your keyboard or click the **Execute Filter** button located on the toolbar. Thirty cases should return to the Matrix.
4. Select **Time Series Analysis** from the Hub's **Analysis** menu or select the **Time Series** button from the toolbar. ATAC will automatically perform a weighted method analysis against 100 cases or fewer. Notice the distribution of events across the hours in the day. (See Figure 14.5)
5. From the **Weighted Method** drop list, select **Temporal Topology**.
6. Click and drag the graph to view the Topology from various perspectives. Pay particular attention to the hotspots that show the times of days and days of week that have the most overlap. (See Figure 14.6)
7. From the **Graph Type** menu on the **Graph** menu, select **Bar**.
8. Continue to rotate the graph using the bar display option.
9. Use the **Graph** menu to modify the graph's colors and labeling. To change other aspects of the graph, simply right-click on the graph. (See Figure 14.7)

Practice On Your Own: Evaluate Time of Day and Day of Week for Various Crimes

Using ATAC and the Sample.atx database select various crime types and run a Temporal Topology against each. Evaluate the results to determine the optimal time to catch a perpetrator or deploy officers. Combine the query

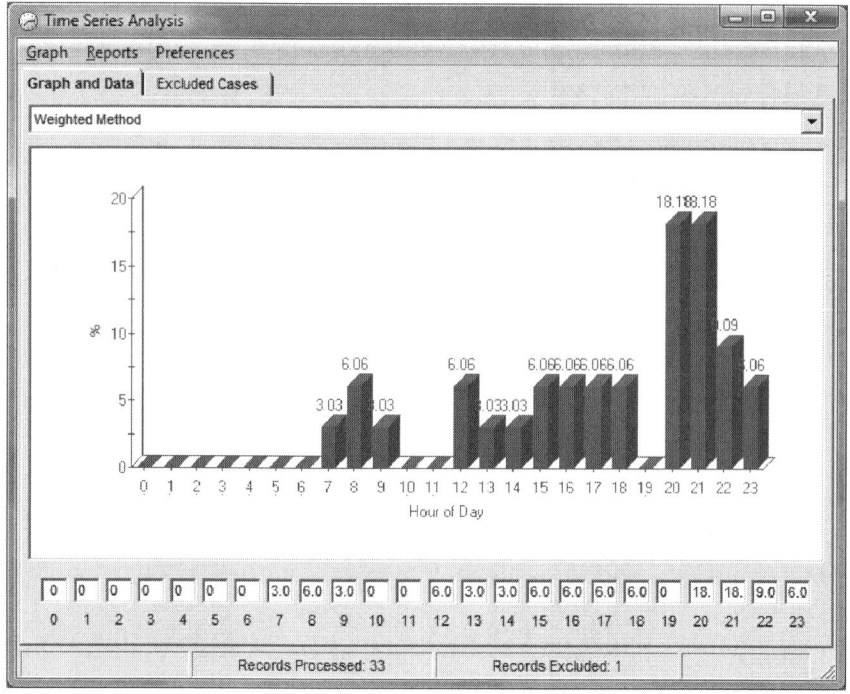

Figure 14.5 Weighted Method in ATAC.

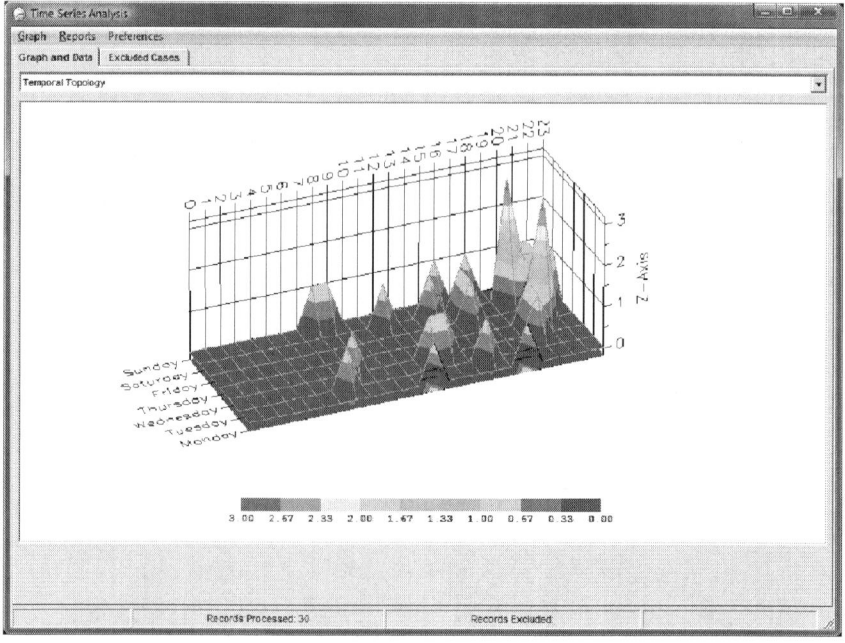

Figure 14.6 Temporal Topology in ATAC.

The Temporal Dimension

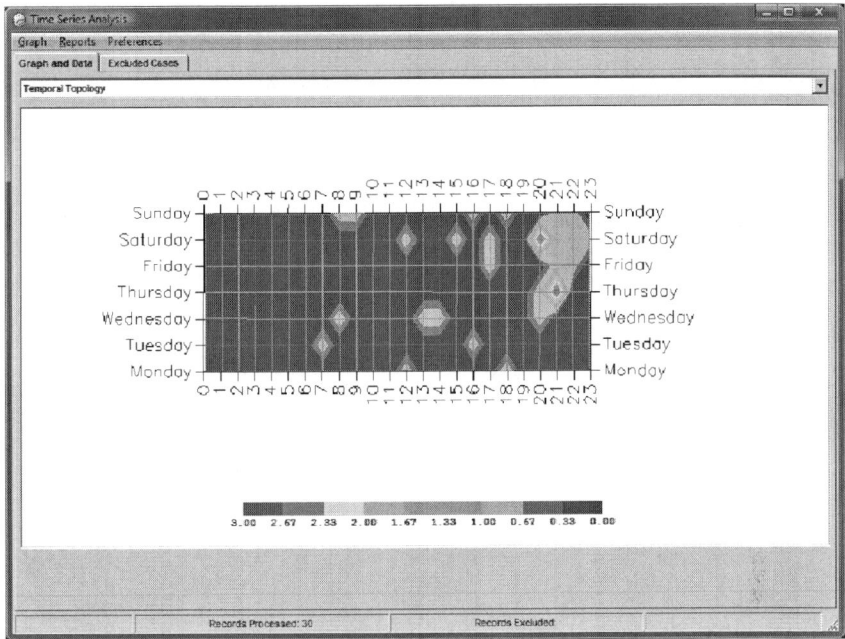

Figure 14.7 Temporal Topology FLAT in ATAC.

capabilities along with the Temporal Topology method in Excel or ATAC to create several temporal topologies against various types of data.

Dynamic Temporal Analysis

With dynamic analysis, instead of studying all events collectively, we examine each case as a unique point in time, and look at how they relate to one another. We are primarily interested in examining the gap between each case and the next, called the Interval. If two cases occur simultaneously, the interval between them is 0. If the second event in a series occurs 3 days and 2 hours after the first, the interval would be 75 hours (3 days plus 2 hours). The following lessons walk us through the study of events using dynamic-based temporal analysis techniques. By studying the change from one event to another, we might uncover hidden motives or reasons for the timing of events.

Temporal Distribution

Just like spatial phenomena, temporal events are categorized into three basic distributions: Clustered, Random, and Uniform.

- **Clustered** events tend to occur in close proximity to one another.
- **Uniform** events tend to occur far apart from one another.
- **Random** events are neither clustered nor uniform.

Tempo

In addition to the three types of distribution, because time only moves in one direction, we can also meaningfully measure that tendency—its tempo. There are three types of tempo: **Accelerating**, **Decelerating**, and **Stable**.

- **Acceleration** occurs when the interval between events decreases as the number of events increases.
- **Deceleration** occurs when the interval between events increases as the number of events increases.
- **Stabilization** occurs when the interval between events neither increases nor decreases as the number of events increases.

Like distribution, tempo can be measured easily as a function of the change in interval over the change in number of events. In other words, the change in X over the change in Y, the same simple calculation for the slope of any line.

It is easiest to visualize the tempo of events using a tempogram, which is a bivariate chart that shows change in time along the X (horizontal) axis, and change in interval on the Y (vertical) axis:

Notice that we can not plot the interval (Y mark) for the last known event because of course we do not know how long it will be until the next (future) event. That is what we will attempt to do in future lessons using correlation.

One of the best features of the tempogram technique is that it allows us to calculate a trend line using a method such as the Least Squares Linear Best Fit method or one of its many variants.

Lesson 23: Create a Tempogram in ATAC

1. Open the **Sample.atx** database and using any of the previous query methods, select the "**Sexual Assault Series**" from the Trend variable.
2. Launch the Dynamic Temporal Analysis Module by selecting **Dynamic Temporal Analysis** from the **Analysis** menu on the Hub or **click** the **Dynamic Temporal Analysis** button on the toolbar.
3. Once opened, you will be taken to the Data tab. This is where you can make changes to the way that the Dynamic Temporal Analysis Module includes or excludes cases.
4. **Click** the **Derive Time Matrix** button. Note the various temporal metrics returned: earliest date, latest date, time span, etc.

The Temporal Dimension

5. Click the **Tempos** tab and then click the **Generate Tempogram** button. Note the "Min Interval," "Mean Interval," and "Max Interval" values at the bottom of the module. Given the lengthy time this series spans, the values are expressed in days and not hours. (See Figure 14.8)

Lesson 24: Create a Tempogram in Excel

1. Open the **Temporal Examples.xls** workbook and make active the **Tempogram** sheet.
2. We'll first need to create an Interval variable to hold the interval values. Right-click on the **E** column and select **Insert** from the popup menu. A new column will be inserted moving the First Time and Last Time fields to the right.
3. Click in cell **E1** and type "**Interval**."
4. Click in cell **E2** and type "**=D3-D2**". This formula subtracts the number of days from the second crime's date from the first crime's date; in other words, the interval in days between the two events.
5. Depending on the preferences already set in Excel, you might have to format column E to display the new interval value as a number. Right-click column **E** and select **Format Cells** from the popup menu.
6. Select the **Number** format from the Category list and click **OK**. The value in cell E2 should now be formatted to show the number of days between the first and second crime in the series.

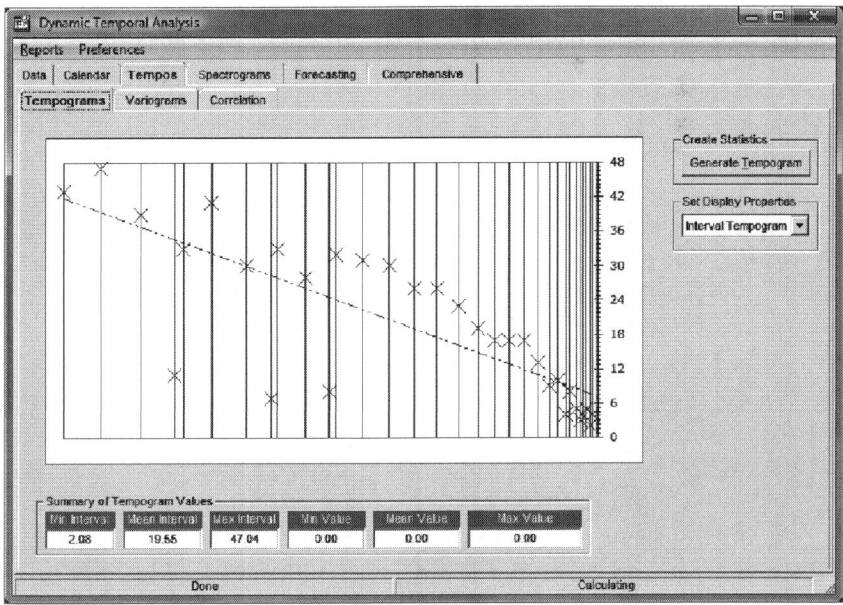

Figure 14.8 Click Generate Tempogram button in ATAC.

7. Click cell **E2**. A black outline should appear around the cell. Double-click the **black square** at the bottom right corner of cell E2. This action will auto-fill the formula in E2 through all of column E. Notice that in the last cell in column E the value is a valid interval. This is obviously because you can not calculate the difference between the last case's date and the next event; it has not occurred yet!
8. Click on cell **E31** and delete its contents.
9. Now, to create the Tempogram, select **D1 through E30**. These are the valid dates and interval values from one case to another.
10. Using Excel 2007, select **Line** graph from the **Charts** area on the **Insert** menu. Using Excel 2003, select **Chart** from the **Insert** menu.
11. From the Chart options, select 2-D Line. Select Finish if using Excel 2003. If using Excel 2007, your graph is ready. Right click on the graph to modify its attributes.
12. Look at the way the line is sloping to identify if this series is accelerating (line goes from upper left to bottom right), decelerating (line goes from bottom left to upper right) or appears stable (line is relatively flat across the horizontal plane).

Using the interval values calculated in the previous lesson, the next lesson takes you through creating a forecast based on the mean interval method. As a reminder, the mean interval method takes the average number of days (or other temporal unit) and "adds" that to the last date to determine a future date.

Lesson 25: Create a Mean Interval Forecast with Excel

1. From the Tempogram spreadsheet and using the Interval values just obtained, click in blank cell **E34**.
2. In cell E34 type "**=average(E2:E30)**". The resulting number is the average number of days between hits.
3. Type in cell **E35** "**=D31+E34**". Depending on the formatting of column E, you may get a strange number. This number is a serial date/time. It simply needs to be formatted as a date instead.
4. Right click **E35** and select **Format Cells** from the popup menu.
5. Select **Date** from the list of Categories on the **Number** tab and click **OK**. The resulting date is the forecast for the next event in the crime series. It should be approximately 21 days after the last event in the series.
6. To determine the reliability of this forecast, we could now calculate the standard deviation for the series. In cell E37 type "**=stdev(E2:E30)**". The resulting value is the standard deviation of days around the mean. Hence, in a normal distribution, 68% of our events would fall (plus or minus) this many days around our forecasted date.

The Temporal Dimension   181

Tip: With a standard deviation so large, we would know the mean was not a good describer of our event's intervals. In addition to the standard deviation, we can use the Tempogram to determine which series are good candidates for Mean Interval method as the Mean interval technique will only work on stable tempos. If you determine that your series is either accelerating or decelerating, as displayed by the Tempogram, then you can use other techniques (e.g., Linear Trend Line or Variogram) to forecast the next event.

Practice on Your Own: Calculate Mean
Interval for Various Other Crimes
In Excel or ATAC and using the **Sample.xls** workbook, select different series to perform tempo and mean interval analysis. Do any of the series lend themselves to the Mean Interval method forecasting?

Variograms

Variograms are one way in which the analyst can perform dynamic analysis. A variogram is a matrix of values that represent change. Traditionally, only interval/ratio values could be subjected to variation analysis using variograms; however, as we shall see, the introduction of the Boolean or Nominal Variogram enables the analyst to study any type of change in any type of activity. Below is an example of a Boolean variogram. (See Figures 14.9 and 14.10)

Examine the variogram displayed above, which shows the change in hunting ground choice of our offender between his three hunting grounds (A, B and C).

Below is an example of a variogram that measures the change in linear distance traveled between cases. At each lag the change in distance is measured. Notice that at lag 5 (comparison of each 5th case) the suspect makes little change in distance. (See Figure 14.11)

Lesson 26: Create a Variogram Using Excel

1. Open the **Temporal Examples.xls** workbook and click on the **Variogram** sheet.
2. Calculate the interval in days between events. Refer to the lessons on Tempograms for a review of the steps.
3. Copy the contents of the newly created Interval variable and paste them into the Metric column. Using this template a maximum of 30 cases and six lags can be analyzed.
4. Review the standard deviations of the 6 lags to determine which has the least deviation (lowest number). The lag with the lowest deviation

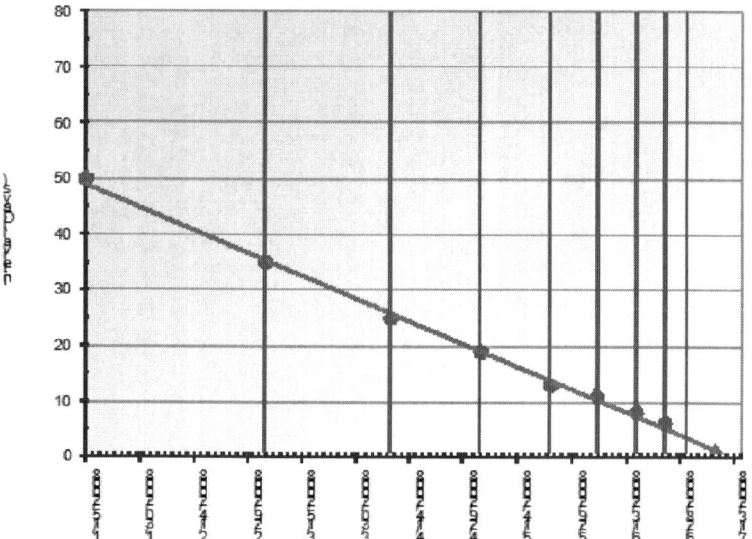

Figure 14.9 Boolean Variogram example in Excel.

is the best predictor. Zero standard deviation is a perfect predictor. In this example, Lag 3 predicts perfectly with a zero standard deviation.

5. Using the last Metric or event in the series, count backward 3 events. So, case 18 is one case, case 17 is two, and case 16 is the third case back. This third case back (case 16) tells us how long the suspect waited in days before striking again. Therefore, three events ago he waited two days (case 16 at metric 2) before striking in event 17. Two days from the last event is the prediction.
6. To calculate the predicted date, add 2 days to the last date in the series by simply typing "=2+G20" in an empty cell where G20 is the date of the last robbery. In the example, the predicted date is 3/26/2008.

Lesson 27: Create a Variogram Using ATAC

1. Open the **Data** sheet in the **Bank Robber.xls** workbook using ATAC. Refer to Section One if you need a refresher on how to open Excel workbooks in ATAC.
2. Launch the Dynamic Temporal Analysis Module by selecting **Dynamic Temporal Analysis** from the **Analysis** menu on the Hub or click the Dynamic Temporal Analysis button on the toolbar.
3. Click the **Derive Time Matrix** button.
4. Click the **Tempos** tab and then the **Variogram** tab.

The Temporal Dimension

Case	Hunting Ground	Lag-1	Lag-2	Lag-3	Lag-4	Lag-5	Lag-6
1	C	0	1	0	1	0	1
2	A	0	0	0	1	0	0
3	C	0	1	0	1	0	1
4	B	0	0	0	1	0	0
5	C	0	1	0	1	0	1
6	A	0	0	0	1	0	0
7	C	0	1	0	1	0	1
8	B	0	0	0	1	0	0
9	C	0	1	0	1	0	1
10	A	0	0	0	1	0	0
11	C	0	1	0	1	0	1
12	B	0	0	0	1	0	0
13	C	0	1	0	1	0	1
14	A	0	0	0	1	0	0
15	C	0	1	0	1	0	1
16	B	0	0	0	1	0	0
17	C	0	1	0	1	0	1
18	A	0	0	0	1	0	0
19	C	0	1	0	1	0	1
20	B	0	0	0	1	0	0
21	C	0	1	0	1	0	1
22	A	0	0	0	1	0	0
23	C	0	1	0	1	0	1
24	B	0	0	0	1	0	0
25	C	0	1	0	1	0	
26	A	0	0	0	1		
27	C	0	1	0			
28	B	0	0				
29	C	0					
30	A						
Prediction		A	C	B	C	A	C
Total Cases		29	28	27	26	25	24
Total Hits		0	14	0	26	0	12
Percentage		0%	50%	0%	100%	0%	50%

Figure 14.10 Normal Variogram example in Excel.

5. Click the **Generate Variogram** button. ATAC provides analysis of up to 12 lags. The lag that predicts best will automatically display in the status information at the bottom. In this example, ATAC predicts that the next event will occur on **3/26/2008 between 0900 and 1100 hours** and displays that lag three is the predictor lag. A literal interpretation of the standard deviation shows that this lag predicts "**perfectly.**" (See Figure 14.12)

Practice on Your Own: Calculate Lag Variograms against Various Other Crimes

In Excel or ATAC and using the Sample.xls workbook, select different series to perform lag variogram analysis. Do any of the series lend themselves to the lag variogram forecasting?

Case	Distance	Lag-1	Lag-2	Lag-3	Lag-4	Lag-5	Lag-6
1	575	-450	375	4445	1940	-10	-440
2	125	825	4895	2390	440	10	820
3	950	4070	1565	-385	-815	-5	4150
4	5020	-2505	-4455	-4885	-4075	80	-2510
5	2515	-1950	-2380	-1570	2585	-5	-1935
6	565	-430	380	4535	1945	15	-425
7	135	810	4965	2375	445	5	820
8	945	4155	1565	-365	-805	10	4100
9	5100	-2590	-4520	-4960	-4145	-55	-2595
10	2510	-1930	-2370	-1555	2535	-5	-1940
11	580	-440	375	4465	1925	-10	-445
12	140	815	4905	2385	430	-5	860
13	955	4090	1550	-385	-820	45	4050
14	5045	-2540	-4475	-4910	-4045	-40	-2525
15	2505	-1935	-2370	-1505	2500	15	-1925
16	570	-435	430	4435	1950	10	-440
17	135	865	4870	2385	445	-5	790
18	1000	4005	1520	-420	-870	-75	4000
19	5005	-2485	-4425	-4875	-4080	-5	-2480
20	2520	-1940	-2390	-1595	2480	5	-1935
21	580	-450	345	4420	1945	5	-460
22	130	795	4870	2395	455	-10	830
23	925	4075	1600	-340	-805	35	4100
24	5000	-2475	-4415	-4880	-4040	25	-2480
25	2525	-1940	-2405	-1585	2500	-5	
26	585	-465	375	4440	1935		
27	120	840	4905	2400			
28	960	4065	1560				
29	5025	-2505					
30	2520						
Prediction	-	2587.00	5269.46	1213.89	195.19	586.00	2607.71
Mean	1842.17	67.07	244.46	253.89	75.19	1.00	82.71
Standard Deviation	1816.69	2402.99	3253.12	3308.41	2380.60	30.14	2414.84

Figure 14.11 Lag 5 Variogram example in Excel.

Lesson 28: Study of Correlation Using Excel

1. Open the **Bank Robber.xls** workbook in Microsoft Excel.
2. Use the steps learned in previous lessons to create a new variable that will be positioned to the right of Property Value. Title it "**Interval.**" Calculate the interval between robberies in days for this new variable. Remember the formatting issue with Excel and how it might display the results initially as dates instead of as a number.
3. Highlight the **Property Value** title and all its column contents except the very last value (we do not know the interval for this property value yet). Continue highlighting to the right to select the Interval column header and all interval values. For the Bank Robber.xls example you should have two columns and 12 rows selected. The last value, $4,400 is not selected. (See Figure 14.13)
4. Using Excel 2007, select **Scatter** graph from the **Charts** area on the Insert menu. Using Excel 2003, Select Chart from the Insert menu.

The Temporal Dimension

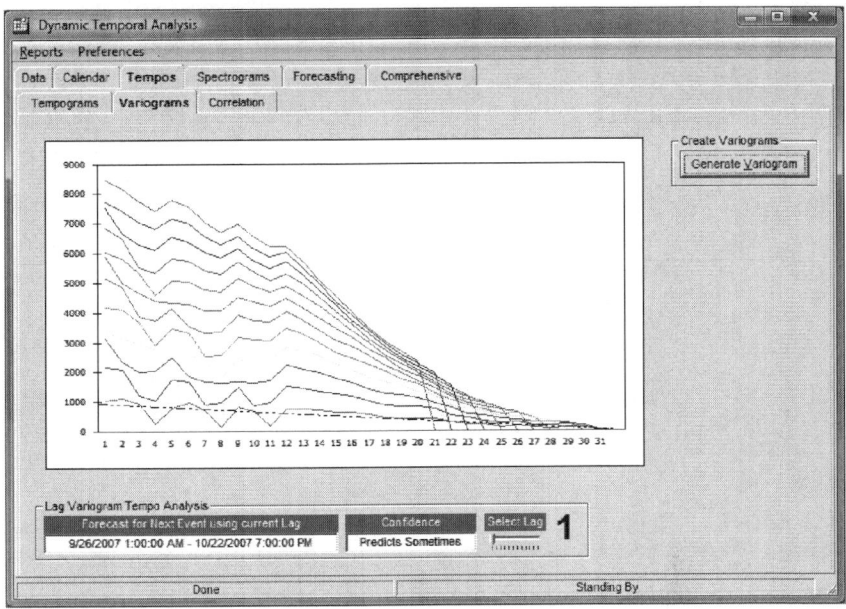

Figure 14.12 Variogram generated in ATAC.

5. From the **Chart** options, select **Scatter with Markers Only**. Select Finish if using Excel 2003. If using Excel 2007, your graph is ready.
6. Right-click on any marker in the graph and select **Add Trendline**.
7. From the list of formatting options, click the checkbox for **Display Equation on Chart** and **Display R-squared value on Chart**. Close out of the formatting dialog.
8. Study the Y equation and the R squared score. Notice this series exhibits a perfect positive correlation! That is, as the property loss increases, so too does the amount of time the bank robber waits to strike. (See Figure 14.14)
9. To calculate the amount of time we anticipate him to wait based on his last $4,400 strike, we must solve for y. Click in cell G13, the interval cell next to the $4,400 property value.
10. Type "=.01*4400-.0343". We simply replaced the x value in the equation with our last known property value. The other two numbers are part of the equation provided in the graph.
11. The result of 43.97 or approximately 45 days is the number of days we expect the robber to wait given his last score of $4,400.
12. To calculate the predicted date, add 45 days to the last date in the series by simply typing "=45+B13" in an empty cell where B13 is the date of the last robbery. In the Bank Robber example, the predicted date is 5/28/2008.

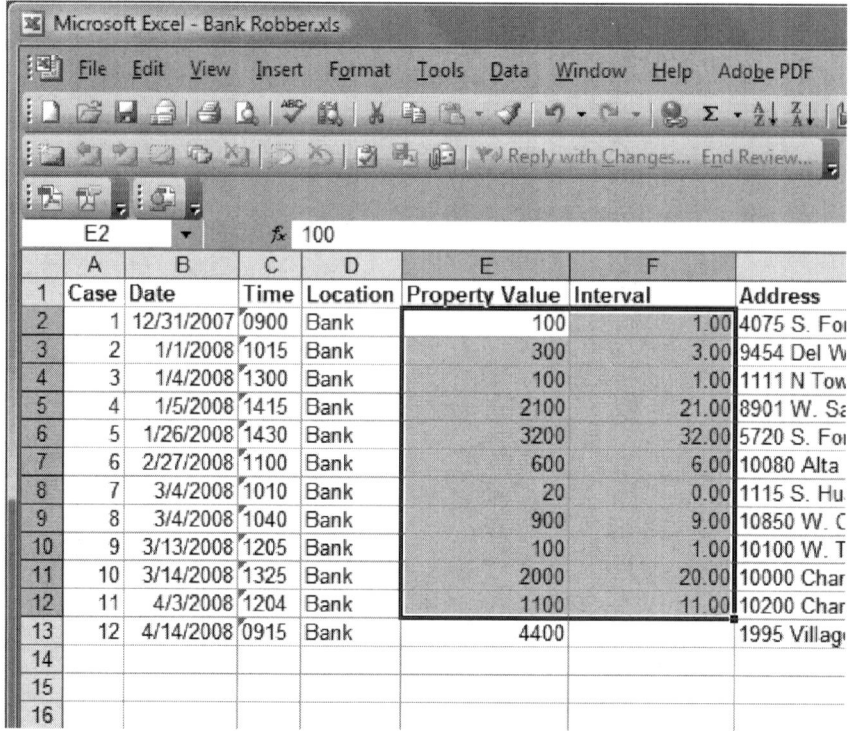

Figure 14.13 Study correlation in Excel.

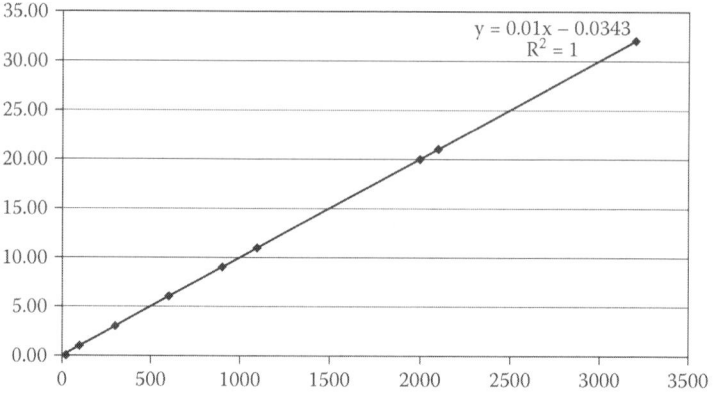

Figure 14.14 Perfect positive correlation in Excel.

Lesson 29: Study of Correlation Using ATAC

1. Open the **Data** sheet in the **Bank Robber.xls** workbook using ATAC. Refer to Section One if you need a refresher on how to open Excel workbooks in ATAC.

The Temporal Dimension 187

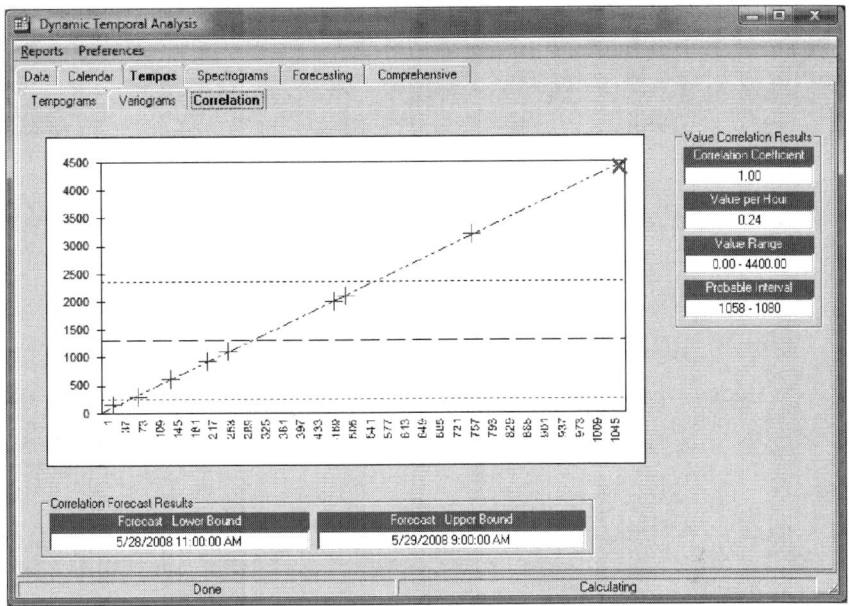

Figure 14.15 Correlation in ATAC.

2. Launch the Dynamic Temporal Analysis Module by selecting **Dynamic Temporal Analysis** from the **Analysis** menu on the Hub or click the Dynamic Temporal Analysis button on the toolbar.
3. **Click** the **Derive Time Matrix** button.
4. **Click** the **Tempos** tab and then **click** the **Generate Tempogram** button.
5. Click the Correlation tab. Note the Correlation Coefficient. Also note the Probable Interval. This is the time range (expressed in hours) for the next event. To express that in days, simply divide either number by 24. The forecast dates are provided at the bottom of the module. (See Figure 14.15)

Review Exercise: Evaluate Other Crime Series Using Correlation
Using ATAC and Excel, perform correlation against the various crime series found in this workbook's sample data folder. In addition to being a forecast technique, you can use correlation to determine other relationships in data as well. For instance, you might find there to be a correlation between population and number of officers a department employs. With the equation, you could then determine how many officers to hire based on a projected population.

Review Questions

1. Does the timing of crimes correlate to the timing of other events objects, such as concerts, holidays, or regular schedules?
2. Describe a statistical technique used to study a crime series. What strengths does it provide and what weaknesses should you be aware of when using it?
3. Describe the difference between static and dynamic temporal analysis.
4. Explain the strengths and weaknesses of the different time analysis methods.
5. When would the mean interval forecast method be a useful time series analysis technique? When would it fail?

The Spatial Dimension 15

Goals of This Section:

1. Learn various static and dynamic spatial analysis methods to identify, analyze, and forecast patterns in spatial behavior.
2. Understand the strengths and weaknesses of the different spatial analysis methods.
3. Use ArcGIS, Excel, Google Earth, and ATAC to create distance and density fields, minimum convex polygons, standard deviation ellipses, perform spider analysis, and uncover a person's activity space.
4. Incorporate previous lessons learned to enhance your ability to query and analyze information spatially.

Introduction

The spatial aspect of a tactical problem is often the first thing crime analysts think of examining. This will consist of looking at what the location of crimes tells us about their relationship to one another and their environment. These usually must be analyzed using a GIS package, but some statistical packages also can be used.

Although analysis of the spatial dimension of a tactical problem can be very powerful, analysts are reminded that this is only one of many equally important dimensions.

The following descriptive factors should be considered for each problem:

Significant Distances: Mean Nearest Neighbor, Mean Inter-point, Mean Q-Range, Mean Shortest Path, Mean Sequential, Mean Triangulated Irregular Network (TIN), and Marauder Circle Diameter are good to know.

Distribution: Clustered, Random, or Uniform—the Nearest Neighbor test is an easy and adaptive tool to determine distribution.

Hunting Grounds: Identify the areas where targets are being attacked. Kernel-smoothed density surfaces, using the Mean Nearest Neighbor distance plus three standard deviations and then contouring by statistical significance, is a good method for identifying hunting grounds.

Hunting Ground Trend: How do hunting grounds change over time? Identify the inception rate of new hunting grounds, how long grounds lies fallow, whether defunct grounds reactivate, their saturation levels, etc. T-coordinate weighting for kernel-smoothed density fields also show trends.

Activity Space: Identify the overall areas where the offender acts.

Sequence of Events: How do the events change in position over time? Connect events with polylines, assigning T-Coordinates to start and end points. These can then be trajected into three dimensions to create a Lund Spacetime Trajectory, analyzed using a Correlated Walk analysis, or Mantel's index for movement path correlation.

Preparing for Spatial Analysis

The next few lessons take us through loading a crime series into ArcGIS, Google Earth and ATAC. Getting a dot on the map is often considered to be the hardest step in performing spatial analysis. Once the crime data are displayed, subsequent lessons will provide details on how to perform a variety of spatial analysis and forecasting techniques.

Lesson 30: Launching ArcGIS and Exploring the Interface

1. Launch ArcGIS and follow the dialog instructions to "Start using ArcMap" with A New Empty map and click **OK**.
2. Explore the menus, table of contents, and data frame of a new empty map.
3. Save the Gotham ArcGIS map document by clicking on **File | Save**.
4. It is recommended to use a WORKING folder as the target destination.
5. Name the map Gotham.mxd and Click **OK**.
6. Add Base Map Layers to your Data Frame by selecting **File | Add Data** or clicking on the Add Data icon **located** on the toolbar.
7. Highlight the layers of choice by clicking on the desire layers (use the control key, "ctrl," to select more than one, or the "shift" key to select sequential files).
8. Select the "base map" layers **gotham.shp**, **parcels.shp**, and **streets.shp** from the GIS DATA folder. Click **Add** to display them in the data frame. (See Figure 15.1)

The Spatial Dimension

Figure 15.1 Layers added in ArcGIS.

Lesson 31: Add the Gotham City Crime Series Using ArcGIS

1. Add the Crime Series to the Table of Contents by clicking on **File | Add Data** or clicking on the Add Data icon located on the toolbar.
2. Navigate to the GIS Data folder, select **SERIES29** and click **Add.**
3. Right-click the SERIES29 in the table of contents and select the **Add X/Y Data** menu option. The 29 points should appear on the map.
4. Change the symbology of the points. Right click on the **Series29** layer and select **Properties**.
5. Left click on the Symbol button.
6. Change the **Color** to **Black** and the **Size** to **12 point**. Click **OK**. (See Figure 15.2)

ArcGIS and the Spatial Analyst Extension

The Spatial Analyst Extension for ArcGIS is a raster analysis suite that extends ArcGIS' capabilities from a simple vector-based environment (points, lines, and polygons), into a raster-based environment where we can approximate field mechanics. This capability is highly desirable, and an integral component of crime analysis. MapInfo software users can use the VerticalMapper extension for MapInfo to perform similar work.

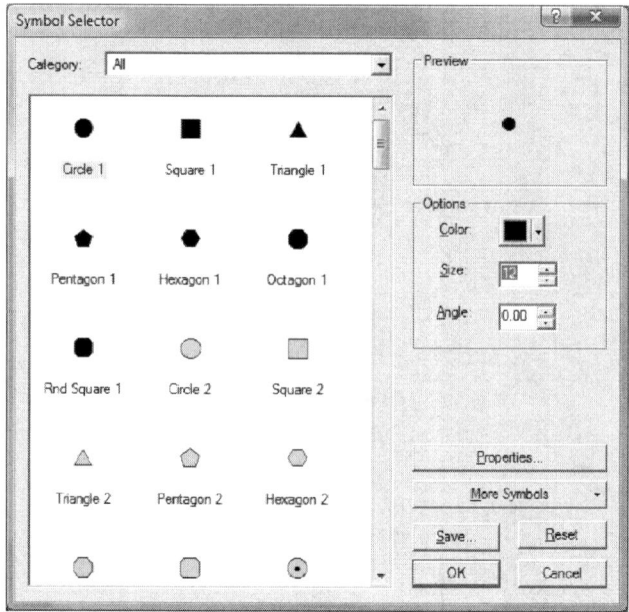

Figure 15.2 Symbol Selector in ArcGIS.

Lesson 32: Loading Spatial Analyst

1. From ArcGIS, click on **Tools** and select **Extensions**.
2. Select on the Spatial Analyst box and click **Close**.
3. Load Spatial Analyst on the toolbar by right clicking **View**, select **Toolbar**, and select **Spatial Analyst**.
4. Notice that Spatial Analyst has a floating toolbar.
5. Drag and dock the floating Spatial Analyst toolbar on the ArcGIS interface.

ArcGIS and SPACE (Spatial Predictive Analysis of Crime Extension)

The Spatial Predictive Analysis of Crime Extension (SPACE) is a tool designed for analyzing serial crime. Specifically, it uses elements of animal movement theories and serial predator activity to develop and interpret patterns associated with the space and time of a serial criminal. Largely based on the Animal Movement & CASE Tools extensions used in previous versions of ArcGIS, it is intended to help Crime Analysts better understand the unique attributes of each crimes series.

The Spatial Dimension 193

Lesson 33: Loading the SPACE Tools in ArcGIS

1. Right-click on **Tools** and select **Extensions**.
2. Select the **SPACE** extension and click **CLOSE**.

Note: Many Extensions need to be loaded on the toolbar. The SPACE Tools automatically loads onto the toolbar.

Preparing for Spatial Analysis Using Google Earth

Google Earth displays satellite images of varying resolution of the Earth's surface, allowing users to visually see things like houses and cars from a bird's eye view. The degree of resolution found in Google Earth varies from area to area, but most area is covered in at least 15 meters of resolution.

Google Earth is not a GIS, but a powerful visualization tool. It is becoming more robust as programmers are introduced to its development tools. It is an easy-to-use and powerful tool for the analysis of crime.

The internal coordinate system of Google Earth is geographic coordinates (latitude/longitude) on the World Geodetic System of 1984 (WGS84) datum. The commercial versions of Google Earth will read ESRI shapefiles.

The following spatial analysis lessons require Google Earth. Visit their Web site to download and install a free copy. If unfamiliar with its functionality, take a few minutes to learn its fundamental pan, zoom and identify functions. It will most likely become an integral part of your analytical toolbox.

Lesson 34: Load Points in Google Earth

1. Launch **GE**.
2. Select **Open** from the **File** menu.
3. Navigate to the sample data folder and open the **Beltway Sniper.kml** file. Google Earth will rotate the earth to focus on the extent of the points in the series. Each point is labeled with its Location Type as designated during the ATAC export. (See Figure 15.3)
4. Click a yellow pushpin to open a particular event's tabular data.
5. Use Google Earth's pan, zoom and rotation functions to view the series from all angles.

Note: GE's native file format is Keyhole Markup Language (KML) files. ATAC can create a KML file if necessary. All that is needed is a valid X and Y coordinate formatted in decimal degrees. Refer to the ATAC help guide for opening and exporting tabular data if desired.

Figure 15.3 Pushpins in Google Earth.

Lesson 35: Export to Google Earth

1. In ATAC, open the **Data** sheet from the **Coffeehouse Thief.xls** workbook. Set the Main Variable to **Case**. The Main Variable contains the text that will be displayed on the pushpin labels in Google Earth.
2. Once the spreadsheet is opened, select **Export Data** from the **File** menu.
3. From the **Files of Type** drop list, specify "**Google Earth (*.KML)**". Name the file "**Coffeehouse Thief.kml**" and place the file in the same directory as the sample data.
4. Launch **GE**.
5. Select **Open** from the **File** menu.
6. Navigate to the **sample data** folder **(directory you installed ATAC)** and open the **Coffeehouse Thief.kml** file. Note how Google Earth displays the "CASE" as designated by the Main Variable in ATAC.

Preparing for Spatial Analysis Using ATAC

ATAC provides a quick means to visualize tabular data that contains X and Y coordinate fields. Any X and Y data will work with the ATAC Map function (e.g., Latitude/Longitude, X/Y, NAD, UTM, or custom coordinates). ATAC

The Spatial Dimension

Map reads ESRI shapefiles for quick comparison of tabular data against the underlying geography.

ATAC Map is not a GIS, but a powerful visualization and analysis tool. Just like Google Earth, ATAC Map does not provide the ability to modify the underlying geographic information nor print cartographic quality maps, such that a GIS would.

Lesson 36: Loading Points in ATAC

1. From **ATAC** and using the **Sexual Assault Series** from previous lessons, select the "**Map**" menu option from the "**Analysis**" menu or click CTRL + M.
2. To load a shapefile from the ATAC Map module, click the **Add Map Layers** button located on the toolbar.
3. Navigate to the **GIS Data** folder in the directly you installed ATAC. Select the Streets.shp
4. Select or type the name of the shapefile you want to open in the "File name" box.
5. Click the **OK** button. Shapefiles will be displayed into the Layer list and map in the order in which they were loaded. (See Figure 15.4)

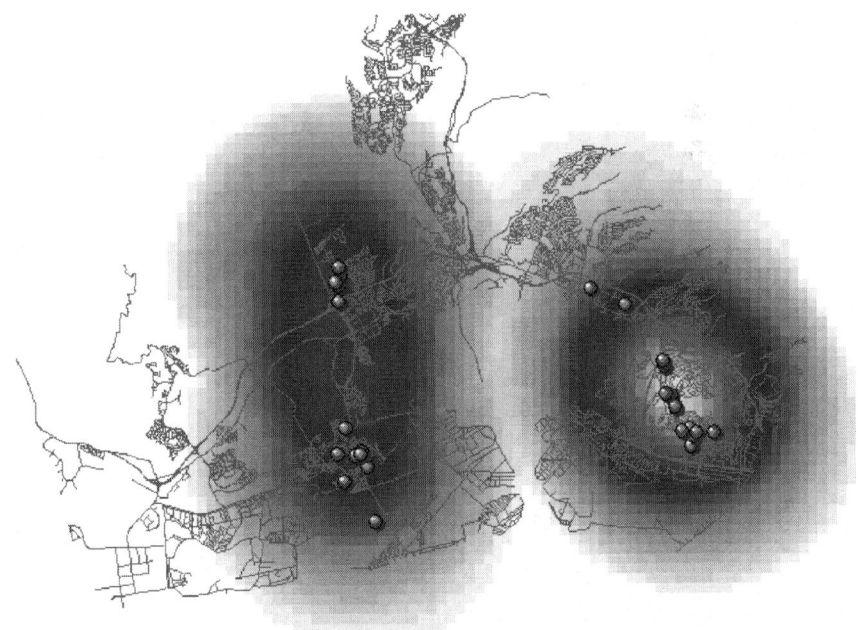

Figure 15.4 Sexual Assault with Street in ATAC MAP.

Point Distributions

Frame of Reference

Analyzing point distributions should be among the first steps in any spatial (or temporal, or behavioral...) analysis routine.

Unfortunately, it is possible for an analyst to perform the mathematics of distribution testing correctly, and still obtain highly misleading results, even with the best tools. This is because all of these tests depend totally on the analyst having the correct **Frame of Reference**.

The Frame of Reference, or **Study Area**, is the zoom perspective that contains all events being studied. For most of us, this area is usually going to be rectangular. This is an unfortunate artifact of working on computer screens and graph paper. Because point distributions typically are not rectangular in nature, this frame shape can result in distortions, most of which can not be helped easily. But the biggest problem with most analysts' Frame of Reference is not its shape, but its size.

Lesson 37: Frame of Reference

1. Left-click on **Activity Space** and select Series29 under "Select Layer."
2. Define the parameters for the Study Area.
3. The layer is **Series29**.
4. Save the layer as **Study Area** to the Working folder.
5. Use **Extent of Points + 10%**.
6. Click **Calculate**. (See Figure 15.5)
7. Right-click on the new layer (Study Area) and select **Zoom to Layer**. Notice that the study area contains all the points as well as buffers the outer most points by ten percent.

Identify Point Distribution

Having organized our crime records into points on a map, the next obvious question should be, "How are these points organized?"

There are three types of point distributions: **Clustered**, **Random**, and **Uniform**. We must determine which of these distributions is exhibited by our data to assist us with the appropriate forecasting methods. For example, trying to identify the hunting grounds would not be useful if the suspect exhibited a uniformed distribution. A clustered distribution would lend itself more to identifying and using Hunting grounds in a forecast and investigative strategy.

Clustered distributions occur when points tend to be located near other points.

The Spatial Dimension

Figure 15.5 Study area in ArcGIS.

Uniform distributions occur when points tend to be located far away from other points.

Random distributions occur when the location of existing points does not influence the location of future points.

The best way to identify a point distribution pattern is with a distribution test. There is an enormous variety of well-known and thoroughly documented tests available to choose from. One easy one is the Nearest Neighbor test.

The Nearest Neighbor test examines the distance from each point to its nearest neighboring point, and from these a mean nearest neighbor distance and standard deviation are computed. These results are compared to the expected random results for this sample size in this study area. This process tests for Complete Spatial Randomness (CSR), meaning that the location of any given point appears to be completely unrelated to the location of any other point or points.

The next lesson uses the SPACE tools to determine the mean nearest neighbor and their point distribution.

Mean Nearest Neighbor

The MNN is average distance between each event and the nearest neighboring event compared to the expected mean distance for a random distribution.

Lesson 38: Calculating Nearest Neighbor Statistics

1. Right-click on the **Study Area** layer and select **Zoom to Layer**.
2. Left-click on **Movement** and select **Nearest Neighbor**.
3. Select the **Series29** layer and choose **View Extent**. Click **Calculate**. (See Figure 15.6)
4. The resulting analysis describes the point pattern, clustered, random or uniform. Scroll down the box to reveal the Mean Nearest Neighbor Distance and Standard Deviation.

Density Fields

By calculating the density of points, rather than their mere locations, analysts can visualize the possible influence of events very clearly; also to convert the

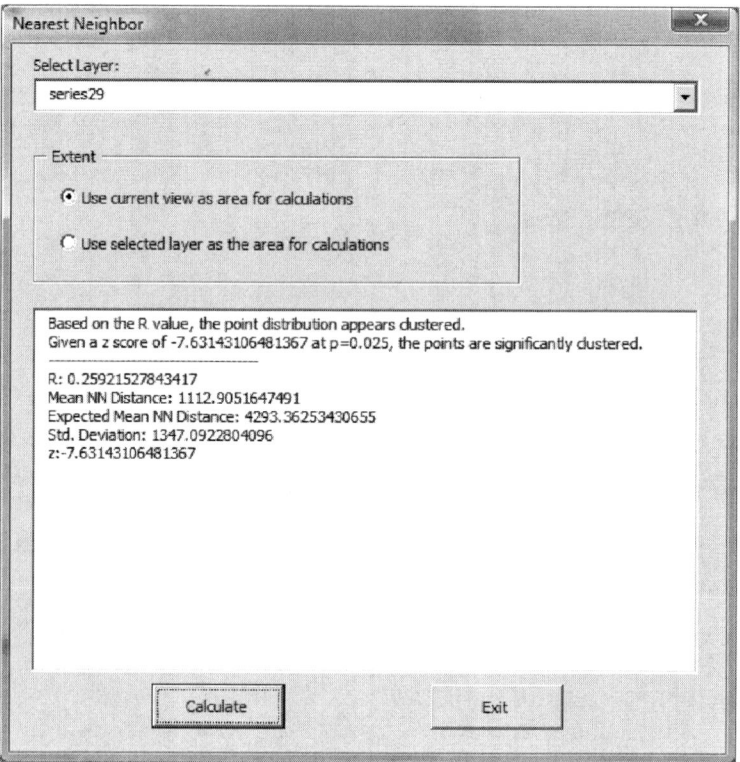

Figure 15.6 Nearest neighbor of Series29 in ArcGIS.

The Spatial Dimension

locations of discrete points into areas such as hunting grounds, home ranges, and so forth. These in turn can give us valuable insight into where the future events may occur, from where they may originate, why certain targets may be selected, and many other things. In order to perform any kind of density analysis, we must count the numbers of points occurring within a certain significant distance of every cell in our raster (or mathematical point in our field). It is important that we choose this distance wisely.

Density is calculated by tallying up the number of events within a selected range of each cell; cells with a higher count of nearby events have a higher density than cells with a lower count. This range, known as the Search Radius, must be chosen carefully. If the Search Radius is short, there may not be any cells that are in range of more than one or two events. On the other hand, if the radius is too large, every cell might be in range of every event, resulting in another nonsensical result. Search Radius selection is the most critical part of performing density analysis.

We must therefore preface any density analysis by calculating Significant Distances. There are several Significant Distances, any of which can result in useful—but very different—density grids. Some of the most significant of these are: Mean Nearest Neighbor Distance, Mean Sequential Distance, Mean Interpoint Distance, Q-Range, Mean Network Distance, Mean TIN Distance, and Mean Spider Distance.

Each of these Significant Distances may have a different potential use for describing various significant factors of our event collection. We will use the Mean Nearest Neighbor distance from the previous lesson.

Lesson 39: Density Fields Using ArcGIS

1. Left-click the drop down menu of Spatial Analyst and select **Options.**
2. Click on the **Extent** tab and scroll down to select "**Same as layer Study Area.**"
3. Click on **Cell Size** and set the cell size to **100** and click **OK**.
4. Left-click on **Spatial Analyst** and select **Density**.
5. Complete the Density parameters. The *Input data:* should reflect the events layer. The *Density type:* should be Kernel. This will provide a smoother transition from one raster cell to the next. The *Search radius:* should be set using a significant distance, for example, the Mean Nearest Neighbor statistic plus two standard deviations.
6. The results are displayed in the data frame and the new layer is added to the bottom of the TOC.
7. Click and drag the new layer near the top of the TOC.
8. Right-click on the new Density layer and select **Properties**.

9. From the **Symbology** tab, change the number of classes to **25**. Also change the color scheme. Left-click on the color symbol for the first class and select the color **White**. Also change the Label to "**Low**."
10. Scroll down to the last class and change the color to **Yellow** and change the label to "**High**."
11. Move the cursor to the scroll bar and **left-click twice** to advance up the list of classes. On the class second from the bottom, change the color to **Red** and remove the label.
12. Right-click on the Red symbol and select **Ramp Colors**.
13. Remove the remaining labels from **ALL** classes (except High & Low). (See Figure 15.7)
14. Click **Apply** and **OK**.

Lesson 40: Calculating Density Analysis in ATAC

1. Open the "Sample.atx" database using ATAC.
2. Select the "Sexual Assault Series" using either the Select Trend function or by simply querying on the series name in the Trend Name field.
3. Click CTRL + M to load the map and display the cases.
4. Click the Identify Hotspots button from the Map's toolbar. (See Figure 15.8)

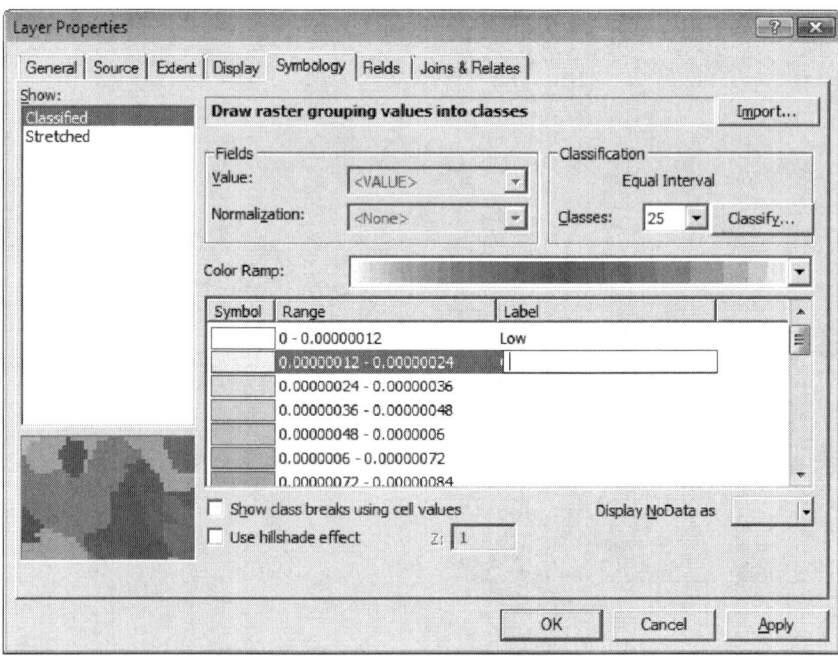

Figure 15.7 Layer Properties labels removed in ArcGIS.

Figure 15.8 Minimum convex polygon of Series29 in ArcGIS.

The hotspot function is optimized to identify statistically significant clusters in data and overcome the difficulties with determining a cell size and proper search distance. Regardless of the zoom level, ATAC Map will configure the optimal search distance based on the current perspective and using the same methods found below.

Study the results of the hotspot map to determine areas of dense activity for this offender. As shown in future lessons, we can begin to determine the offender's hunting grounds. We can use those hunting grounds to select and analyze events that fell within them.

The following lessons introduce students to three techniques useful for describing point distribution as well as uncovering offender home ranges. Minimum Convex Polygon, Standard Deviation Ellipse and Spider Analysis are tools found on the SPACE toolbar.

Minimum Convex Polygon

The minimum convex polygon is a polygon created from a set of points such that it is the smallest polygon that will cover every point without having any concave sides. The minimum convex polygon is one of the easiest means to describe all the events in a series as all events will be contained in the polygon. The polygon can then be used to select collocated data or include in other analytical techniques. The minimum convex polygon can also be used to describe an area if dealing with a marauder type offender.

Lesson 41: Minimum Convex Polygon

1. From ArcGIS, load the **SPACE.MXD** project.
2. Click the **Minimum Convex Polygon** button from the SPACE toolbar.
3. Select **Series29** for the layer of points. Save the new layer as "MCP" in the working folder and click **Calculate**.
4. A polygon containing all points is drawn. The polygon is the smallest it can be while adhering to convex principles.

Standard Deviation Ellipse

A standard deviation ellipse is an ellipse drawn along the Least Squares trend line among a set of points such which bounds determined by the deviation from the mean centroid. It is often used to describe a distribution of events or infer an offender's home range and activity space.

Lesson 42: Standard Deviation Ellipse

1. From ArcGIS, load the **SPACE.MXD** project.
2. Click the **Standard Deviation Ellipse button** from the SPACE toolbar.
3. Select **Series29** for the layer of points. Save the new layer in the working folder. Determine the number of standard deviations (1, 2, or 3). Choose 1 for demonstrative purposes. Click **Calculate**. **(See Figure 15.9)**
4. Based on the parameter setting of one standard deviation, an ellipse is drawn from the mean centroid of all points.
5. Repeat steps 1 and 2 above. Specify a file name and the number of standard deviations. Click **Calculate**.

Spider Analysis

Spider analysis indicates the relationships in distance and direction of a set of study points to their centroid point. There are several possible types of centroids, the most common being Arithmetic or Harmonic.

The Spatial Dimension

Figure 15.9 Standard deviation ellipse of Series29 in ArcGIS.

Lesson 43: Spider Analysis

1. From ArcGIS, load the **SPACE.MXD** project.
2. Click the **Spider Analysis** button from the SPACE toolbar.
3. Select **Series29** as the input layer. Provide a file name. Choose the **arithmetic** centroid type. Click **Calculate**.
4. The resulting spider analysis indicates the relationships in distance and direction of a set of study points to their arithmetic centroid point. (See Figure 15.10)
5. Right-click on the new layer and select **Open Attribute Table**. (See Figure 15.11)
6. Explore the column indicating the length of the line segments for underlying patterns. Close the attribute table. Repeat Steps 1 and 2 above. Instead of Arithmetic choose **Harmonic** and click **Calculate**.
7. The resulting spider analysis indicates the relationships in distance and direction of a set of study points to their **harmonic** centroid point.
8. For comparison, change the color of the harmonic spider analysis by double-clicking the line icon symbol in the TOC and selecting a color such as **Red**, for example.
9 Turn on both spider analysis results in the TOC and compare.

204   Tactical Crime Analysis: Research and Investigation

Figure 15.10 Spider analysis of Series29 in ArcGIS.

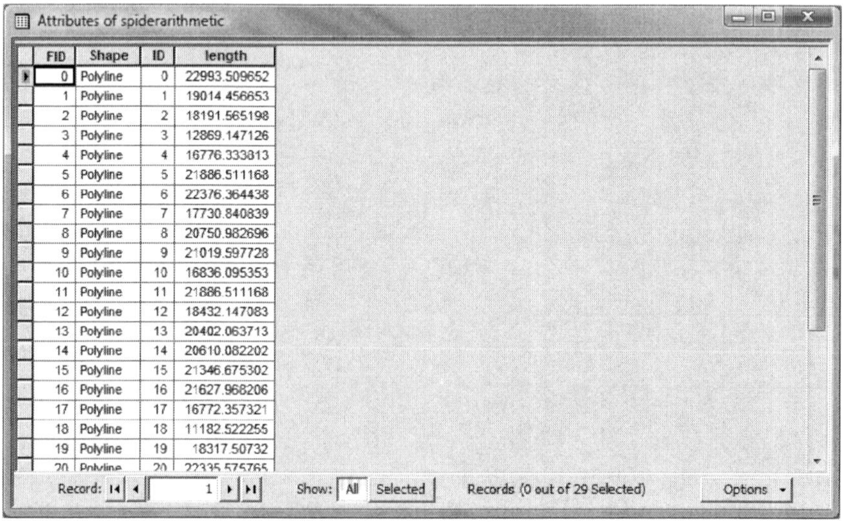

Figure 15.11 Open Attribute Table in ArcGIS.

Lesson 44: Establishing Offender Activity Space Using Spider Lines and Density Fields

1. Add the **Arithmetic Spider layer** to the TOC if needed.
2. Right-click on the Spider layer and select **Open Attribute Table**.
3. Right-click on the **length** column and select **Statistics**.
4. Note the Mean and Standard Deviation of the arithmetic spider line segments. **Close** the Statistics window.
5. Right-click **Spatial Analyst** and select **Options**.
6. Click on **Extent** and choose "**Same as Layer 'StudyArea'**."
7. Click on **Cell Size** and specify the cell size as **100**. Click **OK**.
8. Click **Spatial Analyst** and select **Density**.
9. Complete the Density parameters. The *Input data:* should be **Series29**. The *Density Type* is **Kernel**. The *Search radius:* is determined by a significant measure such as the mean spider distance plus one standard deviation (i.e., **21889** feet). Click **OK**.
10. The resulting Density layer is added to the bottom of the TOC. (See Figure 15.12)
11. Click and drag the Density layer near the top of the TOC.
12. Right-click on the Density layer and select **Properties**.
13. From the Symbology tab, change the number of classes to **25** and click **OK**.
14. Click the **Histogram** icon from the Spatial Analyst menu. (See Figure 15.13)
15. Enlarge the Histogram window and view the breaks in the data distribution. Close the window.
16. Click on **Spatial Analyst** and select **Raster Calculator**.
17. Double-click on "**Density of Series29**." Single click > =
18. Enter a value based on the interpretation of breaks indicated on the histogram.
19. Click **Evaluate**.
20. A new raster layer called **Calculation** has been added to the TOC.
21. Convert the new raster to a feature. Click on **Spatial Analyst**.
22. Select **Convert | Raster to Feature**.
23. Click on the browser button and navigate to the working directory. Call the *Output feature:* **ActivitySpace.shp**. Click **OK**.
24. Right-click on the **ActivitySpace** layer and select **Properties**.
25. Or double-click the polygon icon under the ActivitySpace layer in the TOC.
26. Change the symbol to **Hollow**. Change the *Outline Width:* to **2**. Click **OK**.

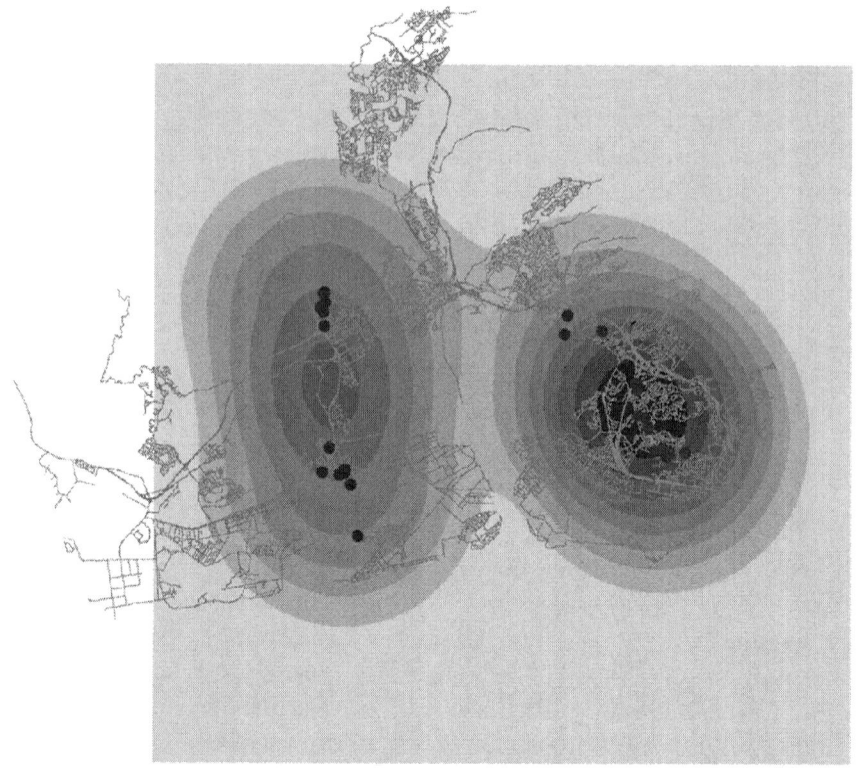

Figure 15.12 Density layer in ArcGIS.

Space-Time Analysis

Predicting future events is a key function of effective analysis. This always involves detecting trends and patterns within the facets of each dimension of the tactical problem, then extrapolating them into the future.

Sequence Lines

Visualizing temporal sequences over spatial positions is a powerful technique that is extremely simple to implement. The addition of temporal to spatial analytical methods to create dynamic spatio-temporal analysis is a needed technique.

There are two easy ways to visualize a combined spatiotemporal analysis: Animation and Sequencing.

Animation is the most obvious, because it mimics reality. Just as we compress miles into inches to make our spatial analysis manageable on our computer screens, we compress days into seconds to make our temporal analysis manageable in our visualization schedules. We can then create a visualization

The Spatial Dimension

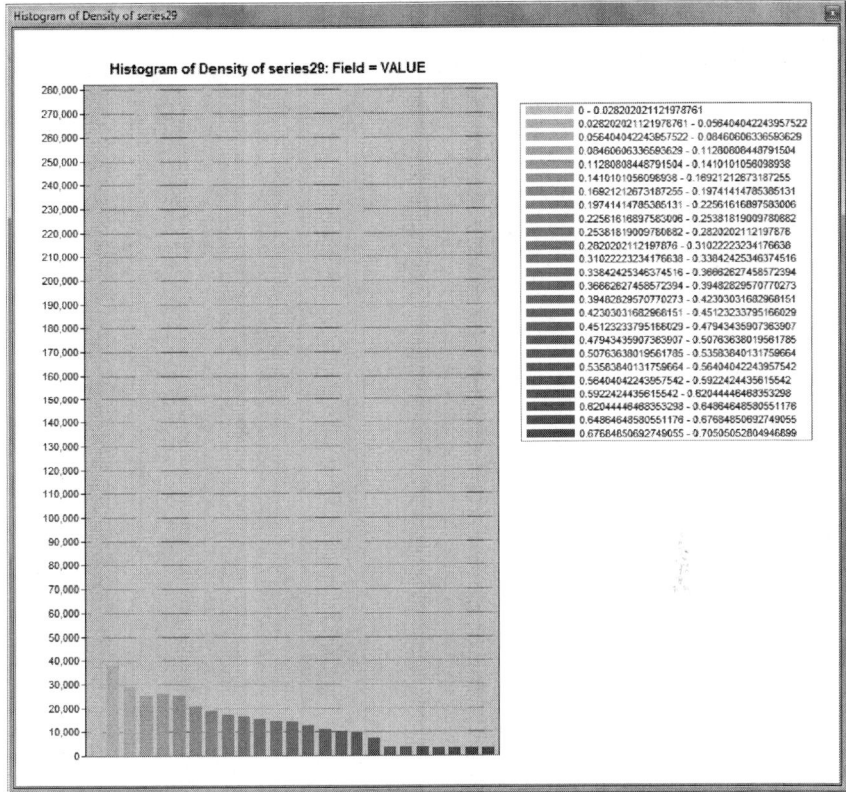

Figure 15.13 Histogram of Series19 in ArcGIS.

that must be experienced in time. An example of an animation would be the nightly weather forecast where the animation of the weather front approaching shows direction spatially as well as speed temporally.

Animation is usually performed by creating a series of static scenes that depict "snapshots" of spatiotemporal activity measured at selected sampling intervals. These can then be combined together using a software package to create an animation file which displays each image sequentially, often helping to smooth transitions from image to image.

An easier and just as useful a method for visualizing spacetime interaction is **Sequencing**. This method consists of drawing lines from event to event in the order of occurrence. Now, in addition to being able to study each event as a discrete phenomenon, we can study the lines themselves. Each line will have important attributes in which we are likely to be very interested—length, direction, angle, bearing, order, and interval, to name a few of the most obvious.

Let us sequence the Sexual Assault Series.

Lesson 45: Sequence Lines

1. Left-click on **Movement** and select **Sequence**.
2. Specify the layer of choice. Save the new file in the working folder. Specify a field which will determine the ordering of events. Click **Calculate**.
3. The new layer is added to the TOC.
4. Right-click on the new layer and select **Zoom to Layer** to see the results more clearly.
5. The symbology can be changed to reveal directional change. Right-click on the symbolic icon listed below the layer, "sequence lines." Scroll down the list of symbol selections and locate the "Arrow at End" symbol type. The color and size can also be modified.
6. Change the color to **Black** and click **OK**.
7. Right-click on the Sequence Line layer and select **Open Attribute Table**.
8. Notice the column of information providing the length of the line segment. This information may reveal underlying patterns.

Geographic Profiling

In Chapter 8, the authors explained how Geographic Profiling attempts to use information about where an offender commits crimes in an attempt to determine his or her most likely anchor points. The results are designed to support investigations into serial crimes, with the purpose of helping to narrow the search area for an offender.

The next two lessons will introduce some simple techniques to help describe an offender as a marauder or commuter, and then actually create a geographic profile from an infamous serial murder series. The first technique, the Great Circle Method, provides the basis for the final technique, the geographic profile. Most proponents suggest that geographic profiling is only supposed to work on offenders classified as "Marauders."

Lesson 46: Calculate the Great Circle against the Beltway Sniper Series

1. First, create a new shape layer. To create a new shape layer select **ArcCatalog** from the **Tools** menu.
2. Navigate to the location where you would like to save the new shape file, and then from the **File** menu in ArcCatalog, select **New** and then select **Shapefile**.

3. In the **Create New Shapefile** box, name the shapefile "**GreatCircle**" and select **Polygon** from the **Feature Type** dropdown menu, then click **OK**.
4. With ArcCatalog still open, click on the **GreatCircle.shp** file, and drag it to the **Table of Contents** in ArcMap. After the layer appears in ArcMap close ArcCatalog.
5. In ArcMap, select **Editor Toolbar** under the **Tools** menu. When the **Editor** box appears, make sure that **Create New Feature** under the **Task** dropdown, and **GreatCircle** under the **Target** dropdown are both selected. (See Figure 15.14)
6. Under the **Editor** menu, click **More Editing Tools** and select **Advanced Editing**. The Advanced Editing toolbar will appear. (See Figure 15.15)
7. Click on the **Circle Tool** button indicated by a small circle, and then create a circle that encompasses your data points. Make sure that the circle encompasses all of the data points, with the edge of the circle touching the outermost points. This may require some editing of the circle.
   a. To move the circle, click on the **Edit Tool** in the **Advanced Editing** toolbar indicated by a small black arrow, then click on the circle that you just created and drag it to its desired position.
   b. To resize the circle, double-click in the circle with the Edit Tool still selected. A small red point located on the edge of the circle indicates that the circle is ready to be resized. Click on the red dot and drag the circle to its desired size.

Practice On Your Own: Are you a Marauder or Commuter?

Create the Great Circle off of your movements in your movement log created in Lesson 19. Based on the confines of the circle, are you a Marauder or a Commuter? Is the area covered by the Great Circle operationally useful? Explain your answer either way.

Figure 15.14 Editor toolbar in ArcGIS.

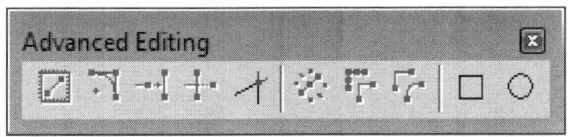

Figure 15.15 Advanced Editing in ArcGIS.

Lesson 47: Create a Newton-Swoope Geoforensic Profile of the Beltway Sniper Series

1. Open the **Beltway Sniper.xls** file in Excel and add an XAverage column and a YAverage column to the right of the X and Y columns in the series. You will be using these columns to find the mean X and mean Y points for our data.
2. In **Cell L2**, begin by calculating the average of the first three X coordinates in the series by using the formula "=AVERAGE(L2:L4)."
3. Now, in **Cell L3**, calculate the average of the first four X coordinates in the series by using the formula "=AVERAGE(L2:L5)." Calculate the average of the first five X coordinates in **Cell L4**, etc., until you have found the average of all of the X Coordinates.
4. In column **YAverage** starting in **Cell M2**, repeat the above process to find the averages of the Y Coordinates.
5. Now, in **Cell N2**, calculate the distance between the westernmost point and the easternmost point in your X Coordinates using the following formula: "=ABS(MAX(J2:J14)-MIN(J2:J14))." The largest X value is the westernmost point, and the smallest X value is the easternmost point. Name this column **XDistance**.
6. In **Cell O2**, calculate the distance between the northernmost point and the southernmost point in your Y Coordinates. The largest Y value is the northernmost point and the smallest Y value is the southernmost point. Name this column **YDistance**.
7. In **Cell P2**, calculate the product of XDistance and YDistance. Name this column **XYProduct**.
8. In **Cell Q2**, calculate XYProduct divided by Pi multiplied by the number of events minus one squared. Use the following formula: "=P2/(3.14159*((MAX(A2:A16)-1)^2))." Name this column **PiFormula**.
9. In **Cell R2**, find the square root of PiFormula using the formula "=SQRT(Q2)." Name this column **Linear Unit**. Linear Unit is the radius that you will apply on XAverage and YAverage points that you calculated earlier. (See Figure 15.16)
10. Create a new worksheet within the Excel document and name the worksheet "**DataAverages**."
11. Copy the XAverage and YAverage columns and paste them into the **DataAverages** worksheet by selecting **Paste Special** and **Values** from the **Edit** menu.
12. Save the Excel file as **BeltwayGeo.xls**.
13. Now create a Geoforensic map in ArcGIS using the Excel file that you just created. In **ArcMap**, create a new empty map. To add the Excel file to the map select **Add Data** from the **File** menu.

The Spatial Dimension 211

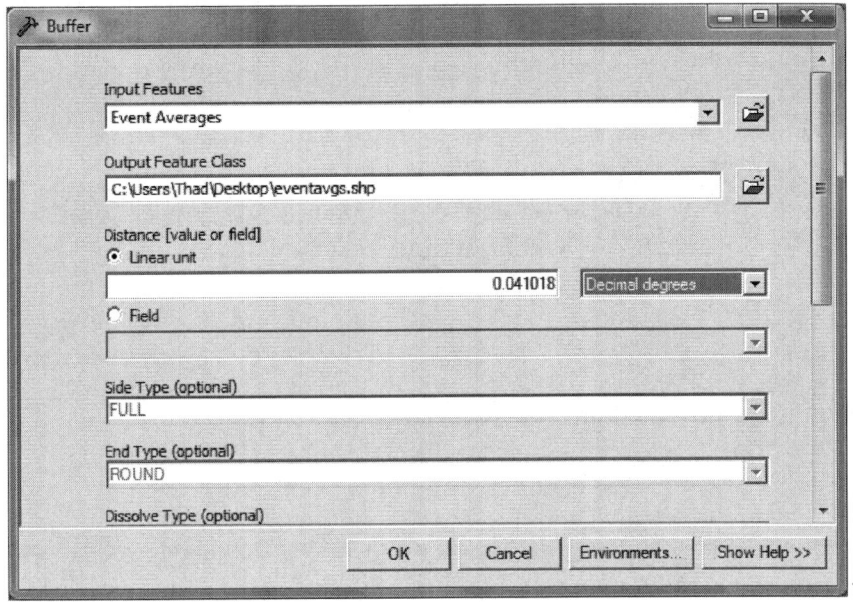

Figure 15.16 Buffer dialogue in ArcGIS.

14. Navigate to and double-click on the **BeltwayGeo.xls** file, then select the **DATA** worksheet and click **Add**.
15. With the **Source tab** selected in ArcMap, **right click** on the layer that you just created and select **Display X Y Data**. Make sure you have specified the fields for the X and Y coordinates before you click **OK** to import the points.
16. Add the mean points created in Excel by repeating steps 9, 10, and 11, choosing the **DataAverages** worksheet and the **XAverage** and **YAverage** coordinates.
17. In the **ArcToolbox**, choose **Analysis Tools** and **Proximity** and double click on **Buffer**.
18. In the **Buffer** box, select the **DataAverages** points that just you added, and then choose a name as your output Feature Class (do not use special characters).
19. Input the **Linear Unit** that you calculated in the Excel file and select **Decimal Degrees**, and then select **OK**. The resulting buffer layer can now be viewed to determine areas of high probability. The area of high probability is where the buffers overlap most.

Review Exercise: Using the Great Circle and Geographic Profiling

Create a geographic profile against your movement log. Does the profile accurately describe where you work, live or play? If so, does your home fall within the marauder circle? If the profile did not describe areas where you have anchor points, were you a commuter as defined by the great circle?

Review Questions

1. Describe the difference between a marauder and commuter.
2. How might geographic profiling be used to resolve a crime series?
3. Explain the three types of spatial distributions and how it would further your analysis knowing which one a series exhibited.

Bibliography

Akers (2008). *Criminological Theory: Introduction and Evaluation.* Los Angeles, CA: Roxbury.
Alston (1994). *The Serial Rapist's Spatial Pattern of Target Selection.* Unpublished master's thesis, Burnaby, British Columbia, Canada: Simon Fraser University, School of Criminology.
Armitage, R. (2006). Predicting and Preventing: Developing a Risk Assessment Mechanism for Residential Housing. *Crime Prevention and Community Safety: An International Journal,* 8(3), pp. 137-149.
Bair, S. (1999). ATAC for analysts: Series breaking. Bair Software, Highlands Ranch, CO.
Bair, S. (2000). Geographic Information Analysis: From GIS to GIA. Crime Mapping and Analysis Program. http://www.iaca.net/resources/articles.html.
Bair, S. (2000, Spring). ATAC: A tool for tactical crime analysis. Crime Mapping News, 2(2), pp. 9-10.
Bair, S. (2004). Getting Started with ATAC. Bair Software. Highlands Ranch, CO.
Bair, S. (2007, January 11). Using your IZE to Identify Crime Series. Keynote address given at the 2nd annual Florida Crime and Intelligence Analysts Association, Orlando, FL.
Bair, S., Boba, R., Fritz, N., Helms, D., and Hick, S. (Eds.). (2002). Advanced crime mapping topics: Results of the First Invitational Advanced Crime Mapping Topics Symposium. Denver, CO: National Law Enforcement and Corrections Technology Center.
Becker (1968). "Crime and Punishment: An Economic Approach." *The Journal of Political Economy,* 76 pp. 169-217.
Bennett, T. and R. Wright (1984). *Burglars on Burglary: Prevention and the Offender.* Hampshire, England: Bower.
Blake, K. (1995). "What you should know about Car Theft." *Consumer's Research,* October 1995, 26-28.
Boba, R. (2001). Introductory Guide to Crime Analysis And Mapping. Washington, DC: U.S. Department of Justice, Office of Community Oriented Policing Services.
Boba, Rachel (2005), *Crime Analysis and Crime Mapping,* Sage Publications.
Brantingham, P. and P. Brantigham, (1991). *Environmental Criminology.* Prospect Heights, IL: Waveland.
Brantingham, P. and P. Brantingham (1993). Environment, routine, and situation: Toward a Pattern theory of crime. In R. Clarke and M. Felson (Eds.), *Routine Activity and Rational Choice: Advances in Criminological Theory, Vol. 5.* New Brunswick, NJ: Transaction Publishers.
Bureau of Justice Statistics (1997). Retrieved from the Bureau of Justice Statistics Website: www.ojp.usdoj.gov/bjs.

Canter, D. and S. Hodge (2000). Criminals' mental maps. In L.S. Turnbull, E.H. Hallisey, and B.D.Dent (Eds.) *Atlas of Crime: Mapping the Criminal Landscape* (pp. 186-191). Phoenix, AZ: The Oryx Press.

Canter, D. and P. Larkin (1993). The environmental range of serial rapists. *Journal of Environmental Psychology*, 13: 63-69.

Canter, D. Coffey, T., Huntley, M., and C. Missen (2000). Predicting Serial Killers' Home base using a decision support system. *Journal of Quantitative Criminology* 16 (4): 457-478.

Carter, R. and D. Q. Hill, (1980). Criminals' and non-criminals' perceptions of urban crime. *Criminology*, 16: 353-371.

Catalano, S. (2004). Criminal Victimization 2003. Bureau of Justice Statistics, National Crime Victimization Survey. Washington, DC.

Central Intelligence Agency, The World Factbook, Downloaded February 15, 2008 from https://www.cia.gov/library/publications/the-world-factbook/fields/2075.html.

Chaiken, J. and M. Chaiken (1982). *Varieties of Criminal Behavior*. Santa Monica, CA: Rand Corporation.

Clarke, R. and P. M. Harris, (1992). Auto Theft and its Prevention. In M. Tonry (Ed) *Crime and Justice: A review of Research*, Vol. 16. pp 1-54. Chicago, IL: University of Chicago Press.

Cohen, L. and M. Felson (1979). "Social Change and Crime Rate Trends: A Routine Activity Approach." *American Sociological Review* 44:588-608.

Cromwell, P., J. Olson and D. Avery (1991). *Breaking and Entering: An Ethnographic Analysis of Burglary*. Newbury Park, CA: Sage Publications.

Cromwell, P. and J. Olson, (2004). *Breaking and Entering: Burglars on Burglary*. Belmont, CA: Wadsworth.

Crow, W. J. and L. J. Bull, (1975). *Robbery Deterrence: An Applied Behavioral Science Demonstration*. La Jolla, CA: West.

Dorbin, A., B. Wiersema, C. Loftin, and D. McDowell (1996). *Statistical Handbook on Violence in America*. Phoenix, AZ: The The Oryx Press.

Eck, J. and D. Weisburd, (1995). *Crime and Place*. Monsey, NY: Criminal Justice Press.

Erickson, R. (1996). *Armed Robbers and Their Crimes*. Seattle, WA: Athena Research Corporation.

Federal Bureau of Investigation (2005). Crime in the United States. Uniform Crime Reports. Washington, DC: U.S. Government Printing Office.

Federal Bureau of Investigation (2007). Crime in the United States. Uniform Crime Reports. Washington, DC: U.S. Government Printing Office.

Federal Bureau of Investigation (2008). Crime in the United States. Uniform Crime Reports. Washington, DC: U.S. Government Printing Office.

Feeney, F. (1986). "Robbers as Decision-Makers." In *The Reasoning Criminal: Rational Choice Perspectives on Offending*, ed. Derek B. Cornish and Ronald V. Clarke, 53-71. New York: Springer-Verlag.

Felson, M. (1987). Routine Activities and Crime Prevention in the developing metropolis. *Criminology*, 25 (4): 911-931.

Felson, M. (1994). *Crime and Everyday Life: Insights and Implications for Society*. Thousand Oaks, CA: Pine Forge Press.

Bibliography

Felson, M. and R. Clarke (1998). "Opportunity makes the thief: Practical theory for crime prevention." Police Research paper 98. London, England: Crown Publishers.

Gabor, T. M. Baril, M. Cusson, D. Elie, M. Leblanc, and A. Normandeau (1987). *Armed Robbery: Cops, Robbers, and Victims*. Springfield, IL: Charles C. Thomas.

Gill, M. (2000). *Commericial Robbery: Offenders' Perspectives on Security and Crime Prevention*. London: Blackstone Press.

Greenfeld, L. (1997). *Sex Offenses and Offenders: An Analysis of Data on Rape and Sexual Assault*. Washington, DC: Bureau of Justice Statistics.

Heineke, J. M. (1978). *Economic Models of Criminal Behavior: Contributions to Economic Analysis*. London: Elsevier Press.

Hickey, E. W. (2002). *Serial Murderers and their victims*. Pacific Grove, CA: Brooks/Cole.

Hipp, J. Bauer, D., Curna, P., and K. Bollen (2004). Crime of Opportunity or crimes of emotion? Testing two explanations of seasonal change in crime. *Social Forces* 82(4).

Hunter, R. and C. R. Jeffery (1991). Preventing Convenience Store through environmental design. In R. V. Clark (Ed.) *Situational Crime Prevention: Successful Case Studies*. New York: Harrow and Heston.

Jeffery, C. R. and D. L. Zahn, (1993). "Crime prevention through environmental design, opportunity theory, and rational choice models." In R. Clarke and M. Felson (Eds.), *Routine Activity and Rational Choice: Advances in Criminological Theory, Vol. 5*. New Brunswick, NJ: Transaction Publishers.

Jeffery, C R., R. D. Hunter, and J. Griswold (1987). Crime Analysis, computers and convenience store robberies. In W. J. Clifton and P. T. Callahan (Eds.) *Convenience store robberies: An intervention strategy by the city of Gainesville, Florida*. Gainesville, FL: Gainesville Police Department.

Kennedy, L. and D. Forde, (1990). Routine activities and crime: An analysis of victimization in Canada. *Criminology* 28 (1): 137-152.

Lemberg, Paul. (2006, March 02). 80/20 Rule - The Vital Few. *EzineArticles*. Retrieved January 16, 2008, from http://ezinearticles.com/?80/20-Rule---The-Vital-Few&id=154867.

Levine, N. (2002). Crimestat: A Spatial statistics program for the analysis of crime incident locations (v2.0). Ned Levine and Associates, Houston, TX and the National Institute of Justice, Washington, DC. Retrieved from the National Archive of Criminal Justice Data Web site: www.icpsr.umich.edu/NACJD/crimestat.html.

Ley, D. (1983). *A Social Geography of the City*. New York: Harper and Row.

Longo, R. and A. Groth, (1983). "Juvenile Sexual Offenses in Histories of Adult Rapists and Child Molesters." *International Journal of Offender Therapy and Comparative Criminology*, 27 (2): 150-155.

Maguire, M. (1982). *Burglary in a Dwelling: The Offence, the Offender, and the Victim*. London: Heinemann.

Messner, S. and K. Tardiff (1985). "The Social Ecology of Urban Homicide: An Application of the 'Routine Activities' Approach." *Criminology*, 23: 241-267.

Miethe, T., R. McCorkle, and S. Listwan (2006). *Crime Profiles: The anatomy of dangerous persons, places and situations*. Oxford, England: Oxford University Press.

Miethe, T. and R. F. Meier (1994). *Crime and Its Social Context: Toward an Integrated Theory of Offenders, Victims, and Situations*. Albany: State University of New York Press.

Morris, N. (1972). Foreword, in *Delinquency in a Birth Cohort* Marvin E. Wolfgang, Robert M. Figlio and Thorsten Sellin eds., University of Chicago Press, Chicago, IL.

Orleans, P. (1973). Differential cognition of urban residents: Effects of social scales on mapping. In R. M. Downs and D. Stea (Eds.), *Image and Environment* (pp. 115-130). Chicago, IL: Aldine.

Paternoster, R. (1989a). "Decisions to Participate in and desist from four types of common delinquency: deterrence and the rational choice." *Perspective, Law and Society Review*, 23: 501-534.

Paternoster, R. (1989b). "Absolute and Restrictive Deterrence in a Panel of Youth: Explaining the Onset, Persistence/Desistance and Frequency of Delinquent Offending." *Social Problems*, 36: 289-309.

Paulsen, D. (2002). "Wrong Side of the Tracks: Assessing the Role of Newspaper Coverage of Homicide in Socially Constructing Dangerous Places." *Journal of Criminal Justice and Popular Culture*, 9(3): pp. 113-127.

Paulsen, D. (2004). "To Map or Not to Map: Assessing the Impact of Crime Maps on Police Officer Perceptions of Crime," *International Journal of Police Science and Management*, 6(4): 234-246.

Paulsen, D. (2005). "Target Profiling: Attempting to Predict Commercial Robbery Victimization using Spatial Modeling." NIJ MAPS Office Annual Conference, September, Savannah, GA.

Paulsen, D. (2006). "Location, Location, Location: Spatial Perspectives on Commercial Robbery." Academy of Criminal Justice Sciences Annual Conference, March, Seattle.

Paulsen, D. (2006b). "Connecting the Dots: Assessing the Relative Accuracy of Geographic Profiling Software." *Policing: An International Journal of Police Strategies and Management.* 29(3), pp. 306-334.

Paulsen, D. (2006c). "Human vs. Machine: A comparison of the accuracy of Geographic Profiling Methods." *Journal of Investigative Psychology and Offender Profiling.* Vol 3, Issue 2, pp. 77-89.

Paulsen, D. and M. Robinson (2009). *Crime Mapping and Spatial Aspects of Crime.* Boston, MA: Allyn and Bacon.

Pyle, G. (1980). "Systematic Sociospatial variation in perspectives of crime location and severity." In D. Georges-Abeyie and K. Harries (Eds.) *Crime: A Spatial Perspective* (pp. 219-245). New York: Columbia University.

Petersilia, J. Greenwood, P. and M. Lavin (1977). *Criminal Careers of Habitual Felons.* Santa Monica, CA: Rand Corporation.

Pettiway, L. (1995). "Copping Crack: The travel behavior of crack users." *Justice Quarterly* 12: 499-524.

Phillips, P. (1980). Characteristics and typology of the journey to crime. In D. Georges-Abeyie and K. Harries (Eds), *Crime: A Spatial Perspective* (pp. 167-180). New York: Columbia University.

Rainville, G. and B. Reeves (2003). *Felony Defendants in Large Urban Counties*, 2000. Washington, DC: Bureau of Justice Statistics. NCJ 202021.

Ratcliffe, J. (2006). "A Temporal Constraint theory to explain opportunity based spatial offending patterns. " *Journal of Research in Crime and Delinquency* 43(3): 261-291.

Ratcliffe, J. and M. McCullagh (2001). "Chasing Ghosts: Police Perception of high crime areas." *British Journal of Criminology* 41: 330-341.

Bibliography

Rengert, G. (1989). "Behavioral Geography and criminal behavior." In D. Evans and D. Herbert (Eds) *The Geography of Crime* (pp. 161-175). New York: Routledge.
Rengert, G. and J. Monk (1982). "Women in crime" In G. Rengert and A. Monk (Eds.) *Women and Social Change* (pp. 7-10). New York: Kendall Hunt.
Rengert, G., Piquero, A. and P. Jones (1999). Distance decay reexamined. *Criminology* 37(2): 427-445.
Rengert, G. and J. Wasilchick (2000). *Suburban Burglary: A Tale of Two Suburbs*. Springfield, IL: Charles C. Thomas Publishing.
Repetto, T. (1974). *Residential Crime*. Cambridge, MA: Ballinger.
Restak, R. (2001). *Mozart's Brain and the Fighter Pilot: Unleashing Your Brain's Potential*. New York: Three Rivers Press.
Rhodes, W. and C. Conly (1991). "Crime and Mobility: An Empirical study." In P. Brantingham and P. Brantingham (Eds.) *Environmental Criminology* (pp. 167-188). Prospect Heights, IL: Waveland.
Robinson, M. (1999). "Lifestyles, routine activities, and residential burglary victimization." *Journal of Crime and Justice* 22(1): 27-56.
Robinson, M. (2002). *Is Justice Blind? Ideals and Realities of American Criminal Justice*. Upper Saddle River, NJ: Prentice-Hall.
Rossmo, D. K. (1994). "Targeting Victims: Serial killers and the urban environment." In T. O'Reilly-Fleming and S. Egger (Eds.) *Serial and Mass Murder: Theory, Research and Policy* (pp.133-153). Toronto, Canada: University of Toronto.
Rossmo, D. K. (2000). *Geographic Profiling*. Boca Raton, FL: CRC Press.
Scarr, H. (1973). *Patterns of Burglary*. Washington, D.C.: Government Printing Office.
Sherman, L. (1989). "Hot Spots of Predatory Crime: Routine Activities and the Criminology of Place." *Criminology* 27: 27-55.
Shover, N. (1991). "Burglary." In *Crime and Justice: A Review of Research*. Vol. 14. Ed. Michael J. Tonry, 73-113. Chicago: University of Chicago Press.
Snook, B. Canter, D. and C. Bennell (2002). "Predicting the Home Location of Serial Offenders: A Preliminary Comparison of the Accuracy of Human Judges with a Geographic Profiling System. "*Behavioral Science and the Law* 20: 109-118.
Snook, B., Taylor, P. and C. Bennell (2004). "Geographic Profiling: The Fast, Frugal, and Accurate Way." *Applied Cognitive Psychology* 18: 105-121.
Snook, B., Zito, M., Bennell, C., and P. Taylor, (2005). On the Complexity and Accuracy of Geographic Profiling Strategies. *Journal of Quantitative Criminology*, 21: 1-26.
Stahura, J. and J. Sloan, (1988). "Urban stratification of places, routine activities and suburban crime rates." *Social Forces* 66(4): 1102-1118.
Stanbrough, J. L. (2007), The Deductive Method, Downloaded from http://www.batesville.k12.in.us/Physics/PhyNet/AboutScience/Deductive.html on January 2nd, 2008.
Taylor, R. and A. Harrell (1996). Physical Environment and Crime: National Institute of Justice Research Report. Washington, DC: U.S. Department of Justice.
Tita, G. and E. Griffiths, (2005). "Traveling to violence: The case for a mobility based spatial typology of homicide." *Journal of Research on Crime and Delinquency* 42(2): 275-308.
Tunnell, K. (1990). *Choosing Crime: The Criminal Calculus of Property Offenders*. Chicago: Nelson-Hall.

Von Luschan, Felix: Van Luschan's Chromatic Scale, Downloaded from Wikipedia http://en.wikipedia.org/wiki/Von_Luschan's_chromatic_scale on March 12, 2008

Wright, R. and S. Decker (1994). *Burglar on the Job: Streetlife and Residential Break-ins*. Boston, MA: Northeastern University Press.

Wright, R. and S. Decker (1997). *Armed Robbers in Action: Stickups and Street Culture*. Boston, MA: Northeastern University Press.

Index

A

Action *versus* reaction by police agencies, 128
Activity schedule, 107
Activity space, 107, 190, 205. *See also* geographic profiling; spatial analysis
Administrative crime analysis, 4, 5
Ambusher, 107
Anchor point, 107
Aoristic analysis, 80–81. *See also* temporal analysis
ArcGIS, 96, 141, 190
   crime series, sample, 191
   Density Fields, 199–200
   Google Earth, analysis with, 193
   launching, 190
   Spatial Analyst Extension for, 191, 192
   Spatial Predictive Analysis of Crime Extension (SPACE), 192, 193
Archetypes, 167, 168
ArcMap, 142
ArcGIS, working with, 190 (*see also* ArcGIS)
Archetypes, creating, 167, 168
   correlation studies, 186–187
   density analysis, 200–201
   downloading software, 142
   evaluating call to service data with, 144
   evaluating crime data with, 142–143
   Excel, utilizing with, 144, 145
   Filter Bar, 156, 157–160
   Layout Organizer, 150–151
   Lesson 1, 142–143
   Lesson 2, 143–144
   Lesson 10, 154
   Lesson 11, 156
   Lesson 12, 157–158
   Lesson 13, 158–160
   Lesson 14, 160–161
   Lesson 15, 161–162
   Lesson 16, 162–163
   Lesson 17, 163–164
   Lesson 18, 168
   Lesson 19, 169–170
   Lesson 20, 172–173
   Lesson 21, 173–174
   Lesson 22, 174–175, 177
   Lesson 23, 178–179
   Lesson 24, 179–180
   Lesson 27, 182–183
   Lesson 29, 186–187
   Lesson 3, 145
   Lesson 4, 145
   Lesson 5, 145, 147
   Lesson 6, 150–151
   Lesson 7, 151–152
   Lesson 8, 152–153
   Lesson 9, 153
   Microsoft Access, opening in ATAC, 143–144
   movement logs, creating, 169–170
   Save Layout, 151–152
   Sorting, 153, 154
   tempogram, creating, 178–179
   temporal typology, creating, 174–175, 177
   variogram, creating, 182–183
   Visual Query Module, 156
Auto theft
   joy riders, 51, 52, 53
   offender types, 52–53
   permanent retention and resale, cars stolen for, 52
   professionals, 52–53
   statistics, 51–52
   stripped for parts, 52
   target selection, 53
   temporary use, cars stolen for, 52
   victim characteristics, 52
ATAC, 141
   activity schedule, 172–173
Automated Tactical Analysis of Crime (ATAC), 58–59

B

Behavioral geography
   forecasting, 26–29
   geographic profiling (*see* geographic profiling)

interview transcript, 36–43
journey-to-crime (*see* journey-to-crime concept)
overview, 25–27
research based on offender interviews, 35–43
spatial behavior (*see* spatial behavior)
tactical crime analysis, tool for, 25
Beltway Sniper, 210–211
Bodnar method for the originator, 92
Brantingham, Patricia, 91
Brantingham, Paul, 91
Buffer zone concept, 33–34, 107
Burglary
  bounded rationality theories, 11–12
  criminal attractiveness correlation to number of houses, 26
  offender profiles, 49–50
  residential *versus* commercial, 49
  statistics, 49
  target selection, 50–51
  victim profiles, 50

C

Canadian School. *See* criminal geographic targeting
Canter school. *See* investigative psychology
Canter, David, 95, 101, 105
Centre for Investigative Psychology, 95–96
Change-based forecasting, 121–122
Clarke, Ron, 19
Coal sack, 107
Community oriented policing (COP), 5
Commuter, 107
Concepts
  development, 74–75
  importance, 74
  Proximity Search, 163–164
  RegEx, in, 162–163
CPTED. *See* crime prevention through environmental design (CPTED)
Crime analysis
  administrative (*see* administrative crime analysis)
  data analysis, importance of, 71–72
  definition, 127
  emergence of field, 3
  importance, 7
  motive (*see* motive)
  operational (*see* operational crime analysis)
  post-secondary curricula, 6
  strategic (*see* strategic crime analysis)
  tactical (*see* tactical crime analysis)
  temporal (*see* temporal analysis)
  who, what, where, when, how, and why?, 60
Crime analysts
  data analysis, importance of expertise in, 71
  expectations of police agencies, 3
  role, 3–4
  skills, 3, 4
Crime decision equation, 128
Crime Mapping & Analysis Program, 118
Crime pattern theory
  complexity of its view of crime, 18
  empirical research, lack of, 18–19
  overview, 16
  propositions of, 16–18
  research on, 18–19
Crime prevention through environmental design (CPTED)
  as strategy for reducing crime opportunities, 5
  impact on crime patterns, 71
  prevalent acceptance of, 5
  target selection factors for burglary, 51
CrimeStat. *See also* journey-to-crime concept
  accuracy, 107–108
  application, 97–100
  software development, 97
  theoretical decay functions, 98–100
  versus Dragnet or JTC, 100
Criminal geographic targeting. *See also* geoforensics; geographic profiling
  algorithm, 93
  application, 93–95
  development, 92, 93
Criminals. *See* offenders
Criminological theory
  crime pattern theory (*see* crime pattern theory)
  overview, 9
  rational choice theory (*see* rational choice theory)
  routine activities theory (*see* routine activities theory)

D

Data analysis

Index

ArcGIS (*see* ArcGIS)
  inference *versus* fact from, 62–63
  RegEx (*see* RegEx)
  SQL (*see* SQL)
Decision models, 113–117
Deductive method, 68–69, 69–70
Defensible Space, 51
Detectives
  assignments, how made, 57–58
  investigative mindset, 62–63
Detention, 131–132
Deterrence, crime, 132–133
  opportunity cost, 135
Discrete choice models, 116
Disintegration, 130–131
Displacement, offender, 129–130
Disruption, crime, 129
Distance decay, 107
Distance Decay Hypothesis, 102–103
Dragnet school. *See* Dragnet software; investigative psychology
Dragnet software, 96–97. *See also* investigative psychology
  accuracy, 105–106
  versus CrimeStat, 100
Dresser drawers theory, 60–62

E

Ecological Fallacy, 103, 118
Excel, Microsoft
  Access data, importing, 145, 147
  ATAC, utilizing in (*see under* ATAC)
  correlation studies, 184–185
  Filter Bar, 158–159
  layouts in, 152–153
  mean interval forecast, creating, 180–181
  tempogram, creating, 179–180
  temporal typology, creating, 173–174
  variograms, 181–182

F

Fleson, Marcus, 19
Forecasting, crime. *See also* prediction, crime
  autocorrelation, 123–125
  correlation, 123
  effective, 110
  ineffective, 110–111
  linear trend estimation (regression), 125–126
  methodology, 120
  overview, 109–110
  percent change, 121–122
  spatial, 112
  temporal, 111–112, 121–122
  utilization, 111
  versus prediction, 109
Forecasting, next-event, 6

G

Geoforensics. *See also* geographic profiling
  application, 102
  overview, 101
Geographic Information System (GIS), 124
Geographic profiling
  accuracy, 105–106
  arithmetic centroid prioritizations, 103–104
  background and history, 91–92
  criminal geographic targeting (*see* criminal geographic targeting)
  geoforensics (*see* geoforensics)
  investigative psychology (*see* investigative psychology)
  line-of-bearing extrapolations, 104
  marauder or commuter, determining, 208–209
  missed opportunity profiling, 104
  movement log, 211–212
  offender travel-demand models, 104
  overview, 91
  philosophy behind, 102–103
  wedge theory (*see* wedge theory)
Geographic targeting. *See* criminal geographic targeting
Godwin School. *See* wedge theory
Godwin, Grover Maurice, 101
Google Earth, 190, 193, 194. *See also* ArcGIS
Gottlieb Rectangle, 117
Gottlieb, Steve, 117

H

Hill, Bryan, 118, 119
Homicide
  arguments, stemming from, 46
  offender profiles, 46
  serial murder (*see* serial murder)
  statistics, 45
  victim profiles, 46

Hunter, 107

I

I-Psy. *See* investigative psychology
Initiative, policing, 128
Intervention, crime. *See also* deterrence, crime
    developing leads, 130
    method-based denial interventions, 133
    objectives, defining, 128–132
    overview, 127–128
    strategies (*see* strategies, intervention)
Interventions, crime
    target-based denial interventions, 133
Inverse time-weighted density analysis, 92
Investigative psychology, 92
    algorithm, 96
    application, 96–97
    development, 95–96
    IOPS, 96–97
ITWD. *See* inverse time-weighted density analysis
IZE method
    categorize, 64, 149
    example, 66–68
    generalize, 64–65, 149
    importance, 138
    maximize, 64, 66, 149
    minimize, 64, 65–66, 149
    organize, 64, 65, 149, 153, 154
    overview, 64, 149
    utilizing ATAC, 150–154

J

Journey-to-crime concept. *See also* CrimeStat
    development, 92
    opportunity structure, 33
    overview, 32
    research on, 33–35
    spatial attractiveness, 32–33
    target attractiveness, 32
JTC school. *See* journey-to-crime concept

L

Lag variogram analysis, 183
Least Effort Principle, 102
Levine school. *See* journey-to-crime concept

Levine, Ned, 97
Linear trend estimation (regression), 125–126
Linkage blindness
    case study, Jane Smith, 58–59
    case study, Sheriff Joe, 59
    deductive method to overcome, 69–70
    IZE method to overcome, 68
    theories behind, 58
Liverpool school. *See* investigative psychology

M

Marauder, 107
Mean interval forecasting, 180–181
Mean nearest neighbor, 198
Mental maps
    criminals' perceptions, 30–31
    overview, 28–29
    research on, 29–30
Method-based denial interventions, 133
Microsoft Access, 143
Minimum convex polygon, 201–202
Missed-opportunity profiling, 92
Modus operandi, 4, 107
MOP. *See* missed-opportunity profiling
Moran's I statistic, 124
Motive
    dresser drawers theory, 60–62
    importance of understanding, 60
Movement logs, 168–169

N

Nearest Neighbor Test, 84–85
Newton, Milton, 101
Newton-Swoope school, 101, 210. *See also* geoforensics
Next-event forecasting, 6

O

Offender travel-demand modeling, 92
Offenders
    motivated, 15–16, 17
    perceptions (mind maps), 30–31
    readiness, state of, 17
    robbery interview, 36–43
    serial, public fascination with, 5
    thinking, 35–43
Operational crime analysis

Index

definition, 4
overview, 5
Operations strategies, 128
Opportunity cost, 135
Opportunity, crimes of, 11–12
    causal relationship, 19
    offenders afforded multiple opportunities, 21
    place, relationship to, 20
    reducing, 22–23
    time, relationship to, 20
    variances by types of crime, 20

P

Pareto, Vilfredo, 58
Pattern theory, crime. *See* crime pattern theory
Patterns in criminal activities, 4
    identifying, 116–117
    linkage blindness to (*see* linkage blindness)
    offender observations, 20
    threshold analysis for identifying, 70–71
Pearson's Correlation Coefficient, 86–87
Percent change forecasting, 121–122
Poacher, definition of, 107
Police initiatives, 128
Predator school. *See* wedge theory
Prediction, crime. *See also* forecasting, crime
    decision models (*see* decision models)
    effective, 112–113
    ineffective, 117–120
    methodology, 120
    overview, 109–110
    versus forecasting, 109
Probability Grid Method, 118, 119–120
Problem oriented policing (POP), 5
Prognostication, 109
Psycho-geographic profiling. *See* wedge theory

Q

Quantitative identification, 70–71

R

Raptor, definition of, 107
Rational choice theory
    bound models, 10, 11–12
    criticism of, 12–13
    definition, 9–10
    limited choice models, 12
    pure models, 10
    victim choice, 10–11
Records Management System (RMS), 57, 62
RegEx
    and expressions, 73
    ATAC, utilizing in, 160–161
    concepts, relationship to, 74–75
    or expressions, 73
    Proximity Search in, 161–162
    proximity searches, 73
    query functions, 72, 74
    versus SQL, 72–73
Regular Expressions. *See* RegEx
Rigel school. *See* criminal geographic targeting
Robbery
commercial victimization profiles, 48
    offender patterns, 47–48
    opportunistic, 47
    planning, 47
    prevalence, 47
    statistics, 47
    street *versus* commercial, 48–49
Rossmo school. *See* criminal geographic targeting
Routine activities theory, 103, 107
    convergence with targets, 14
    criticisms, 15–16
    offender profiles, 13, 15–16
    overview, 13
    research on, 15–16
    VIVA, 13–14

S

Secured by Design, 51
Serial murder
    Hollywood depiction *versus* reality, 45–46
    offender profiles, 46
    rarity, 121
    statistics, 45
    victim profiles, 46
Serial offenders, public fascination with, 5
Sexual assault
    historic levels of, 54
    offender profiles, 54–55
    statistics, 54
    underreportage, 54

victim-offender relationships *versus* stranger assaults, 55
Signature (offender), 107
Space-time analysis, 206–208
Spatial analysis
 activity space, 190, 205
 ATAC, utilizing, 194–195
 density fields, 198–199
 distribution, 189, 196
 events, sequence of, 190
 frame of reference, 196
 hunting grounds, 189, 190
 point distribution, 196–197
 significant distances, 189
 spider analysis, 202–203, 204
 standard deviation ellipse, 202
Spatial behavior
 analysis of (*see* spatial analysis)
 awareness space, 29, 31–32
 mental maps (*see* mental maps)
 nodes, 28, 29
 overview, 27
Spatial Predictive Analysis of Crime Extension (SPACE), 192
Spider analysis, 202–203
Spree-killings, 5
SQL
 data mining sample statement, 71–72
 data searches, 73–74
 versus RegEx, 72–73
 writing, 155
Stalker, 107
Standard deviation ellipse, 202
Statistics, role in crime analysis, 4
Strategic crime analysis, 4, 5
Strategies, intervention, 127
 action plan, 136–138
 denial, 133
 deterrence, 132–133
 interception, 134–135
 investigation, 133–134
Structured Query Language. *See* SQL

T

Tactical crime analysis
 definition, 4
 geographical profiling, 20–21
 increase in departmental hirings, 5–6
 IZE method (*see* IZE method)
 opportunity, impact of, 19–20
 overview, 4–5

specialization in, 5–6
Tactics, 127–128, 135–136
Target-based denial interventions, 133
TDM. *See* offender travel-demand modeling
Technology, role in crime analysis, 4
 tactical analysis, role in, 6
Tempogram, 178, 179, 180–181
Temporal analysis
 activity schedule, 171, 172–173
 aoristic analysis, 80–81, 171
 assumptions, flawed, 78–79
 calendar, 78, 87–88
 clock, 78, 87–88
 clustered events, 84, 177, 178
 correlations, 171, 184–185
 cycles, temporal, 87–88
 date, 78
 date time, 78
 dimensions, 78
 distribution, temporal, 83–85, 86–87, 177–178
 events, 77–78
 midpoint method, 80, 81
 multiple times of occurrence, assumptions regarding, 79–80
 overview, 77
 primary time of occurrence, assumptions regarding, 79
 random events, 84, 177, 178
 study area (range), 82–83
 T coordinates, 78, 82
 tempo, 86–87, 171, 178
 time, 78
 time series analysis (*see* time series analysis)
 timelines, 83
 topology, creating, 173–174
 uniform events, 84, 177, 178
 units of measurement, 81–82
 velocity, 87
 weighted method, 80, 81
Terminal velocity, 87. *See also* temporal analysis
Terrorism, 5
Threshold analysis, 70–71
Tim, transcript of interview with (commercial robbery offender), 35–43
Time series analysis
 extrapolation, 89
 interpolation, 89

Index

linear trend estimation, 89
moving average, 88–89
spectral density, 89
statistical trend estimation, 89
Tobler, Waldo, 102–103
Trapper, 108
Troller, 108

V

Value, inertia, visibility, and access (VIVA), 13–14
Variograms, 181, 182–183
Velocity, 87. *See also* temporal analysis
Victims, crime
    attractiveness (to criminals) factors, 21
    homicide (*see* homicide)
    multi-stage selection of, by criminals, 17
    newness of goods as a victimization factor, 21–22
    rational choice selection, 10–11
    stranger *versus* known, 46
    VIVA, 13–14
    targets, attractiveness of, 21

W

Wedge theory, 92
    overview, 101
Wolfgang, Marvin E., 58

Z

Zipf, George, 102